EATING HEALTHY
for a
HEALTHY BABY

Also by Fred Plotkin

The Authentic Pasta Book

Opera 101

Fred Plotkin
and
Dana Cernea, M.D.

Eating Healthy
for a
Healthy Baby

A Month-by-Month

Guide to Nutrition

During Pregnancy

CROWN TRADE PAPERBACKS, NEW YORK

Published by Crown Publishers, Inc., 201 East 50th Street, New York, New York
10022. Member of the Crown Publishing Group.

Random House, Inc. New York, Toronto, London, Sydney, Auckland

CROWN TRADE PAPERBACKS and colophon are trademarks of Crown
Publishers, Inc.

Manufactured in the U.S.A.

Design by Kay Schuckhart

Library of Congress Cataloging-in-Publication Data

Plotkin, Fred.
Eating healthy for a healthy baby/by Fred Plotkin and Dana Cernea, M.D. — 1st
ed.
p.   cm.
Includes bibliographical references and index.
1. Pregnancy—Nutritional aspects. 2. Mothers—Nutrition. 3. Cookery. I.
Cernea, Dana.
RG559.P56 1994
618.2'4—dc20   93-6458
CIP

ISBN 0-517-88002-4
10 9 8 7 6 5 4 3 2 1
First Edition

This book is dedicated to a few special babies:

Sarah Rhoda Sichel, Sam and Danielle Plotkin, Silvia Anderson,

Madeleine Beard, Silvia Fait-Palazzi, Emily and Patrick Glaessner,

John Isaac Iselin, Phillipe and Julien Mark, Jason and Jenica Rosenberg,

and for many wonderful, healthy babies to come

Contents

Acknowledgments

Fred Plotkin is grateful to Sylvia and Louis Roth, Anthony Pell and Andrei Mark, each in his or her way a modern Medici who made it possible for a writer to write. Thanks to all of them for their caring love and support. And to Bernice and Edward, my parents, whose rendezvous with St. Anthony of Padua in the Adirondacks made me what I am today.

Dana Cernea thanks her husband, Dr. Eric Sichel, and her family, whose support and encouragement were invaluable during the writing of this book. Dr. Judy Gershowitz and partners and Dr. Steven Kandell and staff at the Beth Israel Medical Center in New York all were involved in another first edition, Sarah Rhoda, whose delivery coincided with that of this manuscript. Thanks also to Dr. Richard Schwarz and the attending staff at SUNY-Downstate Medical Center, whose tutelage led to the making of a physician.

Both authors are grateful to Erica Marcus, our wise and patient editor, and David Black, our equally wise and patient agent. Each provided healthy amounts of salt and pepper to our lives and our work. Thanks also to Etya Pinker, Renana Meyers, Pam Stinson, Kay Schuckhart, Beverly Paris, Cynthia Clark, and Zeil Rosenberg for their valuable assistance during the writing of this book.

Introduction

*T*hroughout human history, some of the most ardent dreams and wishes of men and women have involved the birth of a child. The idea of creation, whether in nature or in religion, is connected with thoughts of renewal and, therefore, with hope. In olden days, pregnancy was often surrounded with mystery, superstition, and a great deal of misinformation. The so-called miracle of birth was wondrous because people knew so little about how it happened.

Nowadays, despite all of the knowledge and sophistication we have about conception and birth, there is still a miraculousness and a wonderment that comes with the birth of each child. Many people now plan when to conceive (and some others go through costly, emotionally trying procedures as they struggle to conceive), so the arrival of the child is an event its parents have eagerly anticipated. Although many other pregnancies are not planned, for a lot of these prospective parents the birth of a new baby is also a source of joy. No matter what the circumstances are that attend the conception of a fetus, if a woman chooses to continue the pregnancy, she will need to make certain adjustments in her life to give every opportunity for the fetus to develop into a healthy, bouncing baby.

The first is to find a medical professional who will take care of her and her growing fetus. Too many pregnant women do not see their doctors (or, if they prefer, midwives) on a regular basis, which means that certain typical minor conditions of pregnancy, when left unattended, may develop into serious complications that can affect the health of mother and fetus.

Mothers-to-be need to make other adjustments in their lives, ensuring that particular needs are met, while they still try to lead lives as full and productive as before they became pregnant. For example, snack and rest times must be worked into a daily schedule, whether a woman is at home caring for other children and relatives or whether she must meet the demands of a job. Her social life can be as rich as before, but she might choose, in her later months, to select activities that are less taxing. Similarly, in most cases, being pregnant does not mean giving up exercise and sports, although certain modifications might be in order for pregnant skydivers, scuba divers, and bungee jumpers.

The area in which a woman can exert the most influence over the outcome of her pregnancy is nutrition. The old aphorism "You are what you eat" is especially apt when one thinks of "building" a baby in a mother's womb. In fact, the human organism is a remarkable amalgamation of minerals and chemical substances. When we think of vitamin C (which is essential for many life functions), we do not think of it as ascorbic *acid*. When we look at a piece of copper or zinc, we seldom think of them as substances required for cellular functioning. Water, which is the basic fluid in our blood and cells, is really only a combination of two parts hydrogen to one part oxygen. Yet we could not exist without it.

Throughout the course of her pregnancy (and even before conception, if she plans ahead), a woman can improve her chances of having a healthy baby if she eats correctly. Most women hear their doctors, on the first prenatal visit, say, "Be sure to eat right now because you're eating for two." The problem is that most women—and some doctors—don't know what "eating right" means during pregnancy. Even the many doctors who know about nutrition during pregnancy don't always have the time to dispense this information to each woman when they have a waiting room full of expectant mothers.

Thus came the idea for *Eating Healthy for a Healthy Baby*. By drawing on the combined knowledge of an experienced food writer and a busy physician, readers of this book can learn to eat happily and well while they are expecting and be confident that they are providing optimal nutrition for their fetuses. It is also generally accepted in the 1990s that a woman can, through correct eating, minimize and perhaps remedy many of the typical conditions and complications of pregnancy. For example, numerous studies have shown that women who regularly consume folate (a B vitamin) before and during their pregnancies are much more likely to deliver babies without neurological problems than women who are deficient in folate.

Readers of this book (pregnant women and those who love them) should be sure to read the first chapters about nutrition and pregnancy and about what happens during the nine months before a baby is born. A better understanding of how a fetus develops and what a mother experiences during that period will enable you to make the right choices about your diet. Also, you should take the time to read about conditions and complications of pregnancy (and how changes in what you eat may alleviate these conditions). You will also learn about coping with life-style changes during pregnancy and how to be a pregnant gourmet. Don't forget: Just because you might have to eat different foods, this doesn't mean you can't eat well!

The recipes in this book have been designed to meet the physical as well as nutritional needs of a pregnant woman. By this we mean that you will find very few dishes that require significant bending, lifting, or standing for hours at the stove. This is because the man on this team secured a large pillow at his midsection while devising these recipes so he could have some sense of the changes in gravity and posture that occur when a woman is pregnant. Later on, the woman on this team cooked and ate many of these dishes when she became pregnant. The result was nine months of happy eating and a beautiful baby girl weighing more than eight pounds.

We encourage you to select recipes from all chapters of this book to provide you and your fetus the widest range of nutrients. There is no one simple way to optimal nutrition. This book offers you a wide range of choices to suit your own tastes. Accompanying each recipe is a Doctor's Note that will give you more details about the nutritional content of the food you are eating. Therefore, if you know that you need, for example, to increase your intake of vitamin C or decrease your intake of carbohydrates, you can choose the recipes accordingly.

Finally, you must remember that just as every baby is different and special, so is every pregnancy. In fact, each time the same woman becomes pregnant, it is different and new. Your particular experience will be unique and precious, something you will vividly remember as you hold your child and, for that matter, your grandchild. Therefore, in spite of all the collected wisdom that has come down from centuries of childbearing, *the wisdom that counts most is that of your doctor and of your own good sense.* You should visit your doctor as scheduled, assiduously follow his or her advice, and always ask questions if something is unclear or seems wrong. Share the experience of pregnancy with your child's father; with your other children; and with your parents, siblings, friends, and loved ones. Feel free to seek their support when you need it, and try to be less concerned about being the model friend and relative. Pregnancy is a special time, and you have the right to certain indulgences.

Despite all the technical and clinical information that modern science can make available to you, there is a unique feeling that will sometimes overtake you, when you least expect it; this is also part of having a baby. Science can explain to you what is taking place *physically* during pregnancy, but there is that very special place in the human heart and mind, a place that is not fully captured by any scientific explanation, that gives you a different, equally important, kind of understanding. You will know it when you feel it. It is the joy of motherhood.

That is what this book is about.

Working with Your Doctor

The fact that you purchased this book indicates that you are interested in taking charge of your pregnancy. You will make one step toward your goal by eating right before, during, and after your pregnancy. This book will help you to do this. To have a healthy baby it is crucial to work closely with your doctor. We would like to explore with you how this is done, but first a couple of points:

• Sometimes we refer to your doctor as "he" or "him," other times as "she" or "her." Occasionally, we refer to both genders. This is because of the happy fact that there are talented men *and* women for mothers-to-be to consult about their medical needs. It can be cumbersome in a sentence to always refer to your doctor as "him or her" or "he or she," but we want you to know that there are wonderful female and male doctors. You should select that person with whom you feel most comfortable.

• About the word *doctor*: We might also use the terms *practitioner* or *medical professional*. These are more encompassing, but they may not always accurately convey what we mean. There are people whom you may consult during your pregnancy who are not necessarily doctors. Therefore, in this chapter we will use the term *practitioner* to discuss the various medical professionals pregnant women may visit, but in the rest of the book, the term *doctor* will usually stand for the person who is the primary practitioner for your prenatal care and delivery.

Types of Practitioners

The most familiar type of practitioner for the woman who is going to have a baby is the **obstetrician/gynecologist,** often simply called the ob/gyn. The ob/gyn has board certification in this specialty by the American College of Obstetricians and Gynecologists (ACOG). An ob/gyn is the best choice if you have or expect to have any particular complications of pregnancy (see chapter 4). These might include chronic health problems such as diabetes or a family history of other illnesses. Ob/gyns are specially trained to deal with complications that may arise during your pregnancy. They have admitting privileges at local hospitals and are licensed to perform cesarean sections when necessary. If you choose to use an ob/gyn and do not have a personal recommendation from your personal physician or a friend who was satisfied with her ob/gyn, contact the American College of Obstetricians and Gynecologists, 409 Twelfth Street SW, Washington, DC 20024 (telephone 202-638-5577).

The second type of practitioner is your **family physician,** some of whom provide prenatal care and deliver babies. The advantage here is that he or she knows your medical history and you presumably already have a relationship. The family physician may also have admitting privileges at a hospital and may have an ob/gyn as a back-up if complications arise. Your family physician will also be there after delivery to care for you and your baby. Many women enjoy the continuity that a family physician provides.

The third type of practitioner is the **certified nurse-midwife** (CNM). The CNM is often preferred by women who do not seem likely to have particular complications of pregnancy and want the welcoming, homelike nonhospital setting that a CNM can provide. They work in homes and in birthing centers and often practice what is called "natural childbirth." CNMs offer classes in labor techniques and baby care, emotional support, and often, a particular sensitivity to the pregnant woman's feelings.

CNMs are an enormous help but sometimes not a complete substitute for a physician. If a woman develops complications during her second or third trimesters, she will be referred to an ob/gyn who will be new to her case. Similarly, if complications occur during delivery, the woman then has to be transferred to a hospital, where she will be placed in the care of a doctor she doesn't know and who doesn't know her history.

Selecting a Practitioner

The best way to choose a practitioner is by seeking advice and recommendations from people you trust. Mother, sisters, and friends who have had babies are all good choices. Your family physician should also be consulted, because she or he knows your medical history and can offer valuable guidance. If your family physician suggests that she or he be the practitioner for your pregnancy and you have any reservations, don't hesitate to seek a second opinion and outside counsel.

In selecting a practitioner you must decide whether you want someone who works alone or is part of a group practice. The advantage of selecting a single practitioner is that you will develop a strong relationship with one person. The disadvantage is that this person may not always be available when needed. He or she may be seeing other patients when you have a question, may be out of town or, for that matter, may be delivering someone else's baby when you go into labor.

If you choose a group practice, you are more assured that there will be someone there when you have a need. The disadvantage is that you must take time to develop a relationship with several doctors.

Some pregnant women need the services of special practitioners such as obstetrical endocrinologists and geneticists. These practitioners will be recommended to you by the doctor who is managing your pregnancy.

While we are on the subject of practitioners, we strongly encourage you to take time during your pregnancy to select the **pediatrician** who will care for your baby after it is born. This is the person with whom you will discuss breastfeeding and other types of infant-feeding issues. Your pediatrician can also provide you with information that is not part of the expertise of the practitioner who is responsible for your prenatal care.

Many pregnant women do not realize that the pediatrician they have chosen is not the person who will care for their newborn babies in the hospital. In most cases, hospitals have **neonatologists** (doctors specializing in the care of newborns) on staff.

Your doctor is the person who best knows your case and your particular medical condition. This book is intended to provide background to you, answering many questions you may have about nutrition and pregnancy and giving you hours of eating pleasure. This knowledge will help you take charge of your pregnancy, but you should *use this information in tandem with regular visits to your doctor.*

We cannot emphasize enough how important early and regular visits to your doctor and the careful following of his or her advice are to having a healthy baby.

We also urge you to read the following suggestions and take them to heart.

Once You Have Chosen Your Doctor

- Every pregnancy is unique. This book provides the best and most up-to-date general advice on nutrition and pregnancy plus delicious recipes that you will continue to enjoy long after your baby is born. Yet there may be issues and topics specific to you that we do not cover. While no advice we offer can harm you, it cannot replace the guidance that your own doctor can provide to your case.

- Before calling or visiting your doctor, reread the sections of this book that address issues that concern you. We may likely answer questions to your satisfaction. If you want further information, *write your questions down* and take them with you on your next visit to your doctor.

- Doctors differ in style of practice, philosophy, and the advice they give. Issues such as modes of delivery and whether or not to breastfeed are approached differently by different practitioners. If, for example, your doctor's advice differs from ours, ask him or her about these differences. In most cases, your doctor will be giving you the best suggestions for your needs, and that is the advice to follow. If you have doubts, do not hesitate to seek other opinions from competent professionals so that you may make an informed decision.

- Whomever you choose as your practitioner, remember that you are an equal partner in decision making. This book and books about other topics in pregnancy will help you make informed decisions.

PART ONE

Nutrition in Pregnancy

1

One of the first things everyone will say to you when they learn you are going to have a baby is that "it's time to eat right because you're eating for two now." Yet if you were to ask these people what "eating right" means, they would have difficulty telling you. They may have a little bit of knowledge about food groups but will not be well versed in what a healthy person's daily requirements are. And, of course, when you are eating for two, your nutrient requirements are different from when you are eating for one.

Even if your doctor knows about correct nutrition in pregnancy, he or she will probably not have the time to discuss it with you in any detail. Because proper eating is one of the most important things you can do to have a healthy baby, you need to devote time to learning about nutrition as it relates to pregnancy.

What Food Is Made Of

You may not realize, when you look at a beautiful ripe peach, a fragrant loaf of bread, or a wedge of nutty Parmesan cheese, that food is composed of many chemical compounds that nutritionists place in several categories: carbohydrates (simple and complex), fats, proteins, vitamins, minerals, trace elements, and so on. The human body is also made of these materials and requires a constant replenishment of them to stay healthy. When a woman is pregnant, she shares what she eats with her growing fetus. These chemical compounds (or *nutrients*) provide energy and are the building blocks that make the cells, tissue, fiber, muscle, bone, and organs that form a baby.

Every person needs certain nutrients for energy (carbohydrates, fat, and some protein) and others for growth and well-being (protein, vitamins, minerals, and trace elements).

When nutritional scientists talk about how many nutrients a person needs each day, they use the term *RDA*. This stands for Recommended Daily Allowance or Recommended Dietary Allowance. For the purposes of this book, we can use these two interchangeably. In the United States, RDAs are determined by the National Research Council of the National Academy of Sciences and are carefully researched to reflect the needs of the *average* American. In this book, we are using the 1989 RDA figures (the most recent figures compiled)

It is most important to realize that RDAs vary according to the needs of different groups. For example, women may require more iron than men, the elderly may need a particular nutrient in greater amounts than do babies, and so on. Other variables include weight, body size, climate, metabolism, and how much physical activity a person engages in.

RDAs for pregnant and lactating (producing breast milk) women are different from other RDAs. As a reader of this book, you need to know what the RDAs are for pregnant women and, if you decide to breastfeed, for lactating women. But first you need to learn about the nutrients and how the body uses them.

For every type of nutrient that we discuss in this chapter, we will start by telling you what the RDA is for pregnant and lactating women. In a few cases, no RDA has yet been established, so we will provide you with the most up-to-date medical and nutritional information about how much of this particular nutrient you should have each day. You will notice various types of measurements for different nutrients. Here is a short list of what they are.

UNIT OF ENERGY
- kcal = kilocalorie(s) (1 kilocalorie = 1000 calories)

UNITS OF WEIGHT
- g = gram(s)
- mg = milligram(s) (1000 milligrams = 1 gram)
- mcg = microgram(s) (1000 micrograms = 1 milligram)

UNIT OF BIOLOGICAL POTENCY
- IU = international unit(s) (fat-soluble vitamins)

There is no need to be concerned or confused by the fact that different nutrients are measured with different types of measurements. Your only objective is to get the amount that you need, which you will do if you follow the dietary recommendations we make and those made by your doctor.

After learning the RDA for a particular nutrient, you need to know what foods are the best sources of these nutrients. We list first the foods that are richest in a particular nutrient. In the case of every food mentioned, you should assume that an *average-size portion* will provide you with a goodly amount of the nutrient in question (generally, at least one-quarter to one third of your RDA). Because the notion of what constitutes an average-size portion varies from food to food, you may assume that it is within the range of normal eating: one apple, one potato, one chicken breast, one 6- to 8 ounce glass of milk or juice, and so forth.

We encourage you to eat a balanced diet with a great variety of foods: A nutrient may exist in several foods and the combined intake will supply you with what you need. However, if you need to get more of a particular nutrient (iron, for example), check the listing for that nutrient in this chapter and focus on foods that contain it. If there is a particular food that is a wonderful source of a nutrient, we will tell you.

Following the food sources of a particular nutrient we will present the reasons why you and your baby need this nutrient. Then, for some nutrients, we provide a cautionary word about how a too large or too small dose may affect you and your baby.

There are three types of nutrients that the body uses as sources of energy: **carbohydrates, fat,** and **proteins.** These are quantified in two ways: the number of grams (g) that are consumed and the number of calories these nutrients provide. There are average recommendations for intakes of carbohydrates and fat, and there is an RDA for proteins.

The Department of Energy

We will examine carbohydrates, fat, and proteins individually, but first it is important to define what we mean by energy. Think of your body as a marvelously designed machine that needs fuel to make it run efficiently. This fuel is energy, which is customarily measured in calories. So the first thing you must do is forget the idea that calories are bad for you. *Every body needs calories to function* .

How many calories a person needs depends on several factors:

•*Age.* Children need extra energy to grow. Young adults who are active need sufficient energy to support their activity. Older, more sedentary adults need fewer calories.
•*Gender.* Depending on their activities, men and women have greater or lesser energy needs. Women usually have more energy-containing fat tissue than men, so their intake needs are usually less than those of men. Pregnant and lactating women are a special group with special needs that we will address.
•*Body Size.* A larger body (or machine) needs more energy to power it.
•*Climate.* The body expends energy to maintain a regular temperature. If the weather is particularly hot or cold, the body will use energy to stay at an average of 98.6° F (37.1° C).
•*Physical Activity.* A person who exercises regularly or one who engages in work requiring strenuous manual labor or ongoing movement or activity will burn up calories more rapidly than a sedentary person.

The *average* daily calorie requirements for a woman of childbearing age is 2200 calories a day. This varies somewhat according to some of the factors listed above, but if you are of average size and weight and engage in a moderate amount of physical activity, this is an accurate figure for you.

HOW MANY CALORIES DO I NEED?

Pregnant women's calorie needs are different, because energy is required to build and feed a baby in the womb and to deliver it. Calorie needs are also increased for women who breastfeed their infant. The typical pregnant and lactating woman's needs are

First trimester: 2200–2500 calories per day
Second trimester: 2500–2800 calories per day
Third trimester: 2700–2800 calories per day
Lactation: 2700–2800 calories per day

The extra calories are stored in a pregnant woman's body as fat for use later in the pregnancy and for lactation. During the fourth month, the fetus begins to grow more rapidly and additional energy is required for this process. From this point forward, the typical pregnant woman gains about 1 pound a week. Proper weight gain is normal, important, and healthy during pregnancy, and you should do everything you can to encourage it. The most important point to remember is that *your weight gain must come from healthy eating*. So-called empty calories from cookies and ice cream are not going to do you or your baby any good.

- There are 4 calories for every gram of carbohydrate and protein.
- There are 9 calories for every gram of fat.

WHERE SHOULD MY CALORIES COME FROM?

Here are some rules of thumb that apply to all people:

- Between 55 and 60% of calories should come from carbohydrates (of which one-third should be simple carbohydrates [sugars] and two-thirds should be complex carbohydrates [starches and fiber]).
- A maximum of 30% of calories should come from fat.
- Between 10 and 15% of calories should come from protein.

These proportions are quite important, because all three calorie sources work together to promote good health and, in a pregnant woman, the normal development of her fetus. Let us examine each energy source individually.

Carbohydrates

Somewhere along the line carbohydrates acquired an undeservedly bad reputation among people who thought of themselves as health conscious. In fact, foods that are rich in carbohydrates provide essential energy for the body. As with any nutrient, carbohydrates are bad only if you consume too many or not enough of them.

There are two types of carbohydrates: simple and complex. Simple carbohydrates, also called monosaccharides, are derived from sugar. We think of sugar as coming only in cubes or granules, but it also exists in many fruits and fruit juices, honey, milk, and in many commercially prepared and processed foods. If you read a food label and see a word ending in -ose (such as glucose, sucrose, fructose, and lactose), in most cases that is a sugar. Because fruit and milk contain other important nutrients, you should get your daily supply of sugar from these foods instead of cookies, cakes, ice cream, candy, and other processed foods.

Complex carbohydrates (polysaccharides) come from foods of plant origin: grains, cereals, corn, potatoes, peas, beans, nuts, and seeds. These foods also contain many of the vitamins and minerals listed below and are central to any well-balanced diet. Many complex carbohydrate foods are rich in dietary fiber (also called roughage), which adds bulk to the stool in your intestine and promotes regularity. Because constipation is a typical condition of pregnancy, it is very important for you to get ample dietary fiber.

Both simple and complex carbohydrates convert in your system to a sugar called glucose, which is stored in your liver. Your pancreas produces a hormone called insulin, which helps convert glucose into energy (measured in calories). During pregnancy, the average daily need for glucose is between 60 and 65 g.

If your pancreas does not produce as much insulin as is needed, not enough glucose can be "burned" to create energy. In the case of some diabetics, the body tissues do not use insulin correctly and an excess of glucose circulates in the blood. When either situation occurs in pregnancy, it is called **gestational diabetes** and occurs during the latter stages of pregnancy in about 30% of women. Do not confuse gestational diabetes with regular diabetes (diabetes mellitus)! *They are two different conditions.* Gestational diabetes disappears soon after delivery in most cases. Read all about gestational diabetes on page 61.

Fats (Lipids)

Just the sound of the word *fat* makes many people recoil in horror. Fat conjures up images of obesity and clogged arteries. But that is not an entirely accurate picture. Every person needs some fat (*lipids* is the more technical and genteel term) to provide energy and warmth. In addition, fat transports fat-soluble vitamins (see page 10) into your body through your digestive tract. Because fat contains more than twice as many calories per gram as do carbohydrates and proteins, it is much easier to put on weight with a high-fat diet than with one rich in carbohydrates and proteins. As with all nutrients, when fat is consumed in recommended amounts (no more than 30% of total calories), it plays an important role in your baby's development.

There are two types of fats: saturated and unsaturated. In both cases, 1 tablespoon of fat contains about 120 calories. Saturated fats usually come from animal products (beef, organ meats, eggs, and whole-milk dairy products are major sources) and should be consumed in moderation. Sour cream, ice cream, and mayonnaise are very high in saturated fats and should be had only once in a great while.

The polyunsaturated fats that come in vegetable oils (such as olive and corn oils) are healthier. These contain linoleic acid, which is essential for growth and for maintaining cell structure. Certain vitamins (A, D, and E), known as fat-soluble vitamins, are carried through the bloodstream by fat. Other vitamins are transported throught the bloodstream by water. Polyunsaturated fats are the best conductors of fat-soluble vitamins. You might also come across something called hydrogenated vegetable fat, which is used in commercial baking and in many processed foods. It is not good for you, and in prepared foods, it is frequently accompanied by unhealthy preservatives. So read food labels carefully and avoid hydrogentated vegetable fat.

Nature has devised ingenious ways for pregnant women to use fat. In the early stages of pregnancy, the hormones estrogen and progesterone promote storage of fat in tissues for later use. If there is a shortage of glucose during the second and third trimesters (because much of it is diverted to the growing fetus), the fat stores will be called on to provide energy to the mother and, if necessary, to the fetus.

Needless to say, pregnancy is not a time to diet. Do not be upset if your doctor continues to urge you to gain weight throughout your pregnancy. Fat stores are required to produce milk for breastfeeding and to provide energy to you and your newborn. If you are breastfeeding, you will be pleased to see that you will lose weight naturally as these fat stores are used.

The RDA for protein for pregnant women is 60 g and for lactating women, 65 g. Your best sources are animal proteins that are relatively low in fat. These include lean meat, poultry, most fish, skim milk, and cheese made from skim milk.

Proteins

Proteins are made of small molecules known as amino acids. There are twenty different amino acids, all of which are crucial for development and well-being. You should think of amino acids as the building blocks necessary to make cells and tissues. Not all protein sources contain every amino acid. Proteins from animal sources are often called complete proteins because they contain all or nearly all of the different amino acids.

Protein can also provide energy. It is for this reason that it is especially important during pregnancy to consume sufficient amounts of carbohydrates and fat. If you do not, the energy your body needs will be drawn from protein, which means that there will not be enough of it available to do the necessary building of cells and tissue to make a healthy baby.

Protein consumption must be part of a balanced diet. Women who consume high-protein, low-calorie diets have a higher probability of delivering a low-birth-weight baby that might is more likely to face increased health problems in life. Remember, pregnancy is not a time to diet.

It is important to start consuming protein and calories as soon as you plan to become pregnant. If you unexpectedly learn that you are pregnant, immediately start on a balanced diet rich in protein. It is needed throughout pregnancy not only for your baby but for tissue growth in your breasts and uterus (which expands to accommodate the growing fetus), and for feeding the fetus.

Vegetarians have a much harder time meeting their protein needs than meat eaters. Vegetarians who eat eggs and dairy products still can easily consume sufficient protein each day—for example, 10 ounces of cottage cheese contain 41 g of protein. Otherwise, the highest amount of protein comes from tofu and other soy products, wheat germ, nuts and seeds, beans and legumes, lentils, tahini, whole wheat and enriched pasta, potatoes, and broccoli. Rice and beans are a popular combination in many cuisines. Beans give the eater a good helping of protein.

A pregnant woman experiencing morning sickness during her first trimester may not be motivated to eat during this crucial period in her baby's development. If this is you, try to find protein-rich foods that do not upset your stomach too much. These might include peanut butter, drained water-packed tuna, nuts and seeds, and perhaps, certain dairy products such as hard cheese.

In the latter stages of pregnancy, when the fetus's muscles and internal organs grow, protein continues to be essential. You need to increase protein consumption at the end of your pregnancy and during lactation, because you will be supplying your baby's protein needs in addition to meeting your own.

Vitamins

Vitamins are substances that work in tandem with other nutrients to promote cell growth and functioning. To understand vitamins it is necessary to know the differences between fat-soluble and water-soluble vitamins.

- Fat-soluble vitamins (which include A, D, E, and K) can be dissolved in fat and thus can be stored in the body (more precisely, in the liver). Vitamins A and D can be toxic when taken in very large doses, so it is important to be aware of the RDAs for these two vitamins.
- Water-soluble vitamins (all the B vitamins plus C) dissolve in water and, therefore, cannot be stored in the body. Your body uses the amount of water-soluble vitamins it requires each day and eliminates the rest. Thus you must have daily doses of water-soluble vitamins to keep yourself well supplied.

Vitamins of all types are essential for everyone's good health. Total deprivation or overdosing of certain vitamins can lead to health problems for mother and fetus. For example, vitamin A helps form and maintain healthy skin, hair, and mucous membranes. It is considered essential in maintaining good eyesight, for cell and bone growth, and for general reproductive health. Insufficient vitamin A in someone's diet could result in problems in these crucial areas.

Pregnant women, like everyone else, need vitamins for their own health and well-being. But they have greater vitamin requirements than do other people, because vitamins are essential in the development of the embryo into a fetus and finally into a healthy baby. *All of the requirements (RDAs) we indicate are for pregnant women unless we tell you otherwise.* Where appropriate, we also indicate the RDAs for women who are breastfeeding.

The best way to get vitamins is to eat foods that contain them naturally. During processing of food, naturally occurring vitamins are often destroyed. To make up for this, synthetically produced vitamins are added to the food. The result is called fortified or enriched food. If you could choose between vitamin-loaded wheat germ and a vitamin-fortified or enriched cereal, you would do better by eating the wheat germ. But don't be put off by the notion of "synthetically produced" or "added" vitamins. Milk, orange juice, and margerine are all customarily fortified with vitamins, and you should have no qualms about consuming these foods.

As a general rule, foods in their natural state (such as raw fruits and vegetables, fresh meat and fish, and unprocessed grains) will deliver more vitamins than foods that are canned, frozen, cured, or overcooked. We have emphasized recipes that use raw fruits and vegetables and gently cooked grains and meat so that you will get as much vitamin benefit as possible from every meal.

Exposure to light and air kills vitamins in food. The best way to preserve vitamins in fresh food is to store the food in tightly closed plastic containers or dark glass jars. Of course, the fresher the food is when you purchase it and eat it, the more vitamins and nutrients you will consume. Another hint is not to cut food until you are ready to eat it. If, for example, you chop vegetables for crudités, try not to keep them too long before serving. If you must store them, put them in a plastic container that can be tightly closed. Many people store cut vegetables in water for an extended period of time. This is a mistake: The water drains many of the nutrients out of the food.

Before looking at each vitamin, we must make an important detour into the subject of **vitamin tablets.** In more technical jargon, these are referred to as *vitamin supplements* or simply *supplements* and the giving or taking of these is referred to as *supplementation.*

Whether it is a regular-looking pill or shaped like Fred Flintstone, the typical daily multivitamin that many people take is sufficient for meeting most RDAs. As you have just learned, these RDAs are *not* sufficient for the pregnant woman. For that reason, *many doctors prescribe supplements specially formulated for pregnancy.* These so-called prenatal supplements contain higher doses of certain vitamins and minerals to meet the needs of you and Junior. Prenatal supplements are closely monitored for quality by the U.S. Food and Drug Administration (FDA). Even though prenatal supplements are more expensive than regular vitamins, they contain nutrients in the exact amounts you need. More important, they don't contain certain elements other vitamins have—dyes and colorants, for example—that could be harmful to your fetus.

You should speak with you doctor as soon as you *plan* to become pregnant. You might be advised to start supplementation before conception to prepare your body for pregnancy. If you become pregnant in a less premeditated way, speak to your doctor about supplementation on your first visit. Some women, on their practitioner's recommendation, continue supplementation during breastfeeding.

Please be aware that *supplementation is not a replacement for healthy eating.* You should devote yourself to meeting your vitamin requirements through good eating. Supplements are important if you have particular deficiencies or if you began your pregnancy in less than perfect nutritional shape. For example, many American women are deficient in iron and folate on a chronic basis. Supplements also will see you through days when morning sickness or a hectic schedule prevent you from getting all the nutrients you need. You should not be concerned about overdosing if you are eating ideally and taking supplements. The threshold for an overdose is much higher than anything you would approach in normal eating and daily supplementation.

Supplements should not be taken at mealtime. This way the vitamins will enter your system more quickly, because the supplement will not be mixed with food in a full stomach. An important rule is to not combine supplements with roughage and high-fiber foods. These absorb the vitamins and carry them out of your system before they can be put to good use. Many women take their supplement before going to sleep each evening.

Now let's take a look at each vitamin individually, in alphabetical order.

Vitamin A is a fat-soluble vitamin. The RDA for pregnant women is between 4000 and 5000 international units (IU). The RDA for lactating women is 6500 IU for the first 6 months of lactation and 6000 IU afterward.

Sources: Liver is a superb source of vitamin A, so if you like liver, this is the food to eat. *There are 43,900 IU of vitamin A in 3½ ounces of liver!* Other great sources are fish oil; butter; egg; spinach (7,300 IU in ½ cup cooked), kale and other leafy greens; orange and yellow vegetables such as carrot (11,000 IU in one carrot), squash, sweet potato, pumpkin, and turnip; sweet red pepper; oatmeal and other whole grains; wheat germ; and orange fruits such as cantaloupe (3,400 IU in one-quarter melon), mango, and dried apricot (5,500 IU in eight large halves). You will find several recipes in this book that feature dried apricots. They are a great snack whether cooked or eaten as is.

Why you need vitamin A: This vitamin is crucial for vision and essential life functions of cell development, bone growth and development of immunities to illnesses. During pregnancy, vitamin A is especially important during the third month, when cell growth in the womb is at its highest rate. Pregnant women who are deficient in vitamin A sometimes deliver prematurely or have babies that are smaller in size and weight than normal. While complete deficiency of vitamin A is rare, even a partial deficiency can result in less-than-optimal prenatal growth.

Caution: Vitamin A can be toxic in very high doses. It is believed that prolonged daily consumption of more than 50,000 IU may lead to medical problems. Overdoses may result in liver enlargement, bone fragility, yellow skin, and some birth defects. However, you should not worry if you have a meal of liver and spinach with cantaloupe for dessert. This is a healthy meal that will do you good as long as you don't eat it every day. If you consume vitamin A as part of a balanced diet and in your prenatal supplement, but do not take additional vitamin A tablets, you have nothing to worry about.

VITAMIN A
(ALSO KNOWN TO AS
RETINAL, RETINOL, OR
BETA-CAROTENE)

Special Medical Note: Vitamin A in cream form has become a popular medication for skin problems. None that you can purchase without a prescription has been shown to cause any problems during pregnancy. However, a synthetic copy of vitamin A (retinol) is marketed as a drug called Acutane and is often prescribed for certain forms of acne. Acutane is one of the most teratogenic (damaging to a fetus) drugs that exists. It has been linked to birth defects and a high incidence of spontaneous abortion. If you use Acutane or routinely self-medicate with large amounts of vitamin A, you should consult your doctor before you plan to become pregnant. *If you discover unexpectedly that you are pregnant, immediately stop using Acutane and taking vitamin A tablets.*

B VITAMINS

There are thirteen B vitamins, all of which are water soluble. Many of them are found in the same foods, especially meat and grains. One excellent source of the B vitamins is brewer's yeast. It is an acquired taste, but is almost unrivaled if you need to improve your intake of B vitamins. The typical American diet provides most of the B vitamins we need. There are, however, particular B vitamins that are of paramount importance in particular stages of pregnancy, and these are the ones we will take a look at.

Vitamin B_1 (also known as thiamine)

The RDA for vitamin B_1 pregnant women is 1.5 mg. The RDA for lactating women is 1.6 mg.

Sources: Oatmeal, wheat germ (0.44 mg in ¼ cup), fortfied breads, pastas, and cereals; liver, fresh ham (0.40 mg in 3 ounces), pork; peas; peanuts and Brazil nuts; raisins; and soy milk.

Why you need vitamin B_1: It helps release energy from carbohydrates. An active person with a high carbohydrate intake (such as an athlete) might require more than the usual RDA of vitamin B1. It also helps in the normal functioning of the nervous system. This vitamin is essential for the heart functioning of a newborn baby.

Caution: Vitamin B_1 has been known to cause allergic reactions in a few people. If you think you might be allergic (for example, if you a person who already is allergic to various substances), ask your doctor. Persons who consume large amounts of alcohol often become deficient in B_1. You should devote yourself to reducing or eliminating intake of alcohol during pregnancy (see page 77), but if you have a history of heavy alcohol consumption, talk to your doctor about taking extra vitamin B_1. It is not considered toxic if taken in doses even as great as ten times the RDA, because the body does not efficiently store this vitamin. However, taking such large doses is wasteful, as your body will eliminate most of it.

Vitamin B_2 (also known as Riboflavin)

The RDA for vitamin B_2 for pregnant women is 1.5 mg. The RDA for lactating women is 1.7 mg.

Sources: The best source is liver (0.63 mg in 3 ounces). You may also choose low-fat milk (0.52 mg in 1 cup), yogurt (0.39 mg in 1 cup), cottage cheese, egg, chicken (0.16 mg in 3 ounces), fortified cereals, greens, beans, mushrooms and peas.

Why you need Vitamin B_2: This vitamin helps release energy from proteins, fats, and carbohydrates. It also is important in brain functioning. A deficiency in the fetus may result in poor skeletal development and bone formation. A deficiency in the mother may cause mouth sores and poor appetite.

Niacin (also known as nicotinic acid, or niacinamide)

For some reason this B vitamin never appears with a number attached to it, but it is usually listed third among the B vitamins. The RDA for niacin for pregnant women is 17 mg. For lactating women it is 20 mg.

Sources: Chicken (21.5 mg in one-half breast); veal; liver; pork; lamb; mackerel; swordfish; salmon (9.6 mg in 3 ounces); peanuts and peanut butter (6.2 mg in 2 tablespoons); fortified or enriched breads, pastas, and cereals; and mushrooms.

Why you need niacin: It helps release energy from fats, carbohydrates, and proteins. It also has been shown to foster a healthy nervous system and gastrointestinal tract and good skin in both the mother and the newborn.

Caution: Very large doses of niacin may produce itchy or tingling skin, stomach problems, and low blood pressure. You should have no concern about overdosing on niacin if you have a normal diet and take prenatal supplements.

Vitamin B$_6$ (also known as pyridoxine, pyridox-amine, or pyridoxal)

The RDA for vitamin B$_6$ for pregnant women is 2.2 mg. For lactating women it is 2.1 mg. If you took birth control pills before deciding to conceive, your reserves of vitamin B$_6$ may have been depleted.

Sources: Banana (0.480 mg in one medium); avocado (0.420 mg in one-half medium); blackstrap molasses; wheat germ; brewer's yeast; brown rice; bran; soybean; oatmeal; fortified cereals, grains, and pastas; chicken (0.340 mg in 3 ounces); veal; lamb; organ meats; potato; tomato; and spinach.

Why you need vitamin B$_6$: To release energy in fats and, especially, to help the body use protein to build tissue. It is also essential in pregnancy in reducing the possibility of neural tube defects (see page 36). Its absence may result in skin problems for the newborn.

Folate (also known as folic acid or folacin)

The RDA for this B vitamin for pregnant women is 0.4 mg (or 400 mcg, as it is sometimes listed). For lactating women the RDA is 0.3 mg (300 mcg)

Sources: Brewer's yeast (313 mcg in 1 tablespoon), beef liver (123 mcg in 3 ounces), lentils, black-eyed peas, beans, peas, spinach (106 mcg in 1 cup raw; 82 mcg in ½ cup cooked); leafy greens (especially romaine lettuce), orange and grapefruit juices), and fortified grains and pastas.

Why you need folate: Extensive research has shown that folate is the key weapon that women have in minimizing the possibility of neural tube defects in their babies. (If you begin to take folate *before* you conceive, so much the better.) This subject is addressed fully on page 36. Folate has been shown to prevent premature delivery in many cases. It also helps the body form red blood cells, is used in cell division, and is important in the formation of genetic material within every cell.

Biotin (also known as vitamin B$_7$)

Although there is no RDA established for vitamin B$_7$ during pregnancy and lactation, the RDA for the general population is 0.3 mg (300 mcg). Perhaps a little more during pregnancy is advisable.

Sources: Liver (82 mcg in 3 ounces) and other organ meats; oatmeal (58 mcg in 1 cup cooked); enriched cereals, grains, and pastas; peanuts and other nuts; egg; soybeans (22 mcg in ½ cup cooked); mushrooms; peas; and cauliflower.

Why you need biotin: As with other B vitamins, biotin is important in releasing energy from fats, carbohydrates, and proteins.

The RDA for vitamin B_{12} for pregnant women is 2.2 mcg. The RDA for lactating women is 2.6 mcg.

Vitamin B_{12} (also known as cobalamin or cyanocobalamin)

Sources: Liver (68 mcg in 3 ounces), tongue, and other organ meats; lamb; beef; veal; tuna (2.64 mcg in 4 ounces); mackerel; salmon; trout; and other fish. It is available in lesser amounts in egg (0.95 mcg in 1 cup), milk, cheese, yogurt (1.06 mcg in 1 cup), and brewer's yeast.

Why you need vitamin B_{12}: Vitamin B_{12} is important in the formation of red blood cells, for building genetic material, and for the proper functioning of the nervous system. It works in concert with folate to promote your baby's growth. Fetuses store little vitamin B_{12}, so that the mother should consume this vitamin regularly.

Caution: **Vitamin B_{12} is found almost exclusively in meat and dairy products. If you are a vegetarian who does not eat fish or dairy foods, your only potential source of the vitamin is in brewer's yeast. Ask your doctor if you should be given special vitamin B_{12} supplements to make up for the shortfall in your diet.**

There is no RDA for pantothenic acid, but the generally accepted daily intake is at least 7 mg; perhaps a little more is advisable during pregnancy.

Pantothenic Acid (also known as Vitamin B_5)

Sources: Liver (6.035 mg in 3 ounces), other organ meats, egg (1.1 mg in one medium), orange (0.450 mg in one medium); potato (0.400 mg in one medium), broccoli (0.315 mg in ½ cup cooked), whole grain cereals, beef, mushrooms, and leafy greens.

Why you need pantothenic acid: It helps break down fats, carbohydrates, and proteins, to release energy. It also stimulates wound healing.

Vitamin C is a water-soluble vitamin that plays an important role in the daily diet. The RDA for pregnant women is 70 mg. For lactating women, the RDA is 95 mg.

VITAMIN C (ALSO KNOWN AS ASCORBIC ACID)

Sources: Asparagus, broccoli (52 mg in ½ cup), Brussels sprouts (68 mg in ½ cup), raw cabbage, cauliflower, kale and other greens, parsley, red and green peppers, snow peas, sweet potato, tomato, watercress, apple, cantaloupe, cranberries, grapefruit, honeydew, kiwi, mango, orange (66 mg in ½ cup), papaya, peach, strawberries (66 mg in ½ cup), tangerine, and watermelon. It is also found in juices made of any of the above fruits and vegetables (6 ounces of orange juice has 90 mg). Foods containing vitamin C lose the vitamin easily, so they should be eaten raw or with minimal cooking and should be stored in airtight containers

Why you need vitamin C: Vitamin C is important throughout pregnancy. It helps produce collagen, the protein that gives structure to cartilage, muscles, blood vessels, and bones. This vitamin also helps in the absorption of iron and in resistance to infection. Because the body does not store vitamin C (remember, it's a water-soluble vitamin), it is necessary to consume the vitamin each day. It is particularly important in early pregnancy, when a severe deficiency may lead to spontaneous abortions. A deficiency of vitamin C later in pregnancy may lead to premature delivery. A large amount of vitamin C is customarily lost by the mother during delivery. Therefore, a diet with extra portions of food rich in vitamin C is beneficial a few days before childbirth and in the days after delivery.

VITAMIN D (ALSO KNOWN AS CALCIFEROL, CHOLECALCIFEROL, OR ERGOCALCIFEROL)

Vitamin D is fat soluble. The RDA for both pregnant and lactating women is 400 IU.

Sources: The best source of vitamin D is sunlight: The vitamin is in your system in an inactive form and is activated by exposure to ultraviolet rays. Even minimal exposure should provide a sufficient amount each day, so do not use your need for vitamin D as a justification for long exposure to the sun, which is unhealthy. Other good sources of vitamin D are canned sardines (1150 to 1570 IU in 3½ ounces); fresh mackerel (1100 IU in 3½ ounces), and fortified cereals, milk, and orange juice. Cod liver oil is also rich in vitamin D.

Why you need vitamin D: This vitamin's most important role in your health and that of your fetus is in the absorption of calcium, which is essential for bone and tissue growth and for teeth formation.

Caution: Vitamin D is abundant in the typical American diet and in your prenatatal supplements. There is no need to take additional vitamin D tablets. Average consumption of milk or orange juice along with a small amount of exposure to the sun should be sufficient.

VITAMIN E (ALSO KNOWN AS TOCOPHEROL):

Vitamin E is fat-soluble vitamin. The RDA for pregnant women is 10 mg (15 IU). For lactating, women, the RDA is 12 mg (18 IU) during the first 6 months and 11 mg (16.5) during the second 6 months.

Sources: Wheat germ oil (42.4 mg/63.6 IU per ¼ cup), sunflower oil, safflower oil, wheat germ, fortified cereals, spinach (2.2 mg/3.3 IU in ½ cup), asparagus, prunes (1.22 mg/1.85 IU in ten) almonds, hazelnuts, peanuts, peanut butter, and sunflower seeds.

Why you need vitamin E: Many premature babies are born with a deficiency of vitamin E. There are two reasons for this. The first is that many pregnant women do not have a sufficient intake of this vitamin. The second reason is that because fetuses acquire much of their vitamin E during the last two months of pregnancy, premature babies do not have as much opportunity to store up vitamin E as do those who are delivered at term. Babies who are deficient in vitamin E often have anemia, and some develop even more serious problems such as brain hemorrhages and a lung condition known as bronchopulmonary displasia. As a sort of insurance policy, newborn babies in the United States are routinely supplemented with vitamin E. This vitamin protects vitamin A and essential fatty acids from oxidation (spoilage when exposed to oxygen) in the cells and prevents their breakdown in tissues. A deficiency of vitamin E in adults has also been linked to sterility, but clearly that is not your problem.

VITAMIN K

The RDA for vitamin K in pregnancy and lactation is 65 mcg.

Sources: Vitamin K is produced in the small intestine of the healthy person in sufficient amounts. It is also abundant in broccoli (200 mcg in ⅔ cup), turnip greens (650 mcg in ⅔ cup), kale, and other leafy greens, which is yet another justification for eating a portion of these nutrient-laden vegetables each day. This vitamin is also found in oatmeal, whole wheat, bran, banana, liver, and pork.

Why you need vitamin K: Vitamin K is essential for blood clotting. It also helps prevent excess blood loss after injuries. Newborn babies are routinely supplemented with vitamin K until they start producing it on their own.

Caution: If you are taking antibiotics (prescribed by your doctor, of course), these sometimes inhibit the production of vitamin K, as the flora in your small intestine is altered. After your have completed your medication and are off the antibiotics, yogurt or acidopholus milk may help restore the fauna in your small intestine.

Minerals and Trace Elements

Back in high-school chemistry class we all were introduced to the periodic table of elements. This well-organized chart listed all of the minerals and elements found in the earth and in the atmosphere. Certain minerals and elements are essential to the health and well-being of humans. Some of these (oxygen, copper, iron, and zinc) are familiar to everyone. Others, such as magnesium and phosphorus, may be less well known but are equally important to life.

The term *trace element* may be new to you. These are minerals such as iodine, manganese, and zinc that are found in the human body in an amount of less than 1 teaspoon (so-called major minerals, such as calcium, potassium, and sodium, are found in the body in amounts greater than 1 teaspoon). Some trace elements can be produced by the human body in small amounts for use in various functions. Of course, these trace elements also are available in food and in supplements. Because deficiencies of trace elements are not detectable clinically, it is wise to take your daily prenatal supplement, which contains the trace elements you need.

Here are the minerals most important during pregnancy:

CALCIUM

The RDA for calcium is 1200 mg throughout pregnancy and lactation. You must concentrate on meeting these needs, because many women are deficient in calcium, especially during pregnancy. The average healthy nonpregnant woman has about 2 pounds of calcium in her body, 99% of which is in her bones and 1% is in her bloodstream and in other body fluids.

Sources: Dairy products make up 80% of the calcium sources in the typical American diet. Try nonfat milk (302 mg in 1 cup), buttermilk, uncreamed cottage cheese (146 mg in 1 cup), yogurt (415 mg in 1 cup), cheese, and nonfat dry milk solids (which you can toss into blender drinks and soups or use to enrich skim milk). Calcium may also be found in sesame seeds (329 mg in 1 ounce), tofu (154 mg in 1 pound), tahini, almonds, fortified orange juice, dried figs, parsley, leafy greens, sardines, and canned salmon with bones (167 mg in 3 ounces).

Why you need calcium: This is the most plentiful mineral in the body (and the fifth most abundant substance on earth after carbon, hydrogen, oxygen, and nitrogen). It is also one of the most important as it is essential for strong bones and teeth, muscle contraction, blood clotting, normal heart rhythm, and cell membranes. Recent studies suggest that calcium might play an important role in combatting preeclampsia, or hypertension, in pregnancy (see page 65). Calcium absorption can only happen when the body has sufficient vitamin D. This vitamin can be gotten in ample amounts from fortified milk and orange juice, supplementation, and minimal exposure to sunlight.

> *Caution:* The fetus's need for calcium continues to increase throughout pregnancy. A deficiency will have negative effects for both mother and fetus. Weak bones in the mother may lead to back pain, especially as she needs to support the weight of a growing fetus. If the fetus is deficient in calcium, it will result in a delayed calcification of its skeleton. Pregnant women who are severely deficient in calcium may develop tetany, a condition marked by increased sensitivity in the nerves, resulting in muscle spasms such as leg cramps.

During lactation (not during pregnancy), if sufficient calcium is not available through diet and supplementation, calcium is drawn from a mother's bones to meet the needs of her baby, which, in the long run, is not healthy for the mother. It will result in bone weakness and pain and increase the likelihood of fractures. A high calcium diet and supplementation is crucial to every woman during pregnancy and lactation.

COPPER The estimated daily requirement of copper, a trace element, for pregnant and lactating women is 2 mg.

Sources: Liver (2.4 mg in 3 ounces), lobster (2.45 mg in 1 cup), mushrooms, barley, dried beans, nuts, and seeds.

Why you need copper: Copper works in tandem with iron to form hemoglobin in the blood. A very severe deficiency of copper may result in infertility and, in pregnant women, to spontaneous abortions and stillbirths. You must meet your daily requirement to provide for yourself *and* for your fetus, which will store the amount it needs.

FLUORIDE   There is not an established RDA for flouride, a trace element, although 2 mg is the generally accepted figure.

Sources: Fluoride is routinely added to the water supply of most major cities and towns. The amount in tap water meets your daily need. Fluoride also exists naturally in water in smaller amounts, and it also appears in certain mineral supplements and is added to some brands of toothpaste. If your dentist does fluoride treatments, this is very good for you and your future baby. By the way, be sure to tell your dentist you are pregnant if you go to his or her office for a routine visit.

Why you need fluoride: Fluoride is thought to be the best prevention for tooth decay. It is also thought to be useful in strengthening bones, which makes it valuable in pregnancy.

IODINE   The RDA for iodine for pregnant women is 175 mcg; for lactating women the RDA is 200 mcg.

Sources: Seafood (we advise you not to eat *raw* seafood, which too frequently contains bacteria and toxins), iodized salt (salt to which iodine is added), and foods grown in iodine-rich soil. The typical American diet has sufficient iodine, but you may be assured that you are getting enough if it is part of your vitamin supplement.

Why you need iodine: Iodine is essential for proper functioning of the thyroid gland. This trace element, in the average woman, makes up a mere 20 to 30 mg of her body weight. About 60% of this iodine is in her thyroid gland; the rest is distributed throughout her body, especially in the ovaries, muscles, and blood. A deficiency of iodine during pregnancy may cause severe problems to the fetus, including goiter and endemic cretinism. Studies in animals have shown that an iodine deficiency may result in spontaneous abortions and stillbirths.

The RDA of iron for pregnant women is 30 mg. For lactating   IRON
women the RDA is 15 mg.

Sources: Sources of iron are divided into two categories: *heme*
and *nonheme.* Heme iron usually comes from animal products
(meat, poultry, eggs, and fish). Nonheme iron is derived from plant
products (grains, fruits, vegetables, nuts, and seeds). The body
absorbs heme iron much more efficiently than nonheme iron, so
you should focus on heme iron to fulfill your needs. Liver is the
best source available for iron (7.5 mg in 3 ounces cooked). If you
have been told that you need to increase your iron intake, make
yourself a portion of Chicken Livers (see page 202) or Meat Loaf
with Chicken Liver (see page 213). This latter recipe is for women
who don't like the taste of liver but need it in their diet. Iron is
absorbed better when accompanied by vitamin C. Serve liver or
other heme iron sources with a vegetable containing vitamin C
(read about vitamin C sources on pages 17–18). Similarly, if you are
taking iron supplements, wash them down with orange juice.
Other good sources of iron include ground beef (3 mg in 3 ounces
cooked), dark meat turkey, organ meats, brewer's yeast, blackstrap
molasses (3.2 mg in 1 tablespoon), soybeans, dried beans (2.6 mg
in ½ cup cooked navy beans; 2.4 mg in ½ cup cooked lima beans),
peas (2.1 mg in ½ cup cooked), spinach (2.4 mg in ½ cup cooked),
potato (1.1 mg in 1 medium baked), dried apricot (3.6 mg in ½
cup), prunes and prune juice, pumpkin seeds, lentils, oatmeal,
iron-fortified grains, and juices.

Why you need iron: The average human contains between ½
and 1 teaspoon of this trace element. More pregnant women are
deficient in iron than in any other nutrient. It is essential for the
production of hemoglobin, the part of the blood that transports
oxygen from the lungs to cells throughout the body. The typical
condition of iron-deficiency is called anemia. Anemic pregnant
women feel tired and rundown because their bodies need to work
extra hard to deliver oxygen to their cells and to the fetus. The
need for iron increases as pregnancy progresses. This is particularly
true in the last trimester, as maternal blood volume increases to
meet the needs of the growing fetus. During the last trimester the
fetus stores this element, so if you do not consume enough iron,
the iron you do have will go to meet the needs of the fetus first,

leaving you tired. If you are very deficient in iron, your baby will suffer, too. It may fail to grow adequately or may be born without necessary stores of iron. It is normal for a woman to lose iron along with the blood that is lost during delivery. If she has not had sufficient iron during her pregnancy, she will probably develop anemia during the postpartum period and breastfeeding. If an anemic woman breastfeeds her child, she will share what little iron she has with her baby. Let us reiterate that *you should pay special attention to meeting your iron needs* as you prepare to conceive, throughout your pregnancy, after delivery, during breastfeeding, and for that matter, when your baby is old enough to start scampering around and you need the energy to chase him or her. Meet your iron needs by eating iron-rich foods regularly and, upon the advice of your doctor, by taking iron supplements or prenatal vitamins that are rich in iron.

Caution: Iron can be binding, thus causing constipation in many pregnant women. Read about about constipation on pages 56–57 for strategies to combat it while still getting sufficient iron.

MANGANESE There is no established RDA for manganese during pregnancy, but the RDA for nonpregnant women is 2.2 mg. Perhaps slightly more would be suitable for the pregnant woman.

Sources: Manganese is found in abundance in spinach (0.128 mg in ½ cup cooked), carrot and broccoli (each about 0.120 mg in ½ cup cooked), whole grains and cereal products, nuts, brewer's yeast, wheat germ, banana, raisins (0.201 mg in 1½ ounces), and dried figs, apricots, and dates. Tea also happens to be a good source of manganese (between 0.4 and 2.7 mg in 1 cup), but you would probably have to drink it in larger-than-comfortable quantities to meet your RDA. So focus on getting manganese from food sources, which should easily furnish your daily needs.

Why you need manganese: This trace element is essential in bone development and maintenance. It is particularly important in the early stages of pregnancy as the fetal skeleton develops. A deficiency may result in growth retardation and congenital malformations of the inner ear and the hearing mechanism in the baby.

The RDA for magnesium for pregnant women is 300 mg. For lactating women it rises to 355 mg.

MAGNESIUM

Sources: Wheat germ, bran, millet, peanuts (63 mg in ¼ cup), peanut butter (28 mg in 1 tablespoon) beans, tofu, yogurt, low-fat milk (40 mg in 1 cup), wheat germ (20 mg in 1 tablespoon), fortified cereals and pastas, brewer's yeast, sesame seeds, dried apricot, banana (58 mg in 1 medium), and prunes.

Why you need magnesium: Magnesium is important for building bones and releasing energy stored in the muscles. A deficiency of magnesium may cause the kidneys and the gastrointestinal tract to function poorly. Many women do not consume enough magnesium, so you should remember to look for it in your foods and your prenatal supplement.

The RDA for phosphorus for pregnant and lactating women is 1200 mg.

PHOSPHORUS

Sources: So many foods contain phosphorus that it is difficult not to meet your daily needs. Among the best sources are low-fat yogurt (326 mg in 1 cup), haddock (210 mg in 3 ounces), carp, mackerel, salmon, swordfish, tuna (188 mg in 3½ ounces), soybeans (166 mg in ½ ounce cooked), liver (405 mg in 3 ounces), all meat and poultry, wheat germ, oatmeal, and lima beans.

Why you need phosphorus: This mineral is essential for healthy bones and teeth. Healthy bones have two parts calcium to one part phosphorus. As your calcium intake increases, you should increase your phosphorus intake as well. This will likely occur if you follow a healthy diet. Phosphorus is also involved in releasing energy from fat, carbohydrates and proteins.

There is no established RDA for potassium, although it is generally thought that approximately 2 g per day are fine for everyone, pregnant or not. Some studies suggest that it is wise to increase your potassium intake during lactation to 2.5 g, because the extra amount is used by your baby to build tissue. Most people easily meet their daily requirements of potassium in their normal diets.

POTASSIUM

Sources: Bananas (550 mg in 1 medium) are a famous source of potassium, but this mineral can be found in many foods. These include bran cereal, avocado (604 mg in ½ medium), dried apricots, orange, peach, pear, prune, carrot (341 mg in 1 large raw), lentils, lima beans, peanuts (740 mg in 2½ ounces), peas, potato (755 mg in 1 medium baked), pumpkin, spinach, squash, Swiss chard, tomato, meat, poultry, fish, dairy products, especially nonfat milk (408 mg in 1 cup), and yogurt.

Why you need potassium: This mineral works in tandem with sodium in maintaining fluid balance in cells and throughout the body. It is used to send impulses and is involved in the release of energy from fat, carbohydrates, and proteins.

SELENIUM

The RDA for selenium for pregnant and lactating women is 75 mcg.

Sources: Liver and other organ meats (average 150 mcg in 4 ounces), seafood (average 38 mcg in 4 ounces); lean meat and chicken (average 22.7 mcg in 4 ounces), whole wheat grains and fortified cereals (average 12.3 mcg in 1 suggested serving).

Why you need selenium: Selenium helps prevent cell damage and the breakdown of certain chemicals in the body.

Caution: **Selenium deficiency was particularly widespread in China in the 1970s, where it was called Keshan disease. This deficiency led to myocardiopathy, a potentially fatal disease of the heart muscles. Selenium supplementation in China soon alleviated the problem. Too much selenium (which could only occur with excessive supplementation beyond your prenatal vitamin) can result in nausea, vomiting, loss of hair and nails, and fatigue. You can meet the RDA though a good, balanced diet and, following the advice of your doctor, prenatal supplements.**

SODIUM

Although there is not an established RDA for sodium in pregnancy, as needs vary from person to person, a daily intake of 570 mg when pregnant and 635 mg when lactating are good averages.

Sources: You could almost use the words *salt* and *sodium* interchangeably. The scientific name for salt is sodium chloride and most of the sodium we get comes from salt. Most foods contain salt, so that a balanced diet easily provides enough sodium for your daily needs. We generally discourage you from adding salt to your food, either in cooking or at the table. In most cases, this added salt is unnecessary and, in some cases, may cause you problems.

Why you need sodium: Sodium works with potassium to maintain the proper amount of fluids in your system. It plays a key role in maintaining your increased blood volume in the latter stages of your pregnancy. This increased blood volume allows more oxygen and nutrients to be delivered to your fetus and for waste products to be removed from the womb. If a woman's blood volume does not increase during her pregnancy, this could prove very harmful for her fetus.

> *Caution:* Nutritionists routinely preach against the practice of consuming salt. This is because there is so much salt in the typical American diet that it causes hypertension and other health problems for millions of people. Pregnant women are special cases. Their sodium needs are greater than those of the typical person, so they should not go "no salt" unless instructed to by their doctors. This is not a justification for adding salt to food or indulging in high-salt foods such as anchovies, potato chips, and luncheon meats. You get enough sodium in your normal diet. Of course, if you have hypertension or another sodium-related medical condition, you should closely follow your doctor's instructions.

ZINC

The RDA for zinc for pregnant women is 15 mg. For lactating women it is 19 mg.

Sources: Turkey (3.7 mg in 3 ounces of dark meat; 1.8 mg in 3 ounces of light meat), cooked liver (3.3 mg in 3 ounces), lean pork (2.6 mg in 3 ounces cooked), beef, veal, organ meats, herring, oysters (we strongly discourage you from eating raw or cooked oysters because, unfortunately, many have toxins that can cause serious ailments such as hepatitis A), wheat germ (1.8 mg in 2 tablespoons), yogurt (1.3 mg in 1 cup), oatmeal, corn, and eggs.

Why you need zinc: Zinc is essential in the metabolism of nucleic acid and protein, and therefore, it is crucial in cell division and tissue growth. It works with insulin to ensure the proper regulation of blood sugar, and it helps maintain the genetic code and heal wounds. Zinc also is needed to release vitamin A stored in the liver and to ensure the vitamin's proper use by tissues. It is needed throughout pregnancy from the very early development of the embryo to delivery (in many cases a healthy amount of zinc in the mother's system has resulted in easier labor). A zinc deficiency may be problematic for you, but it is very serious for your baby. At every stage of pregnancy your fetus uses zinc for growth and development. During the last two trimesters, your fetus stores two-thirds of the zinc it consumes. Zinc will very likely be a component of your prenatal supplement, but you should also be sure to eat foods rich in this essential trace element.

Note: **If a woman has a history of delivering babies with malformations, some doctors advise supplementation with zinc before conception. If this applies to you, talk to your doctor.**

Putting It All Together

After reading this chapter, it is probably quite clear to you that there is a direct connection between proper nutrition and the health and well-being of yourself and your future baby. Now that you know about all the different nutrients you need, you might ask how you can manage to get all of these nutrients every day. Don't worry, you do not have to eat with a fork in one hand and a calculator in the other.

Eating during your pregnancy should be a pleasure. Because you are encouraged to gain weight during pregnancy by consuming healthy food, you can devote yourself to the exploration of good recipes and meals. You already know about food groups and about which foods are rich in certain nutrients. You also probably already know how to eat these foods in combinations that please you and provide you with what you need.

To achieve the balance you need, combine foods from the different groups. A breakfast of a bran muffin, fresh fruit, and yogurt or cottage cheese will start your day on the right track. Cereal and a glass of juice also is a good beginning. If morning sickness limits your choices, eat what you can and be sure to read how to minimize the effects of morning sickness on page 50.

A midmorning snack of cut vegetables, a little hard cheese, or a piece of fruit will continue your healthy ways. All the while, you are making sure to consume water, herbal tea, milk, and juice in sufficient quantities to prevent you from becoming dehydrated.

Lunchtime means a good balanced meal: a sandwich made of whole wheat bread and filled with a protein such as salmon, tuna, low-fat cheese, or lean meat. This should be accompanied by vegetable juice or a small salad. Or opt for a hot meal of pasta, fish, or poultry. With your protein you should have a starch such as a baked or mashed potato, brown rice or kasha, and a green leafy vegetable. Dessert could be fresh fruit.

If you want an afternoon snack, there are many foods to choose from. Dried fruit such as apricots are a great pick; so is a slice of one of the homemade breads for which we provide recipes (see page 248).

Dinner should feature all the components of the food groups: protein, starch, fruits, vegetables, and dairy. Start with a soup or pleasing appetizer. Have a protein, starch, and vegetable. Have a fruit for dessert or, perhaps, some frozen yogurt.

At the end of a day that includes this kind of intelligent eating, you will probably have fulfilled your nutritional needs and those of your developing fetus. As an insurance policy, take your prenatal supplement before you go to sleep.

During your pregnancy you should reread the sections of this chapter that will answer questions that may arise. We have given every nutrient you need a separate listing so that it may be located quickly and easily. If you ever doubt the necessity of eating well or assume that one prenatal vitamin will meet all of your nutritional needs, reread any of the cautions in this chapter and think again.

Your job is to get the nutrients you need. Our job is to tell you what they are and to provide you with delicious recipes that deliver the goods. After reading the following chapters on what happens to you and your fetus during pregnancy, you will be ready to get cooking.

The Nine Months of Pregnancy

(2)

*J*f you are already pregnant, then you must know *something* about conception. But somewhere between the birds and the bees, the oblique explanations you heard in hygiene class and any other information you picked up along the way, the basic facts may have become confused. Let us state definitively, in case you haven't yet realized, that a stork has nothing to do with it.

The purpose of this chapter is to examine how the embryo in your womb develops into a fetus which, in turn, becomes a baby. We will pay special attention to the ways that continued proper nutrition during pregnancy helps result in a healthy baby at delivery.

Before Conception

If you are planning to conceive, it is eminently wise to do everything you can to optimize your condition before conception. The better shape you are in, the more suited your body will be for bringing a healthy baby to term. Here's what to do:

- *Get a checkup.* A thorough physical exam will indicate what your health status is. If there are any particular conditions to attend to, this should be done now. Naturally, you should tell your doctor you are considering having a baby. He or she may suggest that you stop taking certain medications and will possibly prescribe special prenatal vitamin supplements.

• *Quit Any Habits That May Harm Your Baby or You.* We address some of these issues in chapter 6. Smoking and drug addiction are bad for you and certainly increase the likelihood of complications during pregnancy. You will need to cut down and preferably eliminate your consumption of alcohol and caffeine. Because you will not be sure exactly when conception takes place, it will be smart for you to have alcohol and caffeine out of your system by the time your pregnancy begins.

• *Start Eating Well.* Unless you are already vigilant about eating a varied diet rich in all the necessary nutrients, it is likely that you need to make some improvements in your nutritional status. Focus on foods rich in folic acid, iron, calcium, protein, vitamin B_{12}, and zinc. Eat a diet that includes all other vitamins and minerals (which may come in your prenatal supplement), and normal amounts of fat and carbohydrates.

Conception

The very beginning of the process that leads to the development of a baby is known as conception. This happens when an egg (ovum) produced in one of a woman's two ovaries is fertilized by one sperm cell that is released when a man ejaculates his semen into a woman's vagina during sexual intercourse. Given the amount of sexual intercourse that many couples engage in, it may seem odd that pregnancy does not occur more often!

Actually, conception occurs despite surprisingly stiff odds to the contrary. A fertile woman produces one mature ovum approximately once a month. This process, known as **ovulation,** happens when the pituitary gland releases a powerful hormone known as luteinizing hormone.

The ovum's journey: After the ovum is produced, it detaches from the ovary and travels into the fallopian tubes. Located on either side of the uterus, these tubes are 5 to 6 inches long and serve as a conduit from the ovaries to the uterus.

The sperm's journey: The tadpole-shaped spermatozoon (or sperm cell) that manages to fertilize the ovum has made a much more arduous trip than the relatively uneventful one made by the ovum. If you have ever seen Woody Allen's film *Everything You Always Wanted to Know About Sex But Were Afraid to Ask*, you will have seen a vivid and funny depiction of the sperm's journey (if you own a VCR, rent this film just to enjoy this episode). Sperm cells are produced in the testes of a man and, during intercourse, they are transported by the millions in a fluid called semen into a woman's vagina. It is assumed that the man and woman were also enjoying themselves during this event.

Of the two to three hundred million sperm cells released during intercourse, less than two hundred hardy cells reach the fallopian tubes. The rest are destroyed in the acidic environment of the vagina.

FERTILIZATION

If one of the sperm cells unites with the ovum in the fallopian tube, than it is said that the egg is fertilized. This can happen if you have intercourse from 3 days before ovulation to 1 day afterward. Otherwise, the ovum will die and be eliminated and you will have to wait about 1 month to bring forth another ovum.

The ovum and the sperm each contain genetic material known as chromosomes. Each has twenty-three, and within the forty-six chromosomes exists all the information about what sort of person these two cells might make. This genetic blueprint contains the future person's gender, eye and hair color, and all sorts of distinguishing characteristics that make each one of us unique. Within hours after fertilization, this genetic blueprint has been established.

The First Month: The Embryonic Phase

Following the establishment of the genetic blueprint, the fertilized ovum, which is a cell, begins to grow. It divides into two halves, which then divide into two more, and so on. This exponential division forms a particle-size clump of cells—called the **embryo**—which will grow, in nine months, to more than 100,000 times the size of the original cluster of cells.

Another journey: As this cell division happens, the embryo slowly moves down the fallopian tubes to the uterus, and implants itself in the uterine wall and begins to grow. Implantation usually happens about 10 days after fertilization.

The amniotic sac: Soon after implantation, some of the cells on the surface of the embryo create a transparent balloonlike covering that surrounds the embryo. This covering quickly fills with liquid from the mother's tissues and ultimately becomes the protected environment in which the embryo will develop. This liquid is known as amniotic fluid; the amniotic sac also is referred to as "the bag of waters."

The Placenta: Placenta is not, as someone once insisted to us, a city in California. The placenta is a vital organ, created by other embryonic cells and maternal tissues, that provides necessary food, liquid, and oxygen to the embryo. The placenta continues to grow for seven months as the embryo (later called the fetus) grows. It is attached to the embryo by a thin tubelike cord, which later develops into the umbilical cord.

This feeding process is quite remarkable: Whatever you eat or drink is digested in your stomach into basic components, which are then absorbed through your intestinal wall into your bloodstream. The blood carries these components to your liver which breaks them down further into essential elements. Your liver sends these nutrients back into your bloodstream. Your blood then carries these nutrients plus oxygen to the placenta, which then passes them through the cord to the embryo.

Similarly, waste products produced in the embryo pass through the placenta to your bloodstream, which carries the embryo's waste to your kidneys, to be elminated in the urine. As you might expect, the blood volume in a pregnant woman needs to increase to do some of this work. This is one reason why you need to focus on drinking water and other healthy liquids and to consume sufficient iron, vitamins B_{12} and C, and other nutrients. You are now eating for two and must eat to help the special functions of pregnancy occur.

It is important to bear in mind that any other substances in your bloodstream can pass to the embryo through the placenta. For this reason, medication, narcotics, recreational drugs, and alcohol should not be in the system of a pregnant woman who wants to do whatever is necessary to have a healthy baby.

Differentiation: As the embryo is nourished through the placenta, growth begins. Only 3 weeks after fertilization, the cells that make up the nervous system of the embryo begin to divide (or *differentiate*) to form the foundation of the brain, spinal cord, and nervous system. At 4 weeks, arm and leg buds appear and the rudimentary heart starts to beat. The beginnings of eyes are already evident. Within the next few days most of the internal organs will be formed through differentiation. By the end of the first month, the embryo will be ¼ to ½ inch long and will have a head, a torso, limb buds, a primitive digestive system, a heart, and kidneys.

WHAT IS HAPPENING TO THE MOTHER DURING THE FIRST MONTH?

Despite all of this activity going on inside her, a woman often does not even know she is pregnant. It only becomes apparent when she notices certain changes. The most obvious, of course, is when she does not menstruate at the expected time. But there are other signs:

- The breasts become slightly larger and firmer.
- Fatigue sometimes sets in.
- Morning sickness occurs in about 50% of pregnant women.

If you experience any of these symptoms, make an appointment to see your doctor. A quicker guide might be a home pregnancy test, but these are not 100% accurate and certainly are not a substitute for seeking medical attention. Once you find out that you are pregnant, plan regular office visits so your doctor can chart your progress. Also take the occasion of your first visit to discuss your nutritional needs. Your doctor may give you several leads that this book will enable you to follow.

NUTRITION DURING THE FIRST MONTH

The 1st month is a crucial period in the development of your baby. The formation of organs (known as *organogenesis*) requires all the necessary nutrients you can provide. Foremost among these is:

- **Protein,** which consists of amino acids, the basic building materials that make up the cells that, in turn, make up the organs. You also need:
- **Iron,** which is necessary in increasing amounts as you increase your blood volume. Remember that iron-rich blood contains more hemoglobin, which is essential for transporting oxygen to the embryo.

• **Calcium,** which you need to begin storing now even though the demands for building your baby's teeth and bones will not come until later. You also need calcium to help absorb iron.

• **Vitamin C,** which is important for blood clotting and for absorption of iron.

• **The other vitamins,** each of which plays a role in making your system function properly.

• **Zinc,** which is crucial for the metabolism (breakdown and use) of protein.

• **Iodine** and **sodium,** which are necessary for regulation of, respectively, your thyroid gland and your retention of liquid. Most readers of the book receive enough iodine and sodium in their normal diets and should not supplement this intake unless told to by their doctors.

The Second Month

Although the embryo only grows to about 1 inch in length and weighs only ⅓ ounce, development continues apace. During this period the head grows more quickly than the body. The rudimentary brain already starts sending nervous impulses to other organs, foreshadowing the responsibilities it will later assume. The brain itself now has five cavities which will later become the ventricles. The following events also occur in the second month:

• Pigment forms in the retina of each eye, making them appear dark. The eyelids also develop.
• The nose and two separate nasal passages are formed.
• The ears develop.
• Lips, teeth, gums, jaws, and tooth buds appear.
• Limb buds start developing into very human-looking but delicate arms and legs.
• The esophagus, stomach, and intestines begin to form.
• Some internal organs start to assume their future functions as the kidneys extract waste materials and the spleen and liver become the sites of formation of the embryo's first blood cells.
• The skeleton is now fully formed, although it is made entirely of soft cartilage. At the end of the second month, the

first bone cells will start creating the bone that will ultimately replace the cartilage.

- The neural tube develops. This is the structure that forms the central nervous system that transmits impulses from the brain throughout the body. Obviously, a healthy neural tube is essential for proper development of the embryo.

WHAT IS HAPPENING TO THE MOTHER DURING THE SECOND MONTH?

The 2nd month is prime time for morning sickness, and if you are going to be someone who suffers with it, you will probably know by now. Interestingly, it seems that women carrying twins do not have morning sickness until the third trimester, if they develop the condition at all. By the end of the 2nd month, many pregnant women have gained a couple of pounds and may notice some tightness across the waist and bust when they wear certain clothes. Now is the time to start thinking about more flexible clothing.

NUTRITION DURING THE SECOND MONTH

At this time it is crucial that pregnant women meet their daily requirement of **folic acid.** This B vitamin is essential for normal cell division and plays the key role in the development of the neural tube. A deficiency of folic acid may lead to all sorts of serious abnormalities in a baby, some of them life threatening. In addition, folic acid is important for blood production, which continues apace.

> *Note:* Women who take oral contraceptives often have a deficiency of folic acid when they give up the pill and become pregnant. If this is you, make certain that you discuss this with your doctor.

Here are some other nutritional highlights during the second month:

- **Phosphorus** works in tandem with **calcium** to stabilize the skeleton and tooth buds. Phosphorus is abundant in the average diet (see page 25) and calcium is available in many foods as well (see page 20).
- **Vitamin D** helps you absorb phosphorus and calcium.
- **Manganese** is directly involved with the development of

the hearing mechanism, which is formed during the second month.

- **Protein** continues to be important because of its essential role in cell development and tissue formation. It also takes part in the development of the skeleton.

Of course, you should eat a balanced diet so that you do not shortchange yourself or your embryo of any nutrients.

Once bone starts replacing cartilage in the skeleton, the embryonic phase is considered to be over and the fetal phase begins. At the start of the 3rd month, the fetus is 1½ inches long and resembles a very frail, delicate human form. Here is what else is happening:

The Third Month: The Fetal Phase

- During the 9th and 10th weeks of pregnancy, fetal muscles and internal organs become interconnected, thanks to the newly formed nerve cell network.
- Some major muscles are fully formed and the fetus can make rudimentary movements.
- The fully formed thyroid gland and pancreas start producing substances similar to hormones.
- The digestive, circulatory, respiratory, reproductive, and urinary systems will all start forming.
- Sexual characteristics emerge as a female forms the urinary bladder and the male starts developing testes and a rudimentary penis.

By the end of the first trimester, the average mother gains between 2 and 4 pounds. Sometimes a lower weight gain is caused by the inability to eat due to morning sickness. A woman who has gained less than 2 pounds should consider slightly reducing physical activity, which burns calories, and should increase intake of healthy snacks such as fruit, especially prunes and raisins, seeds, nuts, peanut butter, shakes made of milk and bananas, and good cheeses such as Parmesan, Cheddar, and Swiss. Some women experience constipation during the third month: the prunes and raisins are recommended with that in mind.

WHAT IS HAPPENING TO THE MOTHER DURING THE THIRD MONTH?

NUTRITION DURING THE THIRD MONTH

Vitamin A and zinc are particularly important.

- **Vitamin A** is crucial for cell development, which happens at a great clip during the third month as many internal organs are formed. The vitamin also helps develop the linings of these organs and is involved in bone growth, a key feature of this phase of gestation.
- **Zinc** releases vitamin A stored in the liver, allowing the vitamin to do its work in cell development.
- **Magnesium** is vital for muscle and nerve membranes as it works with protein for tissue growth. Therefore, as muscle and nerve connections take place, magnesium becomes particularly important.
- **Iodine** is needed now because the fetus's thyroid gland is fully formed and uses iodine to form thyroxine, a hormone that is important for body growth and mental development. Fetuses that are extremely deficient in iodine may result in babies with retarded mental or physical development.
- **Protein** continues to be a necessary nutrient for cell formation.
- **Calcium** is essential to bone growth and hardening, which is a prominent feature this month.
- Calories, in the form of **fat stores**, should be increased during the third month. Fat stored now will provide energy during the latter stages of pregnancy needed for fetal development, during delivery, and for breastfeeding.

The Fourth Month

The 13th through 16th weeks of gestation are characterized by rapid growth in the size of the fetus, although no new organs are formed.

- The fetus grows 6 to 7 inches in length. This lengthening gives the fetus a more human appearance. The head is only one-third of the fetus's total size.
- The heart develops a strong and rhythmic pumping action, pumping between 25 and 30 quarts of blood per day.
- The placenta grows in proportion to the fetus to continue supplying necessary nutrients.
- Facial features become more developed: the eyelids com-

pletely cover the eyes, permanent tooth buds form in the jaw, and the upper lip forms a ridge.

• Ovaries in females will become apparent and the ova (egg cells) that she will need to be a future mother form now.

• Despite its growth, the fetus weighs only 6 ounces by the month's end.

During this month, the blood volume increases. In some women, the first symptoms of high blood pressure occur. If the condition becomes more serious, it is referred to as toxemia of pregnancy. Read about it on page 65.

At the end of the 4th month or early in the 5th month, some women may feel a fluttery feeling in their bellies that is the movement of the fetal legs. This is what people refer to as "the baby kicking."

A key feature during the 4th month is the continued, increasing need for energy.

WHAT IS HAPPENING TO THE MOTHER DURING THE FOURTH MONTH?

• **Complex carbohydrates** (for example, rice, pasta, whole wheat bread, cereals, and grains) will be stored in the liver as glucose to provide energy as needed.

• **Healthy fats** (in some cheeses; in fish; in nuts; and in oils such as olive, corn, peanut, and safflower) also will convert to glucose or will form in tissue. As fat-soluble vitamins (A, D, E, and K) continue to be needed, they will be stored in the fatty tissue.

• **Protein,** at this stage of pregnancy, is more important for the mother than the fetus. It helps blood volume increase, breast and uterine tissues grow, and will be stored in the placenta for later use by the fetus.

• **Biotin** is important for the metabolism of fats and carbohydrates, which are now being consumed in greater amounts.

• **Salt,** although usually thought of as a nutritional villain, is important in pregnancy, and especially during this month as blood volume increases in the mother. Salt should be obtained through consumption of foods that naturally contain it, such as fish, seafood, meats, and vegetables such as celery. Additional salt should be used only if a doctor recommends it.

NUTRITION DURING THE FOURTH MONTH

The Fifth Month

The fetus continues to grow in length and size and more details develop in the face and in certain organs.

- The fetus will be about 12 inches in length.
- It weighs between 1 and 1½ pounds.
- The skeleton is mostly hard.
- The baby moves about more, its heartbeat is stronger, and it can even be felt hiccuping.
- Hair and nails appear.
- A fatty substance known as vernix caseosa is secreted by the fetus's sebaceous glands to protect its delicate skin from the minerals in the amniotic fluid.
- The uterus in the female is completely formed and the vagina is developing.

What Is Happening to the Mother During the Fifth Month?

A woman is generally active, energetic, and enjoys eating. Morning sickness generally disappears.

Nutrition During the Fifth Month

- Potassium is a crucial nutrient at this time. It is important in the transmission of nerve impulses, which occur now that the nerve-muscular systems are connected. This nutrient regulates water flow in the body for the release of energy and for the contractability of muscles. Potassium is lost due to diarrhea, vomiting, and dehydration. A woman experiencing these conditions must redouble her efforts to consume potassium, which is abundant in bananas.
- **Vitamin C** helps form collagen, a binding substance that helps connect muscles, nerves, and blood vessels.
- Certain **B vitamins** (thiamine, niacin, and riboflavin) are needed for the release of energy, and pantothenic acid is needed for healthy muscles.
- **Protein** is still needed. It helps in fat storage and will be built up to be fed to baby during breastfeeding.
- **Iodine** is needed now for the mother's thyroid gland as her metabolic rate soars. Iodine helps regulate the metabolism.

The Sixth Month

The fetus continues to grow and develop, particularly in terms of weight gain.

- The fetus increases in weight to 2 pounds.
- It grows to 14 or 15 inches in length.
- The skeleton starts to calcify, a process that will be completed in the eighth month.
- The fetus accumulates iron in its spleen.
- The heart and liver grow larger.
- The hair is growing longer.
- The skin is red and wrinkled.

WHAT IS HAPPENING TO THE MOTHER DURING THE SIXTH MONTH?

The 6th month marks the end of the second trimester, during which time good nutrition ensured the basic development of the organs of the fetus. Weight gain becomes an key focus as fetal growth becomes as important as development.

At this time women will routinely be given a test for gestational diabetes (see page 61). Increased fatigue may be experienced and should be mentioned to the mother's doctor. This also is the time that toxemia of pregnancy might appear in some women. The woman may feel a dull achiness in the lower pelvis, often the result of the stretching of the ligaments that support the uterus. This is normal and is due to the increased weight of the uterus.

NUTRITION DURING THE SIXTH MONTH

- **Protein** needs are at their highest level. It is needed for uterine growth, which occurs to accomodate the developing fetus. Protein also is needed for storage in the placenta, which continues to grow to serve the fetus's increasing demands.
- **Iron** is crucial during the sixth month. At this point in the pregnancy, iron is stored in maternal tissues in preparation for the blood loss (and accompanying iron loss) during delivery. Iron will be stored by the fetus from now until birth. This is vital, because a baby receives very little iron from its mother's milk during breastfeeding.
- Trace elements such as **copper, zinc, selenium** and **chromium** are stored by the fetus for its needs as a newborn infant.

The Third Trimester: Fetal Growth

The last 3 months (trimester) of gestation are characterized by consistent weight gain by mother and fetus. The fetus typically gains 1 to 1½ each month while the mother gains about 3 to 4 pounds during the same time period. The most notable changes in the fetus are in brain and lung development. It does not move about nearly as much as in the second trimester and, as it grows larger, it settles into the position it will be in at the time of birth.

PREMATURE BIRTH   One of the most serious occurrences that can happen during the last trimester is premature birth (also called prematurity). Babies born prematurely are often nicknamed *preemies*. A baby is said to be born prematurely when it is delivered before the 36th week of pregnancy (a typical pregnancy lasts 40 weeks). In the United States, 7% of all babies are preemies.

Causes of
Prematurity   While doctors and scientists are still searching for precise explanations for prematurity, there is almost universal agreement that some of the following factors are connnected to premature labor.

Drug and alcohol consumption: Drugs and alcohol are the leading causes of prematurity. Read more about them in chapter 6.

Poor nutrition: Women from lower economic groups, who receive the worst prenatal care and nutrition, are the most likely to deliver prematurely. The idea of this book is to promote good nutrition in pregnancy to women of all socioeconomic groups.

Poor health: A mother-to-be who has particular health problems may be more likely to have an early delivery. These conditions include toxemia of pregnancy (hypertension), thyroid imbalance, rubella, diabetes, and venereal diseases.

Mother's age: Girls under seventeen years are still growing themselves and are not always fully ready to bring a baby to term. Women over thirty-five have a greater probability of premature delivery. Good nutrition and medical care will reduce the likelihood of prematurity among women in these age groups.

Stress: Episodes of extreme stress have been known occasionally to bring on premature labor. By extreme stress we do not mean the trials and tribulations of daily life. However, as a general rule, you should seek ways to minimize stress in your life.

Multiple pregnancies: Women carrying twins, triplets, quadruplets, or quintuplets are much more likely to deliver prematurely.

Consequences of
Prematurity   Because it is normal that an unborn child remains in the womb for

40 weeks and develops physically (and perhaps emotionally) during that entire time, it is a traumatic experience to be born before full term. The development that would occur in the protected environment of the womb must take place outside. Preemies often suffer from the following problems:

Insufficient organ development: Underdevelopment is particularly seen in the brain and lungs but also can be evident in the small intestine, causing enteritis.

Insufficient weight gain: Preemies born to mothers who ate poorly and had inadequate prenatal care may weigh as little as 2 pounds.

Greater likelihood of early death: Because of their rough start in life, some preemies simply do not have the physical ability to survive more than a few days.

Greater likelihood of long-term health problems: Because of the inadequate development of certain organs at birth, even preemies who survive stand a greater chance of health problems affecting particular organs (the lungs, for example).

Care for Premature Babies

The earlier a preemie is born, the longer the odds are that it will survive and flourish. Preemies must usually remain in intensive care units, under the vigilant care of specially trained nurses and doctors (neonatologists). During this period, the preemies must continue to gain weight and develop the functions they need to survive. At one time, premature babies had very slim chances of surviving, not to mention flourishing. Nowadays, because of remarkable strides made in medical research and technology, there is a much greater chance of saving a baby born as early as 25 weeks. With proper care and some luck, a preemie will go on to lead a normal, healthy life.

The Seventh Month

The 7th month is a time of accelerated development of the fetal brain and lungs. The outer cortex of the brain becomes ridged, and the so-called gray matter of the brain is formed. Also in the 7th month:

- The central nervous system can direct rhythmic breathing and movement and can control body temperature.
- The fetus moves about and remains active until the end of

this month, when it starts to settle into position to prepare for birth.

• The eyes open.

• Cells in fetal lungs secrete surfactent, which maintains the cells until the lungs will later function. The respiratory system is still inactive.

• The reproductive organs complete their differentiation. The female has produced all of the ova she will need for her reproductive years. In most cases, the testes in the male have descended into the scrotum.

• Some 7-month-old fetuses suck their thumbs.

• The skin, which until now has been wrinkled and reddish, becomes smoother and pinker.

• In the last trimester, most of fetal tissue development takes place.

• By the end of the 7th month, the fetus weighs about 3 to 3½ pounds and the placenta weighs 1 to 1½ pounds.

WHAT IS HAPPENING TO THE MOTHER DURING THE SEVENTH MONTH?

Many women feel the desire to eat less because they think they look and feel heavy. The increasingly large uterus begins to press against the stomach and bowel, which also suppresses the appetite. However, this is a period when ever-increasing intake of nutritious food is essential. If big meals become hard to swallow, switch to eating smaller amounts of food at more frequent intervals throughout the day.

Some women experience gestational diabetes or toxemia of pregnancy (see chapter 4). Constipation also is a common occurrence (see page 56). Some women have backaches and difficulty sleeping because of the increased amount of weight they are bearing.

Edema, or swelling of body tissues, occurs in the majority of pregnant women in the latter stages of pregnancy. Many women experience swelling of the ankles and feet. Mild edema is not a cause for alarm, but more serious cases should be seen by a doctor, who might make a dietary adjustment to reduce salt intake.

Because of pressure against the urinary bladder by the expanding uterus, there is a feeling of needing to urinate more frequently. This will continue until the end of the pregnancy.

From now until the end of your pregnancy you need to consume a large amount of healthy, high-calorie foods. In the second trimester most of your weight gain went to increase the size of your breasts and uterus and to greater blood volume and fat storage. In the third trimester, most of your weight gain will go toward the growth of your fetus as well as an increase in amniotic fluid and, in the seventh month only, an increase in the size of the placenta.

NUTRITION DURING THE SEVENTH MONTH

- **Calories.** As indicated above, an increased intake of calories from healthy, nutrient-rich foods will benefit the growth of your child.
- **Calcium.** Storage of calcium in the fetal skeleton takes place during the third trimester.
- **Folate.** Because folate has been shown in research to be crucial in proper brain development, it is a essential nutrient during the 7th month and for the rest of gestation.
- **Biotin.** This vitamin is required to release energy from carbohydrates. For the rest of your pregnancy, energy requirements are at high levels. Biotin also helps synthesize amino acids in protein.
- **Protein.** Protein is necessary as the building material for developing tissues.

Brain development continues to be the key feature of fetal activity. The brain increases in size and in the number of mature nerve cells it contains. Nerve cells are the most metabolically active of all cells. That is, they require more energy. In fact, while they make up only 2 to 3% of total body weight, they consume approximately 20% of the energy the body manufactures.

The Eighth Month

- The fetus has become larger and has less room to move about. It settles into the position it will remain in until it is born. In 96 to 97% of the cases, it curls up into the well-known fetal position in which it will be born head first. Others assume a "breech" position, that is, a position in which the feet are at the cervix at the time of delivery. There are other intermediate positions as well.
- The fetus drinks increased amounts of amniotic fluid,

which contributes to its weight gain.

• Fat now makes up 7 to 8% of the fetus's body weight. This fat is mostly found immediately under the its skin and is necessary to regulate his or her body temperature once it is outside the womb.

• Weight gain continues; by the end of this month, it should weigh 4 to 5 pounds.

WHAT IS HAPPENING TO THE MOTHER DURING THE EIGHTH MONTH?

Some women eat less for the reasons described in the section on the 7th month (see page 44). They must redouble their efforts to eat well to provide proper nutrients to their fetuses. There are, however, certain women who gain *too much* weight in the latter stages of their pregnancies. This may be a sign of preeclampsia, a condition you should read about on page 65. Women should not gain more than 1 pound per week, and if you find that you are, you should discuss it with your doctor and embark on a diet that is lower in animal fats (found in cream, whole milk, fatty cheeses, and fatty meats). This does not mean cutting back on nutrients. Skim milk will deliver the same amount of nutrients (except fat) as are found in whole milk.

Most women experience "false labor" (also called Braxton-Hicks contractions) during this time. While the scientific reasons for these are not yet known, there are ways to distinguish them from real labor:

• They come at irregular intervals, and these intervals do not become closer in time as they continue.
• The contractions never last more than a total of 20 minutes.
• Whatever pain is experienced is only in the back.

Many women become anxious or impatient about the impending delivery and the changes that a newborn will bring to their lives. If this is you, talk about your feelings with people you confide in rather than keeping them to yourself. Furthermore, some women feel awkward, ungainly, or unattractive. Remember that this is temporary and that you are looking forward to getting back into shape soon (see page 75).

For reasons described in the section about the 7th month (see page 45), **calories, protein, folate,** and **biotin** continue to be important in the 8th month. There are five additional nutrients that are essential now:

- **Iron.** Anemia, a condition characterized by extreme weakness and exhaustion, is a direct result of iron-poor blood. A woman's blood volume naturally expands by 25% during her pregnancy to serve the needs of her fetus. If her supply of iron does not increase correspondingly, she may become a candidate for anemia. The extra blood is normally lost during delivery, which further reduces the iron in a woman's system. Newborn babies are naturally deficient in iron. For all of these reasons, it is necessary for a woman to consume increased amounts of iron during pregnancy, but especially in the last 2 months, when the iron will be stored for use during delivery and breastfeeding. As described on page 23, doctors often prescribe iron supplements to pregnant women and encourage them to eat iron-rich foods such as liver and spinach.
- **Copper.** Research has shown that copper promotes absorption of iron.
- **Vitamin K.** This vitamin is essential for blood-clotting. While most women have sufficient quantities of vitamin K in their bodies, newborns are naturally deficient. Women who consume additional vitamin K now will store it for breastfeeding. In spite of this, most newborns are routinely given vitamin K to use until they consume it on their own or produce it (after one month of age, bacteria in their intestines will produce 50% of their required vitamin K).
- **Vitamin E.** This vitamin is needed to assure the durability of a baby's red blood cells. You will store it during this period to feed to your newborn during breastfeeding.
- **Fat.** You have read about saturated and unsturated fats (page 7) and understand that fats derived from oils such as olive, corn and canola are healthy and essential. The fat you consume now will go toward the increased fat in your baby and you will use it for storage of fat-soluble vitamins (especially E and K).

The Ninth Month

This is it. As you might expect, a lot happens in the last weeks before a baby is born.

- The greatest increase in the fetus's size occurs during the 9th month. It will gain 1 ounce a day and grow, on average, to 20 inches in length.
- The brain, kidneys, liver, and lungs will continue to grow.
- Tiny breasts form on both males and females.
- The circumference of the head and abdomen are about equal.
- The mother's blood begins to deliver antibodies to the fetus, which will provide the newborn with immunity against certain illnesses. Most of these antibodies also are fed to the newborn during breastfeeding.
- The fetus positions itself for delivery. In most cases, the head descends into the birth canal, a process known as *engagement*. It also is referred to as *lightening*, because the unborn baby seems to have dropped, thereby reducing pressure on your abdomen and making you feel lighter. There will be increased pressure on the pelvic area until the baby is born.
- After it has served its purpose throughout pregnancy, the placenta starts to shrivel and becomes harder. This smaller placenta will exit the vagina along with blood and amniotic fluid during the baby's birth.

What Is Happening to the Mother During the Ninth Month?

The mother's body produces **colostrum** in the breasts. This substance is rich in protein and immunoglobins that will, if the mother breastfeeds, be fed to the newborn baby in its first few feedings. The immunoglobins are vital for prevention of infection and disease in the newborn, who will not be able to manufacture its own immunoglobins for 6 to 7 months. Almost all women experience normal leakage of colostrum from the nipple in the 9th month.

Nervousness, anxiety, and excitement are normal as the long-awaited day finally nears. Anemia may occur in women who do not consume sufficient amounts of iron. Women should also consume increased amounts of carbohydrates and vitamin C in the days before delivery.

Because this is the period of greatest fetal weight gain, women must continue to eat abundant amounts of nutrient-rich food. **Calories, protein, iron, copper, vitamins E and K, and "good" fats** remain important. In addition, other nutrients must be consumed:

- **Potassium** helps release energy from protein, fats, and carbohydrates. As you are feeling run-down and will need energy for delivery, potassium will make your life easier. Bananas are the best source.
- Although the thyroid gland in the fetus is already capable of producing its own hormones, it needs **iodine,** supplied by the mother, for this purpose.
- Studies have shown that infants with low levels of **magnesium** are much more likely to suffer convulsions and tremors.
- **Vitamin C** plays an important role in healing, which you will be doing after the birth of a baby. Because you will lose a certain amount of vitamin C during delivery, you should make a point of having extra helpings of citrus fruit and juice in the days before delivery.
- In the days immediately before delivery, a woman should have meals rich in **complex carbohydrates.** These will provide the great amounts of energy needed during delivery. Eating pasta (which runners eat the night before a marathon) is a logical and delicious idea.

The miraculous process of gestation has ended, abetted by intelligent eating and prenatal care, and a baby weighing 6 billion times the amount of the original fertilized egg is about to be born.

NUTRITION DURING THE NINTH MONTH

Typical Conditions of Pregnancy

3

There is no such thing as a typical pregnancy. Your experience as an expectant mother will be something you will recount to other women just as your mother and other relatives and friends probably did to you.

Much of the subject matter in this passing on of experience centers on what we call the typical conditions of pregnancy. These include morning sickness, food cravings and aversions, constipation, diarrhea, and heartburn. Not every woman develops these conditions. If you do, you will be uncomfortable for a while, but it will pass. In some cases there is a nutritional response that may ease these conditions, and you can be sure that we will point you to that response.

Morning Sickness

Morning sickness occurs during the first trimester and typically ends during the 4th month. In some cases, however, it continues throughout pregnancy. If this happens to you, then work closely with your doctor to ensure that you are getting the nutrition you need. The most common symptoms of morning sickness are queasiness and nausea. Many women also experience vomiting and have trouble keeping food down. Not surprisingly, women with morning sickness often have no desire to eat.

One of the chief causes of morning sickness is the accumulation of estrogen and progesterone in the lining of the stomach. Estrogen has been shown to cause queasiness when it interacts with the acid that naturally exists in your stomach. The normal secretion of hormones occurs continuously, but while you sleep the accumulation in an empty stomach results in sickness in the morning. For some women who then eat dry foods, the condition passes in a short time. For others, it may not abate for a few hours and, in a few cases, morning sickness may last all day. A smart way to counteract the hormone accumulation is to make a effort regularly to have food in your stomach to absorb some of the acid. This is just one of the strategies to ease morning sickness that you will find below.

Believe it or not, studies have shown that frequent vomiting by the mother-to-be is often an indicator of a healthy baby. This is because an embryo that secretes a large amount of a hormone called B-Hcg often turns out to be a very healthy baby. This is great news about the baby, but not for the mother. If you are suffering any of these symptoms, take solace in the fact that your baby is probably doing quite well.

Women who experience severe, persistent vomiting during pregnancy may have a rare condition known as hyperemesis gravidarum. This condition is also marked by extreme fatigue and the inability to keep any food or liquid down. If you are showing symptoms of hyperemesis, call your doctor immediately. If not treated, this condition can be very serious for both mother and baby. The usual course of treatment is a brief hospitalization in which the mother receives liquids and food intravenously until the problem passes.

Some studies have shown that vitamin B_6 can help minimize the discomfort associated with morning sickness. While it is not smart to overload on this or any vitamin, we believe that you should try eating foods rich in vitamin B_6 (wheat germ, bananas, and walnuts) if you have morning sickness. It may help, and it can't hurt. Of course, this should be part of a well-balanced diet that you should maintain throughout your pregnancy.

Avoid an empty stomach: When the food's away, the acids play. In addition, the possibility of low blood sugar when you don't eat will make you feel even worse.

Keep food at your bedside: Sometimes morning sickness doesn't set in as soon as you wake up. By eating something right away you are making a preventive strike before the acids in your empty stomach start stirring up trouble. After your snack, stay in bed for a few minutes and then get up gradually. Dry crackers, a muffin, a banana, and some water are good bedside foods.

Eat frequently in small amounts: Instead of sitting down to a big meal, eat lightly (or even just pick) at various points throughout the day. This will bring you a dependable supply of nutrients without burdening you with a full stomach. Emphasize complex carbohydrates and proteins, plus any other healthy food that appeals to you. This is certainly not the time for junk food.

The nose knows: If a particular food smells bad (even if it smells good to you at other times) stay away from it. Greasy and spicy dishes are often particularly repulsive to women with morning sickness. If raw meat or fish repels you but you would gladly eat them when cooked, let someone else do the cooking. And, of course, don't cook foods for others that are a turnoff to you.

The stomach knows, too: You may feel that you must eat something sweet or salty or sour. You should answer your own stomach's call, but do it intelligently. If you want something sweet, skip the candy in favor of fresh fruit, dried fruit, applesauce, muffins, and so on. Saltiness can come without salt. Many vegetable juices have high salt contents. A celery stalk smeared with peanut butter is another good choice. Saltine crackers are a morning sickness standby, especially for an empty stomach. If you are that rare person who craves something sour, any citrus fruit or juice is ideal.

Liquids: If you have difficulty keeping down solid foods, try liquids. Select liquids that are high in nutrients, such as chicken broth, vegetable juices and soups, fruit juices and soups, and any dairy products you can handle. Approach citrus juices with care because they are high in acid. Some women report that they could not stand orange juice while they had morning sickness, but others say that orange juice and bran muffins are what got them through the ordeal. It's up to you.

If you are eating solid foods, then minimize the amount of liquids you have during meals. It seems that liquids and solids in combination are problematic for some morning sickness sufferers. If this true in your case, be sure to have liquids between meals. Remember that it is essential that you not become dehydrated.

Take your prenatal vitamin: When you are eating irregularly, you often miss out on essential nutrients. Therefore, it is especially important that you get these nutrients from the vitamin your doctor prescribes for you. Take your vitamin at the time of the day when you feel that it is most likely to stay down, perhaps just before you go to bed. Remember not to take your vitamin in combination with roughage, because many of the nutrients in the vitamin will be absorbed by the roughage and carried out of your system. And don't forget that your prenatal vitamin is a *supplement* to a healthy diet and not a replacement for eating well.

Take only prescribed medicine: This wisdom applies throughout your pregnancy, but it bears repeating here. You may be tempted to take an over-the-counter analgesic for your stomach or aspirin for your headache, but unless your doctor approves, don't do it. Ask what medical or nutritional response your doctor recommends.

Take advantage of the good days: Even if you have morning sickness, there will be days when you feel fine. On these days make a special effort to eat healthy meals rich in nutrients.

This too shall pass: Take things a day at a time and try to keep a positive attitude.

Food Cravings and Aversions

Earlier we mentioned that you are very likely to hear stories from other women about what happened during their pregnancies. Undoubtedly you will hear about food cravings and aversions that characterized these pregnancies, particularly during the first trimester. Aside from the proverbial pickles and ice cream, there are many foods that women crave. Generally, the foods they hanker for will have a particular characteristic (sweetness, saltiness, or fattiness) or have a particular texture or color.

There are different assumptions made about the causes of cravings and aversions. Some people think that the body is calling out for the particular nutrient it needs, but there is no real scientific evidence to back up this assertion. There may be a psychological component to cravings: Pregnancy is a time of heightened emotions and particular foods can be comforting. Some women are reassured that they are loved when a spouse volunteers to run out at midnight to buy ice cream, but the spouse can show love in other ways as well. If you feel you are not getting the attention you crave, gently bring up the subject. Pregnancy may be a new experience to your baby's father, and he has things to learn just as you do.

HEALTHY CRAVINGS

A craving is not necessarily a bad thing. It is very possible that the foods you crave will be good for you. A woman we know only wanted white foods for a period of time. She was able to have a good diet of chicken breasts; fish; pastas; rice; potatoes; dairy products; bananas, peeled apples and pears. If you crave a healthy food, go for it: You and your baby will be the lucky beneficiaries.

UNHEALTHY CRAVINGS

There might be a food that you crave that simply is not good for you. A pound of cookies or luncheon meat may fill a craving, but the consequences of all that extra sugar or salt are not good. Here are some strategies to use in dealing with unhealthy cravings:

Look at the ingredients in the things you crave and replace them with better foods: Cheese doodles can be replaced by Cheddar cheese and low-salt crackers. Potato chips can be replaced by baked potato skins with a little melted cheese.

Re-create the sensation with something else: Sometimes you don't crave a food as much as a sensation. If you want creaminess, yogurt is just as good as pudding. If you want crunchiness, carrots or breadsticks can do the trick just as well as a bag of pretzels.

Give in a little: If there is a food you crave that your doctor says you can eat sparingly (that is, if it doesn't contain ingredients that will harm you or your baby), eat it as a special event. For example, if you are permitted a little chocolate, have a small piece of the highest-quality chocolate you can buy. Rather than scarfing it down, savor each bite. If you don't feel satisfied, leave the kitchen and change your activity.

Redirect your thoughts: Will power is not only about suffering. If you realize that something you crave will harm your baby, then think about the relative merits of short-term gratification as opposed to the bigger picture. Sublimate your urges, as suggested above, by engaging in an activity that's good for you: shopping for baby clothes, exercise you are permitted to do, seeing a movie, reading a book, cuddling with a loved one, and so on.

AVERSIONS

You should not be unduly alarmed by your aversions. Many women experience them during the first two trimesters and the best advice is to follow your feelings. It is important, though, to be sure that you are getting the nutrients you and your baby require. So if you are turned off by red meat, get your protein from poultry, fish, and beans. If you can't look at meat with bones, eat fillets or cubes of meat. If particular fruits or vegetables don't appeal to you, make note of the nutrients they contain and seek those nutrients from other foods. Of course, if you have an aversion to an unhealthy food, there is nothing to worry about.

PICA

Pica is a special and much more serious form of craving. We are separating pica from our discussion of cravings and aversions because it can have very grave consequences for a woman and her baby. Pica is the craving and ingestion of nonfood substances and certain food substances (such as flour) that are not usually consumed in their original state. Among the most common items favored by women with pica are dirt, paint, clay, laundry starch, soap powder, and tobacco.

Pica affects women in all racial, ethnic, and socioeconomic groups. Although research has been done into its causes, we still do not know why pica happens.

The consequences of pica are clear. Even if a woman only craves nontoxic substances such as flour, she will probably develop deficiencies in nutrients essential to her and her baby because she is filling up on flour instead of a balanced diet. If the woman craves toxic substances such as paint chips containing lead, she puts herself and her baby in danger of poisoning.

We do not bring up pica to frighten you. Most women do not develop pica and they have nothing to worry about. *If you think you have pica, don't panic, but don't ignore it.* Call your doctor and seek his or her help in addressing the problem. For some women, pica may be dealt with by eating healthy alternatives (sour foods or raw vegetables) that mimic the characteristics of the substance they crave. For others it is not this simple. Yet it is necessary—for mother and fetus—for any woman who has pica to face the problem right away.

Constipation   Constipation is a very common condition in pregnancy, especially during the last trimester. In many pregnant women, the internal clock resets, and they have bowel movements less frequently than nonpregnant women. There are four principal reasons why a pregnant woman becomes constipated:

1. The hormone progesterone is released by the placenta. Progesterone acts to stretch the muscle the uterus is made of so that the baby can grow. The hormone also slows muscle contractions so that the uterus will not expel the fetus. The slowed muscle contractions are essential in pregnancy, but the side effect is that the muscle the intestine is made of becomes sluggish and is less capable of moving the stool out of the system. The longer the stool remains in the system, the drier it becomes, making it even more difficult to eliminate.
2. As the uterus becomes large in the last trimester, it presses against the stomach and the intestines, further slowing digestion and elimination.
3. Many women are told by their doctors to take iron supplements to fulfill their iron needs. Iron can be binding in some cases.
4. Reduced physical activity often means that a woman's system does not operate on its usual schedule.

There are some tried-and-true responses for constipation, but before we tell you what to do to relieve your problem, there are three things you should not do.

Do not eat binding foods: Binding foods include hard cheeses, chocolate, and highly starchy foods such as white rice, unripe bananas, and white bread.

Avoid Diuretics: Any substance that can dehydrate you, such as coffee, tea, cola, and many prescription medications, can reduce the amount of liquid that reaches the intestine and make defecation more difficult. As an accompanying strategy, increase your intake of liquids that do not dehydrate, such as water, milk, and juice.

Do not take over-the-counter laxatives, mineral oil, or other medications indicated for constipation: Although they might ease your constipation, they inhibit absorption and deprive you of all the hard-earned nutrients you have eaten. While certain laxatives (such as stool softeners) are acceptable, there are better ways of counteracting constipation.

Eat more foods high in fiber: Fiber absorbs water and, as it enters the intestine, helps move the stool along. High-fiber foods include raw fruits and vegetables with skins left on, whole grains (found in whole wheat bread, oatmeal, grits, bran, and wheat germ), brown rice, nuts, beans, legumes, and dried fruits. Don't eat too much fiber right away or you will overload. If you were not a fiber eater before, gradually increase the amount you consume. Too much fiber will carry nutrients out of your system, especially calcium. Also, do not take your prenatal vitamin with your meal so that the fiber will not absorb the nutrients you get in your vitamin.

STRATEGIES FOR DEALING WITH CONSTIPATION

Look for foods with laxative properties: The star in this category is the prune, a food too many people poke fun at until the time comes when they need it. Prunes are sweet and delicious, and a couple will probably go a long way. Other dried fruits such as raisins, figs, and apricots may also help.

Drink more liquids: As we mentioned earlier, when liquids are combined with fiber, they help move the stool along. Warm liquids such as broth and water first thing in the morning work particularly well. Try heating the Lemon-Mint Water (page 265).

Eat a good breakfast and regular meals: Your system has its own clock. When food doesn't arrive on schedule, some things slow down and others speed up. Your intestine will work more slowly and your stomach will produce more acid, and then you will really feel bad. Breakfast is especially important to provide energy and get the system going.

If you are constipated, try to have a bowel movement in the morning when the reflex in your colon is often stronger: This works for some people. Sometimes the first meal of the day will initiate a chain of events that will result in a bowel movement.

Add exercise to your routine: Many pregnant women

sharply reduce their physical activity during pregnancy. If your doctor says that certain exercise is permissible for you (as it is for most pregnant women), you should make it part of your routine. A brisk walk or a couple of laps in the pool on a regular basis may result in your doing other things on a regular basis too, and you will be happier for it.

Diarrhea   Although not as common in pregnancy as constipation, diarrhea should not be ignored. If it lasts more than a couple of days, contact your physician. Diarrhea may be a product of food poisoning. (You can read about selecting food and storing it properly starting on page 100.) If your stools are bloody or mucusy, be sure to let your doctor know.

The best response to diarrhea is to stop eating and drinking anything but water for about 12 hours and to take it easy. Your system needs to get itself back to normal functioning, so any food you eat will only delay that process. Once you resume drinking other liquids and eating, have warm neutral liquids such as broth and bland foods that bind, such as white rice and a banana. Be sure not to become dehydrated, because you and your baby need liquid. Gradually add other foods to your diet, but steer clear of the high-fiber foods that you would select for constipation. An over-the-counter medication for diarrhea such as Kaopectate is safe for pregnant women. With proper attention your diarrhea should abate within 48 hours. If it persists, call your doctor.

Heartburn   Heartburn, which affects between 30 and 70% of pregnant women during the second and third trimesters, is incorrectly named. Fortunately, it is not the heart that burns, but the esophagus, the canal that brings food from the mouth to the stomach. The effects of progesterone that we described in the section about constipation (see page 56) also come into play in causing heartburn. This same hormone relaxes the muscle that closes the passage between the esophagus and the stomach. This muscle, called the esophageal sphincter, allows food to enter the stomach when you are eating. During pregnancy, when the sphincter is relaxed by progesterone, some stomach acid flows up to the esophagus, causing that burning feeling. Also, as the fetus grows and the uterus is pushed against the stomach, more pressure is created on the esophageal sphincter, letting more acid pass to the esophagus.

Heartburn cannot be fully eliminated, but its symptoms can be alleviated. We suggest that you follow the strategies listed below before considering antacid medication.

Eat smaller, more frequent meals: This way you will not have that overly full feeling that will lead to further discomfort.

Do not lie down after eating: By remaining upright you are allowing your food to move downward and are discouraging the upward flow of acid to your esophagus. Eat your last meal of the day at least 3 hours before going to bed. In extreme cases, sleep slightly propped up by pillows so that there will be less upward flow of acid.

Take a walk after eating: Sometimes this gentle form of exercise is an effective response to heartburn and, at the very least, you are not reclining, which encourages the upward flow of acid.

Eat a diet high in protein and low in fat: This is the best nutritional response to heartburn. Avoid chocolate, coffee, alcohol, fried foods, spicy foods, sour cream, pork products, carbonated beverages, and citrus fruits and juices.

Eat slowly and chew your food: Hurried eating is never healthy, especially when you have heartburn.

Wear loose-fitting clothes: Don't let vanity get in the way of your comfort and well-being. Tight clothing will add to the pushing action of the stomach against the esophagus. Some maternity clothes are designed to expand as you do and these are preferable. Anything that leaves an indentation around your midsection should be put away until after your pregnancy.

Focus on relaxing: Heartburn is often associated with stress. If you reduce your stress you may also reduce your heartburn. Take slow, deep abdominal breaths if you are feeling stressed. Make mealtime a quiet time, accompanied by soothing music. If this is not possible, be sure to find time during your day for quiet moments.

If, and only if, none of these remedies works, take an antacid medication available at your pharmacy. Bear in mind that some antacids prevent the absorption of nutrients and cause constipation, so they should be used sparingly.

STRATEGIES FOR DEALING WITH HEARTBURN

Potential Complications
of Pregnancy

$$4$$

*I*n the previous chapter we looked at conditions that affect many women during their pregnancies. Most of them, while uncomfortable, are not particularly serious if addressed properly in medical and nutritional terms. There are, however, certain conditions—usually referred to as **complications of pregnancy**—that develop in some pregnant women. These complications are more serious than the typical conditions and require special care and attention. In most cases, a woman who carefully follows her doctor's instructions will come through with flying colors and deliver a healthy baby. We shall address the conditions that have a nutritional component.

If you have one of these conditions—**gestational diabetes, preeclampsia (or pretoxemia of pregnancy), intrauterine growth retardation (IUGR)** and **insufficient weight gain,** or a **twin** or **multiple pregnancy**—you will need to make more frequent visits to the doctor's office and follow all the special guidelines, diets, and medication plans your doctor prescribes. These conditions require special vigilance on your part, but you should put things in perspective by remembering that this vigilance is only for a few months, and you are working toward a wonderful goal.

The term **gestational diabetes** is a lot scarier than the condition itself. Gestational diabetes occurs during pregnancy and disappears soon after the baby's birth. Do not confuse it with juvenile diabetes or adult-onset diabetes, which are very serious, permanent conditions that affect millions of people.

Gestational Diabetes

If you are a diabetic—as opposed to a *gestational* diabetic—you must plan carefully before considering pregnancy. Talk with your doctor and be sure to undergo the tests he or she will recommend. Your diabetes may be exacerbated during pregnancy, which means your diet and insulin requirements will require constant monitoring. However, being diabetic no longer means that a woman should forget dreams of having a baby. Nowadays, with proper care and constant attention, the over-whelming majority of diabetic women have successful pregnancies when they work closely with their doctors.

Back to gestational diabetes: *Gestation* is another word for preg-nancy, and the term *gestational diabetes* refers to the change in blood sugar levels that occurs in about 3% of pregnant women. A test for ges-tational diabetes, called the glucose control test (GCT) is usually given between the 24th and 26th weeks of pregnancy, when most cases of the condition are first apparent (the typical pregnancy lasts 40 weeks).

If you have read about glucose, insulin, and energy on page 7, you know that the pancreas produces a hormone called insulin. This hor-mone is used by the body to release energy from glucose (which is stored in the liver) and to provide energy to the cells in the body. Diabetes is a condition in which the insulin cannot act on the glucose. There are two varieties of diabetes: Type I and Type II. Type I diabet-ics normally produce insufficient or no insulin, so they need to take daily doses (orally or by injection) of the hormone to keep their sys-tems functioning properly. Type II diabetics produce insulin but their body tissues do not use it correctly. They usually can control their con-ditions through proper diet and exercise. A few Type II diabetics need to take insulin or oral medication.

Diabetes in pregnancy is a different situation, but it imitates one of the two types of diabetes. Gestational diabetes occurs when a pregnant woman cannot produce enough insulin or her tissues do not respond sufficiently to what insulin is produced to meet her needs and those of her fetus.

There is a reason why this condition occurs in pregnant women. As the fetus grows, it is nourished by the placenta, the organ in the womb specially designed for the baby's nourishment. The placenta produces various hormones that benefit fetal development, but some of these hormones inhibit the action of insulin in the bodies of certain women, which causes a phenomenon called **insulin resistance**. This exists in all pregnant women to a certain degree, but in the more extreme cases, it results in a condition similar to diabetes in nonpregnant women. Because the placenta exits the mother's body during childbirth, the cause of the gestational diabetes disappears after delivery.

Women who have gestational diabetes during one pregnancy are 30% more likely to develop the condition in a future pregnancy. Even if a woman does not have gestational diabetes during her first pregnancy, that does not mean she will not have the condition in a future pregnancy. The older a pregnant woman is, the more likely she will be to develop gestational diabetes. Studies have shown that approximately 50% of gestational diabetic women will develop Type II diabetes later in their lives. If you are a gestational diabetic, make a habit of having regular tests for diabetes tests for the rest of your life.

Gestational diabetes in the mother, *if not properly managed*, may produce certain problems for the baby. These include the following conditions:

Macrosomia: Macrosomia is a fancy term for a fetus that is too big for its gestational age. In other words, if a fetus at a certain point in a pregnancy should weigh 6 pounds and it weighs 10 to 12 pounds, it will be considered macrosomic. Because of all the extra unused glucose in the mother's bloodstream, the fetus has more to feed on and grows much bigger than expected. Depending on the size of the mother and baby, doctors sometimes recommend that large babies be delivered by cesarean section, because a vaginal delivery might be too difficult.

Hypoglycemia: Hypoglycemia is sometimes called low blood glucose, or sugar. Special cells in the fetus's pancreas (called B-cells) produce extra insulin to meet the fetus's needs. Once the baby is born, it no longer gets glucose from its mother. The very high levels of insulin in the baby will further lower the baby's glucose level, resulting in not enough glucose to meet the baby's energy needs. Hypoglycemic newborns are given glucose intraveously until their levels return to normal. Undetected hypoglycemia can be very serious for a newborn baby.

Respiratory distress syndrome: A particular consequence of gestational diabetes in many fetuses is the insufficient development of their lungs. Babies born with respiratory distress syndrome (RDS) need to be kept on respirators until they can breathe well enough on their own. They also will require monitoring of their lung capabilities in early childhood, particularly if asthma develops.

Problems facing mothers with gestational diabetes: Aside from the difficulties that attend the delivery of a very large baby, mothers with gestational diabetes may encounter two other problems: preeclampsia (pretoxemia of pregnancy) and urinary tract infections. The former will be discussed in more detail later (see page 65). Urinary tract infections are usually treated with antibiotics which, of course, should be prescribed by your doctor and not come from an old bottle in your medicine chest.

HOW TO EAT IF YOU HAVE GESTATIONAL DIABETES

Your doctor will probably set up a special dietary program for you. The factors that influence the design of this diet will include your weight, size, age, and medical history as well as the size of your fetus. In the latter stages of pregnancy, the fetus gains ten times as much weight each day as in early pregnancy. Weight gain is normal, natural, and important for both mother and fetus during pregnancy. Your doctor will encourage you to eat well and gain weight. Typically, women should gain 25 to 30 pounds during pregnancy. Aside from the weight of her baby, this weight increase is due to her increased blood volume, the presence of amniotic fluid, the placenta in the womb, and the fat stores the mother develops that will be used in case she decides to breastfeed.

The gestational diabetic should also gain weight, but in a more controlled way. That is to say, she should not have sudden spurts of weight gain that would be the result of vast increases in food consumption. A slow, steady curve of weight gain is the most advisable for the gestational diabetic mother. She must visit her doctor once a week and have her weight and blood sugar levels checked so that her progress can be monitored.

Typically, a doctor will suggest that a gestational diabetic eat between three and five times a day in small- to medium-size portions.

This way, the body will not have to handle so many nutrients at one time and they can be absorbed better. You will likely be encouraged to eat a balanced diet, which you can read about in great detail in chapter 1. This usually is composed of 50 to 60% carbohydrates (especially those from pasta, rice, grain, bread, and potato), 15 to 20% protein (from meat, egg, fish, and beans), and 20 to 30% fat (from oil, butter, fish, meat, and egg). In addition, you will need all the vitamins and minerals available in vegetables, fruits, and all other foods.

It also is likely that a doctor will recommend a diet high in fiber, which recent studies have shown to be effective in controlling glucose levels. Because fiber often absorbs other nutrients, preventing them from being used by the body, you should have your main fiber meal at one sitting and eat meals rich in nutrients at other times in the day. Research has also shown that gestational diabetics require more zinc, magnesium, and vitamin C, so your doctor will encourage you to eat foods rich in these nutrients and to get them through a prenatal supplement.

Most of the recipes in this book are suitable for gestational diabetics. Consult the "Doctor's Note" that accompanies each recipe to see if there is any reason you should avoid it. Otherwise, feel free to eat and enjoy it.

EXERCISE AND GESTATIONAL DIABETES

Exercise, in most cases, lowers blood glucose levels and leads to an increase in insulin secretion. Your doctor may put you on a special exercise routine and diet that are manageable for gestational diabetic women, including walking or swimming as well as measured intakes of glucose.

IF SPECIAL DIET AND EXERCISE ARE NOT ENOUGH

Sometimes all the non-medical responses to gestational diabetes are not sufficient to counteract the problem. In that case, the woman is usually given insulin in amounts measured to her needs. If you receive insulin therapy, you may be told not to exercise, because both the hormone and the exercise lower glucose levels.

Remember . . . gestational diabetes ends once your baby is born.

For more information about gestational diabetes, contact the American Diabetes Association, 1660 Duke Street, Alexandria, Virginia 22314 (Telephone: 800-ADA-DISC; in Virginia and metropolitan Washington, D.C.: 703-549-1500).

If you are familiar with the term **toxemia,** you may confuse it with the term pretoxemia of pregnancy. Toxemia is blood poisoning and has absolutely nothing to do with pretoxemia of pregnancy, which is another way of describing a condition that includes high blood pressure, vision problems, and swelling of tissues in the mother. The preferred term now used by doctors is **preeclampsia** to prevent confusion between this condition and blood poisoning.

The main indicators of preeclampsia, which occurs in the third trimester of pregnancy, are

Preeclampsia (also called pretoxemia of pregnancy)

- A sudden, sharp increase in weight (your weight is monitored at doctor's visits and you may also weigh yourself at home).
- Swelling of face, fingers, and legs and puffiness under the eyes.
- High blood pressure.
- Blurring of vision, especially the contours of the range of view; some women see stars and dots.
- Protein in the urine (detected in urine tests conducted by your doctor).

Women with preeclampsia are usually confined to bed, and take medications, and follow a closely monitored diet to keep their blood pressure down. Long confinement, however, can result in less than optimal conditions in the womb and possible vascular complications for the mother, so additional measures need to be taken. If doctors determine that the baby can survive viably outside of a mother who is past her 32nd week of pregnancy, labor might be induced. Modern hospitals are equipped to care for mother and baby under these circumstances and the prognosis for both is excellent. (If preeclampsia becomes more severe—a condition called **eclampsia** or **toxemia of pregnancy**—there can be convulsions or even coma that are very dangerous to mother and unborn child.)

It is not known what causes preeclampsia, nor are there preventive measures to take aside from being in good physical and nutritional shape before becoming pregnant. You should also know your blood pressure as you plan for pregnancy. Preeclampsia occurs in approximately 5% of pregnant women, 66% of whom had high blood pressure (hypertension) before their pregnancies began. Hypertensive women, many from lower economic groups, often have bad diets with too much salt and fat. Studies of poor women around the world have revealed a direct connection between poverty, poor diet, and incidence of preeclampsia. (Don't forget, though, that pregnant women need salt: It is found naturally in meats and vegetables and is an essential nutrient. We discourage you only from the *added* salt that is found in cold cuts, in fast-food restaurant meals, in commercially prepared food—and, of course, any salt you add to food yourself.)

Women with diabetes and chronic kidney problems are also more likely to develop preeclampsia. This is yet another reason why a complete checkup before or just after conception is a smart idea.

Different studies have shown that increased doses of certain nutrients, especially protein, calcium, zinc, and iron, result in less severe cases of preeclampsia. Thus one nutritional response that doctors take is to increase the level of these and other nutrients through supplementation.

As an educated mother-to-be who is aware of the dietary correlates of preeclampsia, you will better be able to fashion a diet that will suit your needs and those of your fetus. Most of the recipes in this book have no added salt and are high in vitamins and minerals, making them ideal for any woman who may have preeclampsia. If you have this condition, show your doctor some of the recipes you may want to cook so that you both may select the ones that are right for you.

Prematurity and Intrauterine Growth Retardation

A premature baby is one that is born *before term*, before 36 weeks of gestation. Preemies have special health problems because they have not fully developed in the womb. These problems include much higher rates of infant mortality as well as respiratory problems, cerebral palsy, and other forms of damage to the central nervous system. Through advanced medical technology and expertise, more preemies survive today than ever before. The particular subspecialty that deals with the care of the newborn is called neonatology.

The lay term for **intrauterine growth retardation (IUGR)** is *low-birth-weight baby*, one who has not grown sufficiently in the womb. This is a baby who is born *at term* (40 weeks) but who weighs less than 5 pounds. An IUGR baby is likely to suffer many of the same problems as the preemie, but the reasons are different. This is a condition that, in most instances, relates directly to nutrition. An inadequate weight gain by the mother often leads to inadequate development of the fetus in the uterus. Pregnant women who take in more calories and gain more weight are less likely to produce low-birth-weight babies.

IUGR need not happen if you eat properly. Read the recipes in this book, which were designed to be delicious and appealing while delivering the nutrients you need. Select dishes that appeal to you, eat them, and enjoy them.

Although carrying twins is not a complication in the sense that gestational diabetes, preeclampsia, and IUGR are, there are additional things to think about if you are expecting two babies for the price of one. First of all, you should definitely choose an obstetrician/gynecologist as your health practitioner (as should a woman with any complications of pregnancy). These doctors are specially trained to deal with multiple deliveries, which sometimes require cesarian sections. Women expecting twins also have a higher incidence of anemia, gestational diabetes, preeclampsia, and premature delivery. The babies they deliver often are of lower birth weights, even if they are not premature.

Women carrying twins need to gain more weight than the woman carrying one fetus. A total weight gain of 35 to 45 pounds is the current recommendation from most experts. This means a weekly weight gain of 1.5 pounds during the second and third trimesters. If you are lagging behind, select recipes that will provide you with a faster weight gain per portion. This does not mean you should resort to high-calorie junk food, which often contains junk (hence the name) that is bad for everyone, but is especially bad for a pregnant woman with a higher-than-average likelihood of developing certain complications of pregnancy. You have the luxury of indulging in wonderful food, rich in flavor, nutrients, *and* calories, so you should make the most of this opportunity.

Twin and
Multiple
Pregnancies

Breastfeeding and
Postdelivery Weight Loss

(5)

*F*ollowing the birth of your baby, there will be a whole range of issues to deal with regarding the newest member of your family. Because this is a book about nutrition, we will confine ourselves to the topics that relate to that subject.

Throughout your pregnancy you fed your fetus by eating the right foods with the knowledge that you were delivering particular nutrients to your unborn child. Now that the baby has arrived, you should still think in terms of eating correctly to give your baby the best of everything. If you decide to breastfeed your baby—which we encourage you to do—you will continue to supply your baby with nutrients you have consumed. If you choose not to breastfeed, you still need to be in top shape and full of energy to meet the demands of a newborn who requires a great deal of attention.

The first part of this chapter is devoted to women who decide to breastfeed. Most doctors now strongly encourage women to breastfeed, emphasizing that even a short period will offer nutritional, immunological, and psychological benefits to a baby. A woman who consumes a balanced diet and meets her recommended daily allowances (RDAs) for lactation (milk formation that occurs during the breastfeeding period) will provide her baby with all the nutrition it needs. Many physicians will continue to prescribe prenatal vitamins during lactation. This supplement is an insurance policy and should not be viewed as a substitute for a balance diet.

Breastfeeding (also called nursing) is a craft you will need to learn. Ask to be taught while you are still in the hospital or get information from the La Leche League of America. This organization is devoted to the instruction and support of women who choose to breastfeed. You may call them for information and referrals to your local chapter at 800-525-3243 between 9 A.M. and 3 P.M. Central Time. The league's headquarters are in Franklin Park, Illinois (telephone: 708-451-1891), and there are local chapters across the country.

Lactation is a miracle of nature. The mother's body prepares for it throughout pregnancy. Within the breast are **alveolae** (milk glands) that grow under the influence of pregnancy hormones. The alveolae secrete the milk, which flows into the ducts that lead to the nipple. After delivery, there is a sharp decrease in pregnancy hormones and, at the same time, the body produces prolactin (a hormone that promotes milk production) and oxytocin (a hormone that helps the breast release milk).

Breastfeeding

Many women wonder why they cannot simply bottle feed their babies instead of nursing them. The fact is that Nature (a mother herself, after all) has designed things so that breast milk is the perfect food for newborns. Its composition is different from cow's milk and even somewhat different from infant formula that is sold commercially.

WHY IS MOTHER'S MILK BETTER?

- Mother's milk contains most nutrients in the exact proportion that a baby needs.
- Mother's milk contains less protein than cow's milk, but the type it does contain (lactalbumin) is better digested by babies than caseinogen, the chief protein in cow's milk. This particular amino acid profile (from the lactalbumin) combined with high levels of vitamin C in breast milk, promotes good brain and muscle growth.
- Babies who are breastfed tend to not to become overweight

and they do not suffer from constipation or diarrhea.
• Breast milk has only one-third of the sodium found in cow's milk. This is all the sodium a newborn needs.

The most important difference between mother's milk and other foods you could give your baby is that *mother's milk contains immunoglobins and antibodies that help prevent a baby from getting sick.*

The following chart will show you the relative compositions of breast milk found in the average woman, one type of infant formula (SMA) and whole fresh cow's milk. There are more than a dozen different commercial formulas on the market. We are using SMA as a typical example. Infant formulas remain close to the composition of breast milk (which varies a little from woman to woman), but they do not contain the vital antiinfective properties of breast milk.

As you can see, some nutritive values for breast milk are smaller. This is because, at the beginning, a newborn cannot digest a lot of protein and certain other nutrients.

	SMA FORMULA (1 fl. oz.)	BREAST MILK (1 fl. oz.)	WHOLE FRESH COW'S MILK (1 fl. oz.)
Calories	20	24	20
Protein	0.4 g	0.3 g	1 g
Fat	1.1 g	1.2 g	1 g
Carbohydrates	2.1 g	2.9 g	1.5 g
Calcium	12 ml	10 ml	36 ml
Potassium	16 ml	16 ml	44 ml

Here are some other benefits of breastfeeding:

- The psychological benefit that results from the bonding of mother and child is immeasurable.
- Obviously, it is lower in cost than commercial formulas.
- A beneficial side effect of the production of oxytocin is that this hormone promotes the firming of smooth muscle. In other words, oxytocin will play a role in shrinking your stretched-out uterus back to its normal size, helping you to return to your prepregnancy figure.
- Breast milk is about 85% water, a percentage sufficient so that a baby does not need water from other sources even in hot, dry climates.

What breast milk lacks: Forgive us for saying so, but Mother Nature could have improved her recipe for breast milk: It is low in vitamins K and D. Breastfed infants are routinely given these vitamins in drop form.

DISADVANTAGES OF BREASTFEEDING

While we feel that the advantages of nursing substantially outweigh the disadvantages, there are a few problems and particular responsibilities that accompany this activity.

- A mother must assume total responsibility for her baby's feedings. If you decide to breastfeed, you must commit to doing it all the time. This is a big commitment and can be especially difficult for women who work outside the home. A working woman who goes back to work relatively soon after childbirth will have to work out a feeding schedule. Many progressive employers are now making provisions for child care in the workplace that include areas where women may breastfeed their babies. A working woman whose baby is being cared for at home by someone else may consider using a pump (see page 73) so that a supply of breast milk will be available for her baby's regular feedings.
- A woman must continue to be very vigilant about her diet, knowing that anything she ingests can be passed to her baby.
- A breastfeeding mother must continue to avoid substances

such as alcohol, caffeine, and most medications as these would all be passed to an infant who would possibly suffer a severe reaction. (Needless to say, tobacco and all recreational drugs are completely out of the question. These should have been eliminated from your life long before your baby was born and they have no place in your life now!)

• **During breastfeeding, the mother's body gives preference to the newborn in terms of distribution of nutrients.** When a mother does not consume enough nutrients, the nutrients for the baby will be drawn from the reserves in the mother, leaving her with a deficiency. This could have serious consequences.

The best example of a mother being deprived of a necessary nutrient is calcium. The RDA for calcium during lactation is 1200 mg. If a woman does not consume at least this amount of calcium each day, the calcium will be drawn from her bones to be fed to her baby. Bones deficient in calcium become brittle. Years later, this deprivation may show up as osteoporosis, a condition in which menopausal women lose bone mass and are more subject to serious fractures.

In chapter 1 you will find the RDAs for every nutrient you need. You will notice that in some cases the RDA for lactating women is lower than for pregnant women (for example, folate and iron), in some cases the RDA is the same (calcium); and in others the RDA is higher (zinc, magnesium, and iodine). To reiterate what we have mentioned earlier: Your doctor may recommend particular supplements. Do not take vitamins during breastfeeding without medical supervision.

Who should not breastfeed:

• Women with serious debilitating illnesses (heart, kidneys, severe anemia, and in some cases, diabetes) or *any* contagious disease.
• Women who are taking medication for any condition must check with their baby's doctor as to whether that medication might pose risks to the baby.
• A woman whose baby has lactose intolerance or phenylketonuria (PKU).

• Any woman who experiences a profound aversion to breastfeeding.

It is possible to "express" milk from the breast, using a specially designed pump, so that a baby can be fed breast milk from a pre-sterilized bottle. Your doctor or the La Leche League can explain this to you. One advantage of this type of bottle feeding is that a father can participate in the feeding, increasing the bond between father and baby.

USING A PUMP

There are two types of pumps: manual and battery operated. Both are effective. A manual pump costs between $10 and $20, and a battery-powered pump (which works faster) costs between $25 and $50. Battery pumps can be rented. You will also need several sterilized bottles with stoppers as you pump so that you can store extra milk for later. These bottles are either disposable or reusable; the latter must be sterilized before each use, according to the manufacturer's directions or those you receive from your doctor or La Leche League. Someone from La Leche also will explain about dating the milk bottles. Breast milk may be stored in the refrigerator (for up to 48 hours) or freezer (it will be good for 3 to 6 months—assuming the freezer remains at a constant cold temperature—and will not lose any nutrients). Breast milk that has been pumped should always be served at room temperature.

We recommend that all women learn to pump breast milk. It will make their lives easier in that they can be away from their baby for a few hours (assuming, of course, that the baby is being attended to by a caregiver selected by the parents). With this free time the mother can work, rest, give attention to her other children, or spend valuable time alone with the baby's father.

If you choose not to breastfeed:
• Talk to your baby's pediatrician about the best formula for your child if you are not planning to (or cannot) feed your baby breast milk.
• To deal with engorgement of breasts, use ice compresses. Never express or pump milk: This will stimulate production of more milk. Your doctor may recommend a medication that will hormonally suppress milk production.

• You still need to maintain an excellent, nutrient-rich diet. Your body may have lost a lot of nutrients during pregnancy and, especially, delivery, and you need to get back into good nutritional shape, both for yourself and your baby.

Breastfeeding and birth control: There is the mistaken assumption that breastfeeding inhibits ovulation, thus preventing conception. This is not true. We know many women who became pregnant with a second child while nursing the first. If your birth control choice is oral contraceptive pills, you must talk to your physician immediately after the birth of your child to learn when to resume the pill.

Weight Loss After Pregnancy

One of the chief preoccupations of pregnant women is whether they will regain their prepregnancy figures. You should not expect to walk out of the hospital in tight jeans, but there is some encouraging news.

• If your baby was, for example, 8 pounds, you are going to be more than 8 pounds lighter after delivery because the placenta and amniotic fluid left your body as well. The placenta weighs about 1 pound and the amniotic fluid weighs about 2 pounds.
• Within 72 hours after delivery, you will lose more than half of the extra fluid that your body accumulated during pregnancy (a loss of approximately 2 more pounds).
• After delivery you will receive a shot of pitocin (an animal-derived form of oxytocin), a substance that helps shrink your uterus to normal size (the size of your left fist if you are a righty).
• Oxytocin, the hormone produced during lactation, helps tone muscles so that your uterus and abdominal muscles will shrink and become more firm.
• The fat stores (4 to 8 pounds) that you built up during pregnancy will be used for the energy you need to manufacture milk, a highly energy-intensive process that uses 500 to 600 calories per day. If you don't nurse, these stores will have to be eliminated through gradual weight loss and intelligent exercise (see below).

LOSING WEIGHT

If you are breastfeeding, you have some of the natural advantages indicated above. Whether or not you are breastfeeding, you need to focus on ways other than crazy, radical weight-loss schemes to drop poundage.

One of the best choices is *exercise.* If you did not have a cesarean section, you may be able to engage in some forms of moderate exercise (such as swimming and walking) soon after delivery. As always, discuss this with your doctor before embarking on an exercise program.

The postpartum period is sometimes a stressful one that is occasionally accompanied by depression. If your response to stress and depression is to eat less, make sure that when you do eat you have foods that please you *and* that are good for you. Select recipes from this book that were favorites during your pregnancy and make them now. All are rich in nutrients and few are particularly fattening. If your reaction to stress or depression is to regularly reach for the comfort of food, go ahead and eat frequently, but choose healthier foods such as fruit, whole grain muffins, and a chunk of hard cheese instead of junk food.

Set realistic goals. About 1 pound a week for nursing mothers and 1½ for nonbreastfeeding women are realistic expectations.

Weigh yourself every few days, or even just once a week, rather than each day. There is no point in obsessing. Try to weigh yourself at the same hour of day each time you get on the scale. This will present a more accurate picture and might minimize disappointment.

Don't recriminate yourself if you cheat occasionally. Enjoy that forbidden piece of food to the fullest but don't decide that because you have already gone off the wagon you might as well continue. Correct the situation by eating less high-calorie food the next day.

As with any diet, the weight will stay off if you lose it gradually and intelligently. See chapter 1 for listings of foods high in vitamins, minerals (particularly iron and calcium) and low in fat and sugar. Most of the recipes in this book fit that general description. Allow the weight to come off slowly, and it will stay off. *But do not become sick or rundown due to inferior nutrition!*

A special word to any reader who had one or more of the complications of pregnancy described in chapter 4: These complications are often nutritionally based or can be alleviated through carefully monitored consumption of particular nutrients. Be sure to discuss with your doctor what special regime you should follow after delivery. Perhaps you might require more or less sugar or salt or carbohydrates. You need to find out.

Dietary and Life-Style Changes During Pregnancy

6

*H*aving a baby entails a certain amount of behavior modification, most of which is actually very good for the mother too. If you are planning your pregnancy, you should start making changes before conception. If you discover that you are pregnant before you've begun to make your life-style changes, you will need to catch up quickly for the good of your baby and yourself.

The most important thing is that you are in good physical shape for the months ahead. Make a doctor's supervision your first priority. Another goal is to be in top nutritional shape, which is why you bought this book.

For most women, other changes need to take place too. A regular sleeping routine is important, because you need your rest. Adjustments at work (snack breaks and down time) should be considered to make life easier at the office. As the pregnancy continues, women need to purchase clothes that are not only loose and comfortable but attractive as well.

Serious changes: There are many women who need to make

changes of a much more profound nature. If they consume alcohol, caffeine, nicotine, or certain medications that are potentially harmful to their unborn children, they must quickly change their life-styles. All of these substances are known as **teratogens,** which are substances that cause harm to a fetus during pregnancy.

Alcohol

Because many women don't realize they are pregnant until they are in their second month, it is possible that they do not stop drinking alcoholic beverages before receiving the good news. This should not be a cause for much alarm if alcohol consumption stops when a woman learns she is going to have a baby. This is because, during the first 8 weeks of pregnancy, there is no development of the fetal nervous system, which is the part of the fetus most affected by alcohol. However, if a woman continues to drink during pregnancy, the teratogenic effects could be quite serious.

A fetus that is exposed to alcohol for most of its stay in the womb *may* turn into a baby born with fetal alcohol syndrome (FAS). In the United States, 1 or 2 babies per 1000 live births are victims of FAS. Certain ethnic and socioeconomic groups, particularly Native Americans, have a much higher-than-average incidence of FAS. White, upper-middle-class women with good diets tend to have a much lower-than-average incidence of FAS, even if they do consume an occasional alcoholic beverage. It is notable that French and Italian women, who usually have excellent diets and prenatal care, do not have a high incidence of FAS babies even though wine is part of their regular life-style.

Research has shown that there is little correlation between how much alcohol a mother consumes during pregnancy and whether her baby develops FAS, but surely the likelihood of birth defects will increase when women who have other risk factors drink more. FAS babies suffer many complications, including mental retardation, abnormal facial features, heart problems, genitourinary defects, damage to the central nervous system, and insufficient growth before or after birth. Some research has shown that women who drink are more likely to have spontaneous abortions.

Alcohol consumption is sometimes related to a decreased intake of healthy foods, which is a serious problem for mother and fetus. Alcohol also causes dehydration, which is not healthy for pregnant or lactating women. And mothers who breastfeed pass alcohol to their babies. And remember: A bottle of beer, a glass of wine, and a shot of whiskey all contain roughly the same amount of alcohol.

You may say that the percentage of FAS babies is too small to worry about. The point is that some babies *are* born with FAS, and you don't want yours to be one of them. Simply stated, it can generally be said that alcohol can't help and could hurt pregnant women and their fetuses, so it should probably be eliminated from your routine. Many women naturally lose a taste for alcoholic beverages when they become pregnant, so they do not have to worry about this problem.

If you still want a drink, check some of the recipes in the beverage chapter for possible substitutes. Or see if any of the alcohol-free wines or beers now on the market are pleasing to your palate. If you are a person who equates a drink with winding down or calming your nerves, try to find other ways to relax. These might include exercise (see page 85), music, conversation, meditation, or whatever works for you.

Try to get the baby's father and other loved ones you spend time with to share delicious nonalcoholic drinks with you. We want to emphasize that drinking intelligently and in moderation away from pregnancy is fine if a person is not an alcoholic and if that person does not drive or in any way endanger people near them by drinking. Wine, in particular, is one of life's great pleasures and, in nonpregnant adults, is thought to have healthful properties when consumed moderately. In pregnancy, however, doing without alcohol is a wise move.

There is one small exception to these sweeping suggestions. A couple of the recipes in this book call for wine in cooking. If you bring the wine in a sauce to a boil, most of the alcohol will evaporate and leave the good flavor of the wine. *If you crave the taste of wine, then cooking with wine is the way to go.*

Caffeine

There is a divergence of opinion among doctors and experts as to whether caffeine is harmful to the fetus. Some say that moderate consumption of caffeine (which is found in large amounts in coffee, tea, chocolate, and cola) will cause no problems. Many others assert that, although there is little conclusive evidence about caffeine, it is still best to avoid anything containing this substance. Coffee and tea contain xanthines, which narrow the blood vessels and could, therefore, cut off oxygen to the fetus. It is also well known that caffeine elevates blood pressure, which could pose potential complications to mother and fetus.

What is certain is that caffeine is not healthy for most people. It has a diuretic effect, which means that a heavy caffeine consumer (six or more cups a day) should worry about dehydration. Caffeine also causes the heart rate to speed up and is a leading cause of tension, irritability, and insomnia. Don't you have enough to think about without adding these problems to your busy life?

During breastfeeding, caffeine in mother's milk goes directly to the newborn, making it cranky and inhibiting its ability to sleep adequately. This is not a good way for a baby to start life.

Make it your goal to gradually cut caffeine out of your diet, at least for the duration of your pregnancy and breastfeeding. Many pregnant women develop an aversion to caffeinated drinks, so they do not have to think about quitting. However, if you still want caffeinated drinks, follow some of the suggestions below.

If you are a regular drinker of caffeinated drinks, you should try to reduce your intake *gradually*. Going cold turkey will make you even more irritable and jumpy than you were before. Therefore, attempt to cut back a little at a time. Here are some tips:

- Skip the second cup in the morning. Have juice or a fruit on a coffee break.
- If you crave the taste of coffee or tea, look for high-quality decaffeinated coffees and teas, including coffee decaffeinated by the so-called Swiss water process. These are not caffeine-free, but they contain approximately one-quarter of the caffeine found in regular coffee or tea.
- Seek healthy alternatives that may taste good. Juices, cold or hot herbal teas (read about herbal teas on p. 274), hot cider, and warm milk are all possibilities.
- If you must have "high test" coffee, at least cut back on the amount of caffeine in your cup. For example, chicory or Postum blended with coffee will reduce the percentage of straight coffee in your drink, resulting in less caffeine.
- Make your coffee a *café au lait*. Instead of a cup with a splash of milk, make it half coffee and half milk. Warm the milk and, if you want, add a dash of cinnamon before blending with the cof-

fee. Gradually change the proportion until it becomes warm milk with a splash of coffee.

• You may feel sluggish as you cut down on caffeine. Habitual coffee drinkers do not realize the kick the drink gives them until they stop drinking it. If you feel run-down, slightly increase your consumption of healthy carbohydrates (rice, pasta, and healthful muffins) to make up for the energy you lack. Remember that healthy carbohydrates provide a much better "high" than the one you would get from a cup of coffee.

Cigarettes

With all the negative publicity that cigarette smoking has received, it is remarkable that some people still think it is chic or desirable to smoke. In case you have missed all the news about smoking tobacco (in cigarettes, cigars, and pipes), let us be the ones to tell you: **Cigarette smoking is dangerous to your health and can harm your unborn child.** The long-term effects of cigarettes on your health may result in terrible diseases and early death. (We are being especially blunt here because the problem is so serious.)

Here are just a few complications the smoking mother may face:

• Smoking reduces the flow of oxygen to the womb and increases the amount of carbon monoxide. Such an environment is no place for a fetus to develop healthily.

• Babies born to smoking mothers usually are smaller in weight and less healthy at birth. Their likelihood of survival and normal development is lower than babies born to nonsmokers.

• Smoking depletes the levels of vitamin B_{12}, vitamin C, and certain amino acids in the mother, often resulting in fetal deprivation of these elements.

• If you smoke, the poisons in tobacco will be passed directly to your baby during breastfeeding.

• Passive smoking, that is, when people around you smoke even if you don't, can still cause problems. You will breathe in some of the more than 2,000 compounds in cigarette smoke that are harmful. Ask those you live and work with to smoke outside the house or office or at least in another room. Restaurants, airplanes, and most public places have smoking sections as well. Make a point of staying away from concentrations of smoke.

The sooner you stop smoking, the better for you and your baby. If you stop before conception, your body will be better prepared for pregnancy. If you stop as soon as you learn you are pregnant, the harmful effects on your fetus will be minimized.

People usually smoke for a particular reason. Once you can identify the reason, it will be easier to come up with alternatives. For example, if you are accustomed to having something in your mouth, you might feel awkward without a cigarette dangling from your lips. Put a toothpick there instead and whirl it around to your heart's content. Chew on a carrot stick, pop some raisins in your mouth, or slowly eat a breadstick. Junk food is not an acceptable alternative.

Other people enjoy smoking because it keeps their hands busy. If this is you, focus on doing other enjoyable things that are tactile: piano playing, typing, letter-writing, playing board games, baking, knitting, weaving, sculpting, playing cards, and so forth.

If you find tobacco stimulating, slightly increase your intake of healthy carbohydrates (rice, pasta, and healthful muffins), which will give you an energy lift when you are dragging. Get involved in other activities that are stimulating that take place in smoke-free environments: movies, concerts, theater, swimming, and brisk walking.

If you smoke to calm down, find other ways to relax: listen to music, meditate, get a neck rub or a massage, or take a walk. If smoking is associated with particular activities or places, such as a coffee break in the employees' lounge, avoid those activities and places.

Do not go it alone. Seek help and support from friends and family who will keep you busy with other things so that smoking will not be your focus. Ask your doctor for suggestions and help. You might be advised to join a therapy group dedicated to stopping smoking. You can contact your local branch of the American Cancer Society or call 800-4-CANCER for tips about how to quit smoking.

Recreational Drugs

Let there be no mistake about it: Any recreational drug that a pregnant woman uses during pregnancy is unhealthy for her and potentially life threatening for her fetus. When a pregnant drug addict experiences convulsions, oxygen is cut off from her fetus. A baby born to a drug-using mother faces many obstacles to normal growth and development that other newborns never encounter.

If you are using any recreational drug, you must immediately stop for your good and the good of your fetus. However, *it is important that you do this under medical or professional supervision.* Going cold turkey when you are addicted to a drug may have serious consequences that you can not foresee, including fevers and chills, accelerated heartbeat, convulsions, and inability to eat or drink. Any problems you experience may have a negative effect on your fetus, which will go throught the same withdrawal you do, but without being monitored by a doctor. Candidly discuss your drug use with your doctor and seek his or her help in kicking the habit.

Because studies of children born to drug-using mothers are only relatively recent, it is difficult to document the long-term effects their mothers' actions will have. However, there is abundant knowledge of how newborns and young children suffer because of a drug-influenced prenatal period. Read the following if you still think you can use recreational drugs during pregnancy.

MARIJUANA   Don't assume that smoking marijuana is not as bad for your fetus as more "serious" drugs such as cocaine and heroin. Marijuana, even if smoked once or twice a month during pregnancy, can lead to serious problems for the fetus: premature birth, IUGR (see page 66), facial deformities, and difficult deliveries.

Carbon monoxide levels in the womb are much higher among women who smoke marijuana, which means the fetus is not getting the oxygen it needs. Because the component in marijuana that gets you high (called tetrahydrocannabinol, or THC) is fat soluble, it can be stored in the tissues of the fetus, giving it an intensive high that may leave lasting damage. Babies born to mothers who smoked marijuana during pregnancy are more likely to have neurological and emotional problems.

Some people mistakenly suggest that because marijuana often stimulates appetite pregnant "pot" users will eat better. This is a fallacy. Even if drug use brings on the munchies, a woman will likely eat the wrong foods and deprive her fetus of the nutrients it needs that only healthy foods would provide.

It does appear that marijuana use before conception (which is thought, in fact, to make conception more difficult) will not have harmful effects on the fetus if it is stopped once conception has occurred. However, a breastfeeding mother should not use marijuana.

Studies have shown that use of these pills during pregnancy may cause IUGR (see page 66) and all of its attendant problems. Babies born to mothers who took barbiturates often suffer seizures and have difficulty breathing. They experience a neurological slowdown and absorb nutrients less effectively.

BARBITURATES

This drug, whether inhaled as powder or taken in the form known as "crack," is potentially lethal for you and your fetus. It is easily absorbed by the placenta, which means that any cocaine you use will be fed to your fetus as well. Cocaine remains in the fetus twice as long as it does in the mother's system.

COCAINE

Among the most dangerous consequences of cocaine use is a complication known as **abruptio placentae**. This is the separation of the placenta from the wall of the uterus. The result is that a fetus will be denied food, oxygen, and the ability to eliminate waste. The result is almost certain death for the unborn child.

Even if abruptio placentae does not occur, cocaine may also cause IUGR and prematurity (see page 66), birth defects, brain damage, and difficult delivery. A baby that does survive may experience seizures, eating problems, irritability, and even sudden death. "Crack babies" who are now entering preschool and kindergarten have shown severe behavorial and learning problems (especially the inability to focus and concentrate) that will plague them for the rest of their lives.

In the very worst-case scenario, a heroin-using mother who shares needles may contract HIV, the virus that can cause AIDS. This tragic occurrence inevitably leads to premature death for mother and child.

HEROIN

Even if a heroin user does not share needles, there are enough disastrous things she can do to herself and her unborn to warrant great concern. Heroin use can cause abruptio placentae (see above), spontaneous abortion, IUGR and prematurity (see page 66), and death to the newborn. Babies who survive are often addicted to heroin and must be weaned of their "habit" in their fragile early days of life. This may cause seizures, vomiting, diarrhea, dehydration, sweating, and feeding difficulty. These traumatic first days of life may have lasting, long-term consequences, although this has not been sufficiently studied.

We have outlined all of the dreadful results of drug use to make it very clear to you that there is absolutely no justification for even the occasional toke on a joint if you plan to have a healthy baby. If you use drugs, "just saying no" may not be enough to get you to stop. Tell your doctor the truth and seek help in quitting.

Prescription and Over-the-Counter Drugs

There are many jars, bottles and containers in your medicine chest that contain prescription drugs and medications that you routinely take for small ills or more serious ongoing medical conditions. Examples include aspirin, cough syrup, sleeping pills, antihistamines, antibiotics, ointments, salves, and lotions. Although many of these are safe for use by pregnant women, others should not be used until after the baby is born and breastfeeding is completed.

As a general rule, you should not take medication during pregnancy unless specifically instructed to by your doctor.

This includes aspirin and ibuprofen (Advil and Nuprin are two over-the-counter brands of ibuprofen). Always take a moment to read the label or package of a medication before taking it (this is a wise move even if you are not pregnant). Many labels contain cautions that advise pregnant women not to take that particular medication.

As often as not, there may not be specific knowledge as to whether a certain medication may be harmful to a pregnant woman or her fetus. All medication taken by a mother crosses the placenta and can be ingested by the fetus. In the *Physician's Desk Reference*, a comprehensive directory consulted by doctors, many medications are described as follows: "The safety of [name of medication] in human pregancy has not been established. The use of this drug in pregnancy requires that the expected therapeutic benefit be balanced against possible hazard to mother and infant." In other words, check with your doctor before taking any medication.

It is especially important that unprescribed medication not be taken during the first trimester, when the embryo is developing. Past experience has shown doctors that certain drugs (such as Thalidomide and Acutane), when taken during the embryonic phase, can cause birth defects in most cases.

There are a couple of instances in this book in which we encourage you to take medication without calling your doctor (for example, Kaopectate for mild diarrhea). This advice is based on extensive medical research, and you may feel safe in following it. Similarly, if there *is* a medication that your doctor recommends you take for whatever reason, it is wise to follow his or her advice. Failure to take that medication correctly may cause other problems.

If you are being treated by a specialist for any condition not related to pregnancy or are having dental work done, tell that doctor that you are pregnant and mention any medications you are now taking.

Exercise

Unlike every other activity in this chapter, we do not want you to avoid exercise. Pregnant women who exercise correctly do themselves and their fetuses some good. Exercise promotes general physical health and well-being, good muscle tone, better functioning of the heart and respiratory system, and often results in psychological well-being too. During pregnancy, there are other specific benefits:

- Aerobic exercise will increase your intake of oxygen, crucial for your fetus' development.
- Exercise is good for your self-image: If you feel good, you look good.
- It may offer relief of the discomforts of headaches, backaches, fatigue, and shortness of breath.
- It will help you develop better posture (as your stomach and breasts enlarge, the demands on your back will increase).
- Better fitness may make delivery easier and certainly will make you more fit for postpartum recovery.
- The energy gained is needed for the demands of caring for a newborn.

As with most other activities in pregnancy, you should discuss your exercise goals with your doctor during one of your first prenatal visits. He or she will assess your current condition and determine what exercise is good for you and which ones you should abandon. If you are in superb shape due to regular exercise or if you are a professional athlete, discuss with your doctor the extent that you can continue your participation in your sport. If you are in poor physical shape, this is the time to engage in *moderate* exercise rather than starting an ambitious workout program.

Most exercise can be safely done until the 30th week of pregnancy.

Studies have shown that permissible exercise by mothers has had no negative effects on their fetuses.

Here are exercises and physical activities that are safe for most pregnant women:

- Aerobics, low-impact, low-intensity
- Aquacise and water aerobics
- Bicycling (to protect your back, adjust your bicycle seat so that your heel is 2 inches below the pedal when your leg is fully extended. You may be more comfortable riding a stationary bicycle because there is no risk of falling)
- Cross-country skiing
- Dancing (if not too frenetic)
- Golf
- Nautilus (upper body and leg lifts only, of no more than 10 pounds and under supervision)
- Pregnancy-conditioning exercises
- Prenatal exercise programs
- Rowing

The best two exercises of all are

- Swimming
- Walking

The exercises indicated below should be avoided during pregnancy. In general, they involve too much impact on the body and could result in injuries, muscle strains, and back pain.

- Bowling
- Bungee jumping
- Calisthenics (except for nonimpact)
- Contact sports
- Dancing (break dancing and other strenuous types)
- Downhill skiing
- Diving
- Gymnastics
- Horseback riding

- Ice skating
- Mountain climbing
- Racquet ball
- Roller skating
- Running and jogging
- Scuba diving
- Sky diving
- Softball
- Surfing
- Water skiing
- Weight lifting (of more than 10 pounds)

RECOMMENDATIONS FOR EXERCISING

As with anyone who does exercise, there are certain intelligent guidelines for pregnant women to follow. The first is to *always stretch and warm up* for at least 10 to 15 minutes before engaging in more vigorous activity. *Check your pulse rate periodically* during your workout. The ideal rate as you reach your exercising peak is between 120 and 140 beats per minute. During exercise, *never allow yourself to become too breathless*. This indicates that you are overdoing it. More important, the limited oxygen you take in goes to you first rather than to your fetus.

As your pregnancy advances, you should decrease the intensity of exercise. Following each exercise session, *cool down* for at least 15 minutes. To enhance uterine blood flow after a workout, *rest on your left side* (to take pressure off the vena cava) for 10 minutes.

EXERCISE PRECAUTIONS

Stop exercising and contact your doctor if any of the following occur: dizziness; numbness; pain in the chest, back, hip, or pubic area; contractions; nausea; vaginal bleeding; headaches; or muscle weakness.

Do not exercise if you are subject to any of the following conditions: Hypertension or pregnancy-induced hypertension, severe anemia, a history of three or more spontaneous abortions, severe infection, uncontrolled diabetes, ruptured membranes, bleeding, heart disease, or thyroid disease.

If you have gestational diabetes: speak with your doctor. He or she will devise a special diet and exercise program so that your glucose and insulin levels remain within a safe range. Read all about gestational diabetes on page 64.

Remember, you are not exercising to lose weight right now. Exercise in pregnancy is meant to keep you healthy, fit, and relaxed. If you find that you are losing weight as your pregnancy progresses, this requires immediate attention from you and your doctor. The probable cause is insufficient caloric intake. Remember, a calorie is a unit of energy. You consume calories in food and you burn them during exercise. If you burn more calories than you consume, you lose weight. As we have already made abundantly clear in this book, you should gain weight in pregnancy at a steady pace by regularly eating healthful, nutrient-rich foods.

As a general rule, eat some complex carbohydrates (cereal, rice, or pasta) or milk or fruit 1 or 2 hours before exercising and again 1 or 2 hours after exercising. This will keep your nutrient, glucose, and fluid level up.

Many people who exercise become dehydrated and dizzy if they do not drink enough fluids. This is particularly true for pregnant women, who must think about their fetuses as well as themselves. Always have some water nearby when you exercise and be vigilant about consuming healthy liquids (water, milk, fruit juice, broth, and seltzer) on a regular basis. Coffee, tea, and alcoholic beverages actually cause dehydration when consumed heavily; sugary or chemical-laden sodas are never recommended.

One Last Thought About Dietary Changes and Life-Style in Pregnancy

Once upon a time, when a father-to-be with a starched wing collar was likely to say, "The missus is in a delicate condition," pregnancy was viewed as a state of fragility and infirmity. We now know that most pregnant women can maintain normal busy lives as long as they make the necessary adjustments required for the well-being of themselves and their fetuses. In modern times, when many women are out of the home for much of each day, they often become so active that they fail to get adequate rest.

We want to encourage you to get sufficient rest and find time for yourself as a part of your daily routine. Chances are you will feel better and will be in a better frame of mind if you take a portion of each day to pamper yourself with luxurious moments of quiet relaxation and reflection.

PART TWO

Nine Months of Good Eating

On Being a Pregnant Gourmet

As we began our thinking and research for this book, it became very clear to us that the prevailing attitude about women and what they eat during pregnancy was one of "confinement." This old-fashioned expression used to be a common euphemism for pregnancy, but many of the assumptions that clung to that term still persist. Many pregnant women are treated with the respectful distance that is a product of people's (especially men's) lack of knowledge about pregnancy. We hope that fathers will read this book as diligently as mothers.

Pregnant women work, raise families, run households, travel, socialize, entertain, and exercise; they have good days and bad days. In effect, they are like everyone else in most ways except one. They need to learn how to combine the needs of their daily lives with the special needs of their pregnancies. An essential aspect of this is good nutrition. The well-worn maxim that if you eat well you feel well is, in most cases, true. The body is a functioning organism that requires fuel to power it. This fuel comes in the form of fresh, healthy food that is free of artificial additives. What we propose to you is that this food need not taste like fuel. Every recipe in this book delivers the nutritional goods and is delicious as well. They contain a great variety of ingredients so that there will always be some dish in the book that will suit your mood. Each recipe is simple to prepare, will appeal to everyone in the family and, with a few exceptions such as salads and pastas, may be stored as leftovers for snacking or for another meal. You should note that many recipes are for one serving. The reason is that you might choose to prepare something for yourself at the moment you want it. If you are cooking for more than one person, simply multiply the amounts by the number of people being served. The recipe will indicate if there are any adjustments you need to make if you are multiplying the ingredients.

In planning this book, we paid special attention to the way people live now. Many recipe books assume that people have huge kitchens, every fancy piece of equipment, and unlimited time and money to shop and prepare meals. We realize that the busy woman does not want to devote precious time to complicated, time-consuming cooking when she only has so many hours in a day. And you know very well that being pregnant is expensive. There are doctor's bills (it is essential that you work closely with your doctor from the beginning of your pregnancy), maternity clothes, and all the purchases that you make in anticipation of your baby's arrival. The recipes call for very few costly ingredients.

The philosophy that informs this book is one of combining time-tested wisdom that has been handed down through human history with the most up-to-date medical and nutritional research. All the recipes are doctor-approved and feature notes that indicate whether the dish is recommended or discouraged for women with particular needs or conditions of pregnancy. There are many dishes suitable for women who observe the special dietary laws of Judaism and Islam. Many are indicated and others will be easy to discover. If you are a vegetarian, you will have no trouble fashioning a delicious nine months for yourself if you select from the many dishes that are suitable for you. Just be sure to focus on getting sufficient iron and protein from nonmeat sources such as dark leafy greens, beans, tofu, and if you eat them, dairy products and eggs.

Ingredients to Consume with Caution

Salt and Sugar: You will notice that almost every recipe in this book lacks added salt and sugar. Both of these are essential for good health, but they exist in significant amounts in our food already. If your doctor tells you to cut back even further on salt and sugar, you will have to avoid foods that naturally contain high amounts of salt and sugar. Recipes that are good for people on low-salt and low-sugar diets are indicated throughout the book. Get in the habit of not salting water for pasta; don't reach for the saltshaker while eating your main course. Learn to read labels in the market. If a package lists salt or sugar as one of the first ingredients, you should put that package back on the shelf. Look for foods that are low-salt or low-sodium. For example, in choosing between vegetable juice that is "regular" or "low salt," opt for the latter and enliven it with fresh lemon or lime juice and some pepper. There are many recipes in this book that contain freshly squeezed lemon juice. You will find that vitamin C–rich lemon juice is a delicious flavoring for many foods and, somehow, reduces the need for salt to give food that extra something. Peppercorns that are freshly ground also give distinctive flavor to food.

Alcohol: At various points in this book you will see cautions about alcohol. The prevailing medical wisdom has been that alcohol consumption by a pregnant woman will cause harm to her baby. Some experts say that moderate consumption of alcohol is permissible. You should remember that the idea of what *moderate* means when discussing alcohol consumption varies greatly from person to person. See page 77 for a full discussion of alcohol and pregnancy. If you are skipping alcoholic beverages during your pregnancy, drink alcohol-free wine and beer if you want that type of beverage. Otherwise, take a look at the section about beverages (pages 261) for other ideas. What you *can* do is use wine in cooking. There are a few recipes in this book that call for wine. During cooking, most of the alcohol evaporates and the flavor remains.

Caffeine: Another component in food that you should consume in moderation during pregnancy is caffeine. It is found primarily in coffee, tea, chocolate, and colas. Most decaffeinated coffee has undergone too many processes to be good for you, so skip coffee altogether. There is the so-called Swiss water-process decaffeinated coffee, which its makers claim has no additives. Read the label well, as all brands are different. Regular tea contains caffeine, so you should minimize your consumption of this beverage. You may drink herb and fruit teas, but heed this caution: *Do not buy* loose teas of the type that are sold in health food stores and certain specialty shops. Many of these loose teas contain ingredients of unknown origin and have made many people ill. You may feel perfectly safe buying packaged, well-known brands of herbal teas and infusions from the United States and Europe. Herbal teas come in many varieties, so you should sample different types and select those that appeal to you. Almost all of these come in the form of tea bags. While purist tea drinkers pooh-pooh tea bags, they are a useful convenience for you. Keep a couple in your purse, so that you may have an herb tea break at work or at the end of a restaurant meal. Take a box with you when you travel.

Food Preservatives and Other Additives: There has come to be a much greater awareness of food additives in recent years. Many foods are vitamin enriched and these vitamins, technically, are additives. Vitamin- and nutrient-enriched foods are good, but they are no substitute for fresh foods that naturally contain nutrients. As for preservatives, gums, stabilizers, colorings, and flavors (whether artificial or "natural"), they do nothing to nutritionally enhance your food. Avoid packaged and prepared foods that contain these additives and opt for foods in their natural state. Fresh food or "fresh frozen" food contain more nutrients and tend to be less expensive than foods that claim to offer convenience. Frozen dinners and canned entrées do not give you nearly the quality of nutrition that you get from fresh foods. A preferable way to get flavor and nutrition from nonfresh foods is to use frozen foods that are staples. These packages contain only the food, without preservatives, flavor enhancers, or additives. Good examples of these staples include frozen spinach and squash, juice concentrates and frozen fish fillets. Remember: This fish is only fish—no breading or prefrying should be have been done before you buy it. Use frozen fish fillets according to the recipes in the fish and seafood section (page 181).

Cooking Equipment

In keeping with our supposition that you probably don't have money to burn right now, the recipes in this book do not require all sorts of fancy utensils and gadgets. There are a few essential pieces that we encourage you to acquire now if you don't own them already. They will always be useful to you and are necessary for any cook.

Blender: Probably no piece of equipment is more useful to the pregnant gourmet than the blender. It facilitates the preparation of soups and is the key to blended drinks and smoothees that you will favor during your pregnancy. If you want softer food for whatever reason, the blender is your tool. It can also chop nuts and grind vegetables. The typical blender is quite inexpensive and is easily maintained. Just be sure to clean the container well after each use and to wipe away any pieces of food that have dropped to the base of the blender. The obvious safety tip is to never stick your hands in the blender while it is running. If you own a food processor, it can perform many of the functions of a blender, but there is no need to buy a food processor for the purposes of this book. If you do own a food processor, it will take care of many of your food preparation needs, but will probably be inadequate for making blended drinks. Also, a food processor can be a nuisance to clean, and you don't want to waste time and energy. Invest the approximately $30 for a blender and save your food processor for when you need it for a function the blender can't perform.

Rubber Spatula: Use a spatula to scrape ingredients from the side of the blender container. The rubber sptatula may also be used to push ingredients down in a blender, but make sure that the blender is not operating when you do this.

Cutting Board: Purchase a high-quality plastic or polyurethane cutting board for food preparation. Wood blocks may look more attractive, but wood absorbs and holds bacteria that can prove harmful to you. Marble is not an acceptable alternative either. Although it is pretty to look at, it is heavy to lift and shows cut marks when you use a knife on it. Also, marble dulls knives, which means you must sharpen them more often.

A Large Pot for Soups and Pasta: In general, you should have a good set of pots and pans (with covers) for successful cooking. Stainless steel and glass are the best materials to use. Although copper equipment destroys vitamins C and E and folic acid when used in cooking, copper is an excellent conductor and distributor of heat. An ideal choice is a set of copper-clad stainless-steel pots and pans that use the copper to distribute heat and the steel to be in contact with the food. Many stores put starter sets of these pots and pans on sale for reasonable prices. If you don't already own them, now is a good time to buy them. Beyond this, you should purchase a large pot (6 quarts is a perfect size) with a lid for use in making soups, pasta, and steamed foods. Despite what you might have heard, it is necessary to use a large pot of boiling water to make pasta even if you are making only one portion. To be cooked successfully, the pasta needs a lot of room to move about. You might be tempted to buy a much bigger pot, but heed a word of caution: You do not want to do heavy lifting and, if you are not the strongest person, a large full pot may be too much for you. When it is time to drain pasta, if you find the 6-quart pot too heavy, you have some alternatives. Use a spaghetti fork, a skimmer, or a slotted spoon to fish the noodles out. With soup, you can ladle out portions into bowls or containers until the load lightens.

Large Metal Colander: This is essential for draining pasta once it is cooked. The colander should be large enough that you can easily set it in an empty sink and then pour in the ingredients of a pasta pot without having to aim for it. Even if you fish pasta out of the pot using one of the means suggested above, you should put the pasta in a colander for a few moments to let extra water drain off. Use a colander when you wash fruits, vegetables, poultry, and fish. If anything drops, the colander will catch it, and the food won't fall into the sink. You also may use a colander for steaming if it fits neatly over your large pot. Remember to use oven mitts or pot holders to lift the colander out of the steaming pot.

Steamer: If you have the extra money and if you eat a lot of steamed foods, you might want to invest in a steamer.

Good Sharp Knives: Good knives make difficult tasks easy and allow you to control the size and shape of foods you cut. Get a sharpening rod to keep your knives in good condition. A couple of small paring knives are important for cutting vegetables and fruit and for general food preparation. So is a serrated knife for slicing breads and loaves. A large carving knife is necessary for roasts and many cooked foods.

Other Utensils: Here are some other utensils that you'll find handy: a slotted spoon, a ladle, a pitchfork, and a metal spatula.

Pepper Mill: Every time pepper is called for in a recipe in this book, you will see the words *freshly ground*. Store-bought shakers of ground pepper do not compare with fresh pepper in terms of flavor. You do not have to buy a gaudy pepper mill that is the length of your arm. A simple palm-size pepper mill made of wood or plastic is all you need. But it makes a world of difference in your enjoyment of food. Buy peppercorns only as needed.

Cheese Grater: Calcium-rich Parmesan and Romano cheeses taste their best when freshly grated. You need to purchase imported cheese from Italy if you want the flavor and nutrients they offer. Versions of these cheeses from other nations are not worth eating. To get the best out of these ingredients, which are not cheap, they should be wrapped tightly in aluminum foil and stored in the refrigerator until you are ready to use them. At that point, a little flat hand grater or one with a small crank will enable you to have freshly grated cheese that practically bursts with nutty flavor. You may also use a grater for Cheddar, Swiss, and other cheeses in recipes that call for them. Do not grate cheeses in your blender. It tends to overwork the cheese, making it gummy.

Salad Spinner: A salad spinner is not an essential, because you can wash greens in your colander. But it is nice to have if you eat salad frequently. Nothing else gets leaves of lettuce or spinach dry so effectively.

Plastic Containers for Food Storage: There are several well-known brands of storage containers (you know, the type some people purchase at parties) which are made of durable plastic and are designed to seal tightly. These are necessities in any cook's kitchen, but especially when that cook is a pregnant gourmet who plans to make leftovers a major part of her repertoire. You should not reuse the flimsy plastic containers that held food you bought at the supermarket. The type of container you need must be of thick enough plastic that it cannot be punctured or torn. Of course, wash your containers in hot soapy water after each use.

Shopping for Food

In many cultures it is customary to shop once or even twice a day for food. The idea is that you can select the freshest, most appealing food for your meal and answer your particular craving of the moment. It is also typical in these cultures that food is sold in a central marketplace and part of the shopping ritual is tied to the pleasurable social interaction that occurs when you go to market.

Unfortuately, the dictates of living in a busy, modern society tend to interfere with this delightful activity, but there are things to learn from it. The first is to develop relationships with the people who sell you your food. They will save you that special cut of meat or will hang on to those special items you requested if they know you are coming for them. The impersonal world of many supermarkets separates the seller from the consumer, which is unfortunate. Even at a huge market, you can get to know the people behind the counter, the butcher, the manager, and the buyers. Make a point of doing this. While you might pay a little more in small produce markets and specialty shops, the trade-off is good service and the knowledge that you have dependable suppliers who are responsive to your needs.

There are two other benefits to be learned from daily shopping. The first is that it helps you be in tune with what you feel like eating and what looks good that day. Fresh food always has more nutritional value than that which is stored for a few days. The second is that you are less likely to impulsively buy certain foods that will wind up being long-term residents at the bottom of your pantry or the back of your refrigerator.

How do you fit the daily market idea into your busy life? If you live close to a farm where many of these ingredients are available to you fresh, you are particularly fortunate. If you live in a city where it is convenient to pass a market on your way home to pick up what you want, take a few minutes to make it part of your routine. Stock up on staples on the occasional big shopping trip and only buy the protein and produce you will want in the next 2 days. Naturally, you will not shop every day. Sometimes you will eat out. On other days you will have the ingredients in your pantry or freezer that are necessary to make a superb meal. But the thinking will be the same: Do I want a nice turkey breast with fresh lemon or shall I make pasta with canned San Marzano tomatoes? After asking yourself what you want, you will know if it's is a shopping day or not. Aside from these daily wishes, most of the foods you consume are staples. These include items that need to be replaced frequently, such as milk, and those that are replaced once in a while, such as oil or flour.

Once you have learned that you are going to have a baby, it is a good idea to go on a big shopping expedition to stock up on staples for

Your First Shopping Trip

your pantry. Take somebody along to help, if possible. This may seem like a large initial outlay of money, but you will be glad to have made these purchases. This way, you will then only need to buy the fresh foods you require at any given time and to replace the items listed below as you use them up. Aside from the staples in your pantry, you should also put foods in the freezer such as vegetables, fruit juice concentrates, and plain fish fillets to have available for days when you are not able to shop. The idea in putting this larder in the cabinets and freezer is that you always have a great variety of healthy foods around for meals and snacks. Replace items as they are consumed and arrange them in storage so that the older items will be used first. Take this book with you to the market and consult this shopping list.

STAPLES

- Butter or margarine, unsalted (whipped or stick): 1 pound
- Cinnamon, ground: 1 container
- Fines herbes, imported from France (such as herbes de Provence): 1 container
- Flour, unbleached, all-purpose: 1 pound
- Milk, nonfat, dry solids: 1 box
- Mustard, Dijon: 1 jar
- Nuts, unsalted (walnuts, almonds, or cashews): 1 container
- Oil (corn, canola, or safflower): 1 bottle
- Olive oil, extra-virgin: 1 quart or liter bottle
- Parmesan cheese, imported from Italy: 1 chunk (wrap tightly in aluminum foil)
- Peanut butter, freshly ground, with no added salt or fat: 1 jar
- Peppercorns (for your pepper mill): 1 jar
- Tomatoes, crushed (preferably imported from Italy): eight 28-ounce cans
- Vinegar (red or white wine): 1 bottle
- Vinegar, Balsamic: 1 bottle

BEVERAGES

- Herbal tea in tea bags, a selection of your favorites, including mint for the occasional upset stomach: 3 boxes of approximately 25 bags each

- Juice cartons (individual cartons with straws, for travel and bag lunches): 18
- Juice concentrates, frozen (apple, cranberry, grapefruit, orange, etc.): 12 small cans
- Milk, low-fat or skim: 2 quarts
- Orange juice, fresh (not from concentrate): 2 quarts
- Prune juice: 1 bottle
- Water or seltzer, bottled (if you have good tap water, it is still wise to buy seltzer for use in making sparkling drinks): 6 quarts or liters

CARBOHYDRATES AND GRAINS

- Bread, whole wheat (may be frozen if not eaten quickly): 1 loaf
- Breadsticks with sesame seeds
- Cereal, bran (sugar and salt free): 1 pound or large box
- Cereal, granola (sugar and salt free): 1 pound or large box
- Cereal, hot (sugar and salt free, such as oatmeal, farina, cream of wheat, or grits; you may consider buying instant cereal if it does not have added chemicals or sugar): 2 one-pound boxes
- Pasta, long (spaghetti or linguine; imported from Italy): 4 one-pound boxes
- Pasta, short (penne, rigatoni, or maccheroni; imported from Italy): 2 one-pound boxes
- Rice, brown: 1 pound
- Sesame seeds (for sprinkling; a great calcium source): 2 ounces
- Wheat germ (store in refrigerator after opening): 1 jar

FRUITS

- Bananas (for snacking, smoothees, or freezing): 5
- Grapes, seedless (for freezing): 1 pound
- Lemons, fresh: 4
- Pineapple, unsweetened, packed in juice: 2 cans
- Prunes, pitted: 1 box or container

- Raisins: 1 box or container
- Raisins, small boxes for bag lunches or pocketbook snacks: 12 boxes

PROTEINS

- Chicken supremes or turkey fillets: 1 pound
- Chicken wings (for stock): 4 to 5 pounds
- Cottage cheese (low-fat, low-salt): 1 24-ounce container
- Eggs, preferably organic: 1 dozen
- Fish fillets, plain, unbreaded frozen fish (cod, flounder, perch, salmon, sole): 2 pounds
- Salmon: 8 cans (7 ounces each)
- Tuna, packed in water: 12 cans (7 ounces each)
- Yogurt (plain, lemon, or vanilla): 1 16-ounce container

VEGETABLES

- Beans (kidney, chickpeas, white beans, etc.): 6 15-ounce cans
- Carrots, fresh: 1 pound
- Garlic: 2 heads
- Greens (lettuces, etc.): 2 heads
- Onions, yellow, medium-size: 1 pound
- Parsley, fresh: 1 bunch
- Potatoes: 2 pounds
- Spinach, leaf or chopped; frozen: 8 10-ounce packages
- Squash, cooked, frozen, with nothing added (a quick, easy delicious vegetable, loaded with vitamin A. Leftover cooked squash is very tasty and silken when served cold): 4 10-ounce packages

Be a selective shopper. This means being a smart consumer who clips coupons, buys staples on sale, checks labels and expiration dates, and only purchases the highest-quality foods. When you read the label of a packaged food, the first thing to remember is that ingredients are listed by the percentage in which they exist in a package. If, for instance, the label on a bottled drink shows that it contains "water, sugar, fruit juice, corn syrup, natural coloring, and artificial flavoring" you will know that this is probably not worth buying. It means that there is a hint of real fruit juice in a solution of sugary water that is further sweetened with corn syrup and "enhanced" by coloring and flavoring. If a drink's label says, instead, "100% fruit juice, not from concentrate," this is the one to buy. You will notice that many juice cartons specify whether or not the juice is made from concentrate. It is always better to buy fresh juice because concentrated juice had to be reduced and then reconstituted with water before being packaged. Many of the nutrients will have to be added in packaging the juice. Fresh (not from concentrate) packaged juice is the best. The next best is to purchase frozen concentrate of 100% juice and reconstitute it when *you* are ready to use it. It is wise to store reconstituted juice in a dark jar or opaque container because clear glass will admit vitamin A–destroying light.

Labels also list the presence of different nutrients and elements in the food that is in the package. These include protein, fat, cholesterol, sodium (salt), carbohydrates, calories, vitamins, and minerals. You must remember that a label indicates how many nutrients exist *per serving*. Even experienced label readers fail to make this distinction. It is further complicated by the fact that what the manufacturer considers a serving may bear little relation to what you consider a serving. For example, you may want more than 1 ounce of dry cereal for breakfast even though the package says the serving is 1 ounce. So you will need to do some quick arithmetic to figure out the amount of nutrients you are receiving for *your* portion. In truth, for you it is more important to check the ingredients to determine whether the food contains junk that you don't need. Reading the nutrient information will help educate you about the nutritional content of foods (such as "which has more fat: frozen sole or frozen flounder?"), which is good knowledge to have. Also, if your doctor tells you to stay away from a certain item (such as salt) or to have more of something (calcium or iron, for example), labels will guide you toward the right foods.

There are two types of expiration dates. Foods such as ground meat, chilled juice, eggs, and dairy products have dates that relate to spoilage. You should use these foods by the date indicated or they will likely be spoiled. Always examine and smell perishable foods for freshness. Frozen foods such as frozen yogurt or fish fillets also are dated, and it is best to use those foods by the date indicated. Packaged foods such as baked goods contain the words "best if consumed by" and give a date. This is an indicator of freshness. Bread eaten after the date may be a little stale but might not be spoiled or moldy. Examine it carefully before eating it. Older bread is good for toast, bread crumbs, and French toast.

When shopping, carefully examine every item you buy. After reading the label and checking the expiration date, see if the package is in good condition. Dented cans or those that are swollen or rusted should be avoided. Never buy a jar or package that seems to have been opened. If there is even the smallest tear in the plastic wrap of an item, put it back on the shelf. Check meat and fish for freshness. If they smell stale or funny, don't take them. If they are discolored, blotchy, or bloody, they should not be used. If, after you get home, you find a little blood on the poultry near a joint, wash that area well with cold water and cut away the immediate site before cooking.

A word about shellfish and sushi: Long before there were bacteria scares about raw fish, crustaceans, and mollusks, people were getting sick from these foods. Nowadays, unfortunately, food poisoning from these products has become common. So a rule for the pregnant gourmet is to skip all sushi and raw shellfish. In fact, it is wise to avoid cooked shellfish as well, as it is too often subject to mishandling. We do have a couple of recipes that call for cooked shrimp. Simple boiled shrimp is probably not a problem if you know and trust your supplier. Frozen cooked shrimp (without sauce or breading) available in the United States also is of high quality. Needless to say, raw meat should never be eaten.

When shopping for fresh fruits and vegetables, the logic you apply to other fresh foods still obtains. Produce that smells strange or is discolored should be left in the bin. Pick the ripest, most richly colorful and fragrant fruit and vegetables you see. Fresh produce that is stored for a few days loses some if its nutritional punch, so don't buy more than you think you will use in 2 days. Thick-skinned fruits such as lemons, limes, oranges, grapefruits, tangerines, and bananas last longer. If they start to age in your home, use the citrus to make some fresh juice before they spoil. Bananas should never be refrigerated. If they get a bit mature, freeze them as described on page 245.

Of course, staples such as onions, garlic, shallots and potatoes have longer shelf lives, so you may buy these in greater quantities. When they start sprouting little shoots, it is time to throw them away.

A lot of money is wasted by people who impulsively buy food and forget about it. Great amounts of food are also wasted by cooks who store foods incorrectly. Unfortunately, poorly stored food often becomes a breeding ground for bacteria that will result in poisoned food and sickness for those who eat it. You should always practice the safety precautions that follow.

Storing Food

Rotate all stored foods: Bring that which is older to the front of the shelf and put newer food behind it. This applies to the refrigerator, the freezer, and the pantry. Place labels on packages of foods (and foods that you have wrapped) to indicate what the food is and the date that it was put in the package.

Store food in proper containers: To maintain freshness and nutrients, food must be well stored. Use durable plastic containers (not flimsy supermarket packaging) that seal tightly to keep greens and some leftovers. Glass jars that close tightly or glass dishes with secure lids may be used to store liquids or cooked foods. Leftovers should be wrapped and should be among the first foods you eat. Any raw food that goes into the freezer should be neatly, firmly wrapped in aluminum foil and labeled. As a general rule, all meat and poultry that will not be used within 24 hours should be frozen. Fish that you are not about to eat should be frozen immediately. If you have purchased fresh meat, poultry, or fish, *never* freeze it in the package from the market. These packages were not designed for freezing. Always rewrap meat in foil. If you buy a large amount of these foods (more than you will consume at one sitting) wrap them in separate packages that approximate one portion so that they may be used as necessary. Fresh meat or fish that has been frozen by you should be used within 3 weeks.

Thaw frozen foods in the refrigerator: If you plan ahead, you might decide to thaw your meat for dinner before you start your day. Place the wrapped package in a bowl (removing the label that contains ink) and let the food defrost in the refrigerator. Some people add a little cold water to the bowl to keep the food cool. This is only necessary if you will be out for a long time or if the food is rock-hard, as liquid will escape during thawing. If you prefer to add water, that is fine. Owners of microwave ovens use them to thaw their food. Please read our cautions about microwave ovens on page 105. If you still choose to use them, they are effective for thawing frozen food. Some packaged frozen foods, such as spinach and squash, are not supposed to be thawed before cooking. Read labels.

Keep food at the proper temperature: Food that should be kept cold or frozen should not be left at room temperature for more than 30 to 45 minutes. Bacteria will grow easily once the food is at room temperature. Foods in cans or unopened jars should be stored in cool, dark pantries and closets. The same applies for flour, sugar, salt, oil, vinegar, and most cereals. Read labels carefully for guidance. Wheat germ, for example, should be refrigerated after the jar is opened.

Wash or clean all foods carefully: Most foods, except for those that come in tough natural packages such as bananas and citrus fruits, need to be carefully cleaned. Each recipe details how this cleaning should take place. As a general rule about vegetables, they should be washed in abundant cold water and any blemished parts should be cut away. Remember that the darker, outer leaves of many greens have the most nutrients, so be sure to use them. The chapters about poultry and fish include descriptions about washing those foods.

Cook meat, poultry, and fish thoroughly: The minifad of serving meats and fish pink or nearly raw has spawned a lot more than a fashion trend. When these foods are not cooked at a temperature of at least 160° F, bacteria still remain.

This does not mean that steak cannot be eaten rare. But it should be hot and dark red in color on the inside to be safely consumed. If you are eating out and get undercooked meat, poultry or fish, send it back.

Do not overcook produce: With produce, we have the opposite problem of meat. How often have you pushed away cafeteria-style cooked vegetables that have been boiled to oblivion? All the flavor, color, and nutrients go out with the wash. Cook vegetables and fruits so that they still retain flavor, color, and texture. When you see recipes in this book that call for cooking liquids or leftover vegetables that will be puréed for soup, they sometimes add flavor, sometimes nutrients, sometimes bulk. But they all fill a role in good cooking and eating, and you should never let any produce go to waste.

About the Recipes

The idea behind the recipes in this book is that you eat well without spending too much time on your feet preparing and cooking meals. If you are tired or have children or another adult you need to be with, lengthy cooking should not be in the cards. Very few recipes here call for a great deal of work.

Most of the recipes that require cooking in this book call for stove-top preparation. The simple reason is that at a certain point you will find it more difficult to bend, kneel, and lift heavy pans from an oven or broiler. Also, stove-top cooking usually means that the meal will be done more quickly. For dishes that do require oven or broiler cooking (meat loaf, broiled or baked fish, muffins, breads, and loaves are a few examples), they are not so heavy that they should pose serious problems, at least during your first two trimesters. If you feel you can't bend or lift, ask someone to help you. For baked goods such as muffins and loaves, bake a lot in advance and freeze them for use during the last part of your pregnancy.

MICROWAVE
COOKERY

You will notice that there are no recommendations in this book for microwave cookery. The philosophy behind this is that there has not been enough research done on what effect, if any, rays from microwave ovens may have on pregnant women and their babies. Until more definitive knowledge exists, we feel it is wise to discourage you from using your microwave oven to cook or, as is more commonly said, to "nuke" food. It is true that the microwave oven is a great convenience for busy people but, more often than not, the foods they cook in these ovens are the prepared frozen meals we have discouraged you from buying. Such foods are expensive, not very nutritious, and certainly don't taste good. If you choose to use your microwave oven, do so sparingly and only make foods that are healthful. Another word of caution: Many new mothers heat baby food jars in the microwave oven. The contents of the jar become scaldingly hot and many infants have had serious damage done to their lips, gums, and palates by eating microwaved food. Make the extra effort to heat baby food jars in boiling water and always test the temperature of food before feeding it to your child.

With your busy schedule and everything you have to think about, we do not expect you to devote endless attention to cooking and nutrient counting. We encourage you to follow the nutritional guidelines of this book and those laid out by your doctor. Eat a balanced diet, drawing from all the food groups and avoiding the few items (caffeine, alcohol, excess sugar and salt, deep-fried foods) that you know are not good for you. In selecting recipes from this book, you will naturally be drawn to certain dishes more than others. Because these recipes contain a wide range of nutrients, you will probably get the nutrition you need as long as you don't binge on only a few items. If you eat with the idea of balance, you will have to spend less time actually counting how many nutrients you have had from this or that food group. Of course, if you are a gestational diabetic or have some other medical condition that imposes restrictions on what you can eat, you should closely follow the instructions of your doctor. But even if you have special conditions, there are many recipes in this book for you to enjoy. Consult the doctor's notes for further guidance.

LEFTOVERS

Another cornerstone of the philosophy of this book is the use of leftovers. Most dishes (except for salads and pastas) may be prepared in larger quantities. This means that your snack or next-day lunch is already cooked and requires only wrapping or reheating. Therefore, you will have a saving of time that can be devoted to other things. Don't forget that many cooked foods—including meat, poultry, fish, vegetables, fruit, and some soups—are delicious when eaten cold.

The Working Woman

The customary definition of the working woman is of someone who has a full-time job away from the home. Because this applies to more than half of all American women and large percentages in other countries, the traditional definition encompasses a lot of women. However, women who run homes; raise children; have responsibilities to parents, church, synagogue or mosque; do volunteer work; and/or go to school are also working women by any fair definition.

The pregnant working woman is often away from her home and kitchen for significant periods of time and must not forget her nutritional needs. What follow are suggestions for putting all the pieces of your busy life together without sacrificing the nutritional needs of your baby and you.

LUNCH AND SNACKING AT WORK

Part of the notion of cooking in a way that will yield leftovers is that, in effect, you will have made your lunch the night before. Wrap your lunch well and keep it in a refrigerator at work. Bring muffins, fruit, little boxes of raisins, and individual servings of juice to answer the call when you are hungry at work. Do not put yourself in the position of having to buy a candy bar or junk food because you don't have good food nearby. If your office has vending machines, buy 100% juices instead of juice cocktails and sodas. Purchase raisins and unsalted nuts. If these machines don't have nutritious foods, make note of the supplier and make suggestions. You will be surprised how receptive suppliers are when they know they have steady customers. It is important to keep bottled water around (or make periodic visits to the drinking fountain) and drink frequently. Closed office environments have very dry air that will dehydrate you. It is necessary to replace liquids, and there is no better choice than water. If you are in a business meeting or with a client and you get hungry, assess if it is an appropriate time to have a snack. It might be the right moment to excuse yourself for a break to have that snack in peace and quiet and come back with your best ideas. If you are with a client and develop a little hunger, mention that you would like a nibble because you are eating for two and then offer some to your client as well. Whether he or she accepts or declines, you will have made the gesture and explained sufficiently why it's time for that banana.

DINING OUT

Whether you eat at restaurants for business, for pleasure, or out of necessity, you must follow the same rules of balanced nutrition you would otherwise. Opt for dark breads, food that is prepared as you would at home, and select drinks that are permissible for you. You should feel no pressure to drink alcohol just because other people are having it. Get in the habit of asking the waiter to instruct the chef to hold the salt, whether you are having a hamburger or a fancy dish. Many cooks, especially in ethnic restaurants, use salt quite liberally unless they are told otherwise. Similarly, certain restaurants, especially those making Chinese food, use monosodium glutamate (MSG). Ask that MSG be omitted. By now, many restauranteurs recognize that *most* diners have special needs and are willing to accommodate them. Most people you dine with also realize that there is nothing strange about having particular food needs. So do not feel awkward about making any special requests. A general rule about salad dressing: If you think the restaurant makes its own good salad dressing from quality ingredients, ask for some on the side and use it sparingly. Otherwise, ask for lemon wedges to squeeze over your salad.

Aside from the well-known fast-food restaurants that are frequented daily by millions of eaters in a hurry, there are two particularly popular ethnic cuisines which deserve some attention on their own. Chinese food as served in the United States ranges from the authentic to food that a person from Shanghai, Canton, or Beijing would not even recognize. The pregnant diner in a Chinese restaurant—no matter what her ethnic background is—should bear certain things in mind as she looks down column A and column B. Aside from asking that MSG be withheld from all food, she should avoid soy sauce, which is essentially a highly salty liquid with added coloring. For the same reason, dishes with clear sauces are preferable to dishes with brown sauces. You should opt for chicken or beef instead of pork or seafood, as you are not sure how well handled the food is or how long it has been cooked. Soups often sit for a while in Chinese restaurants and are kept lively by added MSG. As a general rule, this course is probably best avoided when you eat Chinese food. Conversely, vegetable, noodle, and rice dishes are good choices, and any permissible food that you order steamed is the best choice of all.

Italian food as served in the United States falls into two categories: authentic Italian cuisine and that peculiar hybrid known as Italian-American cooking. Each style has its virtues, but you should never confuse one with the other. Authentic Italian cooking is often very light, uses fresh herbs and flavorings and ingredients that are at their peak. As often as not, authentic Italian dishes need only rapid preparation. Italian-American cooking, in contrast, often features slow-cooked sauces, overcooked spaghetti and meatballs, lots of frying, and rivers of melted cheese. It is delicious, but it very high in salt and fat. If you order a pizza, bear in mind that while it offers great taste and a good helping of protein, it also has a lot of salt and fat. Maximize your pizza choice by having it topped with appealing vegetables such as mushrooms, eggplant, zucchini, broccoli, or spinach. Avoid sausage, pepperoni, chopped meat, or salami, all of which increase the fat content and often contain salt, colorings, and preservatives. In the general area of Italian restaurants, try to select ones that cook food the way it is served in Italy and go for the pastas with vegetable or cheese sauces and main courses that are grilled or sautéed in olive oil and accompanied by good fresh vegetables and salads. An Italian restaurant that serves Americanized Italian food will probably serve slow-cooked tomato sauces thickened with various ingredients. While this is not as nutritious as authentic Italian cuisine, it is tasty. Enjoy this type of Italian food periodically, and make your menu selections wisely.

In dining out, you will find that most restaurants have desserts that are not in your repertoire. Ask if they have any plain fruit or *fresh* fruit salad for you to eat. Make note if there is a half grapefruit or a piece of melon among the appetizers and ask the waiter to set aside a piece for you to have for dessert. The occasional sorbet or piece of plain, unfrosted cake (pound cake, orange savarin, and tea loaves are good picks) are fine unless you are on a sugar-restricted regime.

In fast-food restaurants (which you should steer clear of anyway), avoid the overdressed, the overfried, and the oversalty. This probably leaves you with little choice, so you should ask for a *grill order*. This is a fast-food term for a dish that has to be specially made. Many of these restaurants have eggs in the refrigerators for breakfast. The grill person can always prepare scrambled eggs if you ask for it. The person at the cashier will probably have to ask for approval to place this order, so be patient. The decision will probably come from the manager. Corporate policy moves slowly, but fast-food franchisers are eager to serve the customer, and they want return business. A simpler grill order is a plain hamburger, cooked without salt and free of ketchup, pickles, special sauces and other fillers. Have a plain burger on a bun with lettuce and tomato. Use mustard if you like it and, if you must, a little ketchup that you add yourself. Avoid fried fish fillets or chicken breasts, shakes, french fries, pickles, and special sauces.

Salad bars seem easy, healthy and inviting, but they are fraught with hidden problems and should be approached cautiously. When visiting salad bars, ask the manager if the food is sprayed with sulfites. This happens more often than you might think. Sulfites preserve color and the semblance of freshness, but many people get allergic reactions to them. At the sulfite-free salad bar, first make sure the foods are kept cold and are fresh. Check that there is the glass or plastic "sneeze shield" that is supposed to keep the food protected from the people who hover over salad bars all day. If you have decided to eat at a salad bar, go for the foods you know to eat anyway. Lettuce, tomatoes, cauliflower and broccoli florets, grated carrots, sprouts, beans, and chick-peas are fine. Other fresh vegetables in good condition also are decent choices. If there are hard-boiled eggs that have not been opened and they seem fresh, have one. Pieces of real cheese (not "cheese products") are fine if they are cool and in good condition. If cut fresh fruit is in good shape, eat it. Whole fresh fruits are a superb choice. Stay away from egg salad, tuna salad, chicken salad, and any other food suspended in mayonnaise. For that matter, skip any food that has a creamy base. Freshness is not guaranteed and the food could make you sick. Also, skip any artificial food (such as bacon bits); they are no good. Cold pasta or rice that is not already dressed is fine if it appeals to you. If there are bottles of oil and vinegar nearby, make your own dressing. Otherwise, skip the gloppy, preservative-laden prepared dressings and opt for a squeeze of fresh lemon. Select fresh wheat bread, good packaged wheat crisps, or sesame breadsticks instead of commercially made croutons. Do not bother with salad bar soups. Too many people have been near them (they are often kept in tureens to the side of the bar), and if they have sat for a period of time, they have probably cooked down to a salty liquid devoid of all nutrients.

In all restaurants and salad bars, drink water, juice, milk, or ask for hot water and take a bag of herb tea out of your purse. At more formal meals, start with a cocktail of citrus or cranberry juice that is mixed with some sparkling water and garnished with a lemon or lime slice.

If you are a guest for dinner in someone's home, politely tell that person when you receive your invitation what foods you can enjoy. You don't need to go into great detail. Simply say that "I can eat any grilled, broiled, or baked fish, poultry or meat and all fruits and vegetables as long as these foods have no added sugar or salt." This should give any good cook plenty of latitude. If there is anything particular you cannot eat or something that you really enjoy (provided that it is not expensive or difficult to prepare), let your host know. Any good host wants to please a guest, so it is incumbent on a guest to help his or her host meet that goal. And carry that herbal tea bag in your purse, just in case. By the way, if you are asked to bring a dish, why not make something from this book? You know that you will be able eat it, and you will be pleased to see how much everyone else enjoys it too.

COCKTAIL HOUR

Whenever you are having drinks for business or social purposes, you know that you can partake if you follow some basic rules. Opt for the juices, water, seltzers, and alcohol-free beverages that appeal to you. Nibble on crudités, unsalted pretzels, unsalted nuts, or hard cheeses and crackers, if they are available. Stay away from all the chips, salted pretzels, beer nuts, popcorn, and other salty noshes that represent empty calories to anyone who eats them. Also steer clear of most dips. Commercially prepared dips may not have been stored in ideal conditions. Sour cream and soup mix dips are high in fat, salt, and artificial ingredients. A good, easy dip is plain yogurt combined with fresh dill. Everyone will love it with crudités.

ENTERTAINING

Entertaining is quite easy. All the recipes in this book are delicious and will please other people as much as they please you. Prepare some foods in advance if you can and have other people help you cook if you are not particular about working alone, as some cooks are. Remember that other people may want cocktails, wine, beer, and coffee, so have these beverages on hand for your guests while you enjoy your own drinks. Don't be surprised if they want to try your spritzers and sangria (see pages 263, 267).

TRAVEL

In the first two trimesters of your pregnancy you might have the need to travel for business, family obligations, or pleasure. Follow the advice about eating out that you have just read. Airlines and railway dining cars don't necessarily serve food when you want to eat. Similarly, your flight or connection may be delayed, which means that you will need to wait even longer to eat. Carry snacks and herbal tea bags for the trip. You might also want to bring along a couple of frozen juice packs, which will thaw during the day and offer you a refreshing serving of juice. Remember that tomato and vegetable juices served in little cans on planes are often high in sodium.

Ask your airline if it has special meals (salt-free, sugar-free, kosher, vegetarian, etc.) that suit your needs. Normally, special meals need to be ordered 24 to 48 hours before departure, so plan accordingly. Better still, bring along your own meal, if possible.

You never know where or for how long a meal has been sitting before it gets to you or how many times it has been handled in between. More and more flyers now travel with their own meals. Good choices are whole fruit, muffins, and hard cheeses. If you need to snack in airline terminals, buy a plain or lemon yogurt at a concession stand in the terminal. If this is inconvenient, take the time to arrange for a special meal.

In booking a seat, ask for an aisle seat in the nonsmoking section—as far as possible from the smoking seats (many international airlines still have smoking sections). An aisle seat will enable you to go to the restroom easily and also means that you can stretch your legs or go for a walk, which is very good for you. Be sure to drink a lot of liquids when you fly. The air is very dry in the cabin of a plane, and you can become easily dehydrated. Tell the cabin attendant of your needs as you enter the plane (and, for that matter, the reservations clerk when you book your flight), and you will receive special attention. Cabin attendants are very good at providing special service when they know in advance that they will need to do so. Wear comfortable, sturdy shoes that you can slip on and off easily. Feet expand during flight (and yours might be swollen anyway) so that you should pick your footwear carefully. If you have trouble bending, especially in a tight spot such as an airline seat, wear roomy shoes that don't need to be laced up. Travel as light as possible. Always carry any medication prescribed for pregnancy along with refill prescriptions in your carry-on baggage. If you use eyeglasses or contact lenses, put them in your carry-on luggage (if you are not wearing them), and have a copy of your prescription just in case. If you can keep all of your luggage in the overhead compartment, this will get you out of the airport sooner and save you the walking, standing, waiting, and lifting that occur in the baggage claim area. Prearrange your ground transportation to your flight and from your flight in your destination city to save stress once you start traveling.

When staying in a hotel out of town, ask for a room that is in a quiet part of the hotel but not too far from the entrance. This way you will not have to walk far to reach your room, and you will have a good night's rest when you are there. Have the bellman carry your luggage if you are tired or if it is too much for you to handle.

Keep your ice bucket full and drink a lot of water. As usual, conditioned air is very dry. If you are having room service, advise them of the same nutritional needs you would in any restaurant. If you have breakfast in the hotel restaurant, use the same good sense in ordering that you would anywhere else. Skip those frosted Danishes and go for dark loaves made of bran, oats, carrots, or bananas. If you want an egg, have one that is boiled or fried. You would be surpised how many of these places use powdered eggs for scrambling. Also, unless you see the eggs in front of you that will be used for your omelet, give it a pass. Some restaurants ladle prebeaten eggs out of a metal cannister at the side of the grill. Also, skip bacon and sausage. They are loaded with salt, fat, and preservatives and are often served undercooked or precooked. For hunger when you are in your room, keep healthy snacks there if your hotel does not have food available at all hours. You may put foods that need refrigeration in the minibar in the room. They will be more appealing than the overpriced contents the hotel has stocked it with.

Use the concierge or desk clerk in your hotel as a source of information and guidance about where to eat, how to get about easily and let him or her know of any special needs or requirements you might have. It is a good idea to carry your doctor's name and phone number if you have any special questions or needs. It also is smart to ask your doctor to suggest the name of a doctor or hospital in the city you are in if there is any reason you need medical assistance.

As you have learned, the pregnant gourmet can lead a full and happy life in most circumstances if she takes certain sensible precautions. This might be a stress-filled time full of eager anticipation about all the changes that will take place in your life, but it can also be a happy time full of learning, discovery, friendship from strangers, and love from people you know. It is also a time when you can savor wonderful foods and establish good eating habits that will serve you and your family for the rest of your lives.

Let's start cooking!

ach recipe in this book was designed to meet the special nutritional needs of pregnant women. Some recipes are unusually rich in a particular nutrient and were created specifically for the woman who has a special need for that nutrient. For example, frozen bananas (page 245) should be of particular interest to the woman who needs potassium; the chicken breasts featured in the poultry section (page 194) should interest the woman trying to meet her daily need for niacin.

A Word About the Doctor's Notes

On the other hand, many pregnant women need to restrict their intake of certain foods because of particular conditions or complications of pregnancy they may have. For example, the gestational diabetic must limit her intake of sugar and carbohydrates. Many recipes in this book are geared to her needs, including most dishes made with meat, chicken, fish, or leafy green vegetables. Starting on page 286, you will find five charts that indicate recipes suitable for women with different conditions or complications of pregnancy: morning sickness, need to gain weight, need to lose weight, gestational diabetes, and preeclamspia.

Each doctor's note contains an approximate calorie count per serving and indicates which nutrients this dish offers in abundance. To arrive at the calorie and nutrient values indicated in the recipes, we consulted Handbook Numbers 8 and 456 published by the U.S. Department of Agriculture (USDA). Bear in mind that calorie and nutrient counts will change if you eat more or less than the portion size indicated in a recipe or if you add or subtract ingredients in that recipe.

A final word of caution: The doctor's notes are not a substitute for your own doctor's advice. If you have any questions, particularly if your doctor recommends a certain diet, bring this book to his or her office and confirm that the recipes you are drawn to are suitable for your needs.

BREAKFAST

You have always been told that breakfast is the most important meal of the day. The simple reason is that you have probably gone for 8 to 10 hours without eating by the time you sit down for breakfast, and you need to power up for the day. This is especially true for pregnant women because, of course, they are eating for two. Although your baby might be receiving its nutrition as necessary, you need to replace enough nutrients to nourish the two of you.

The problem for many pregnant women, especially in the first trimester, is that they don't want to eat anything when they wake up because of morning sickness. A pregnant vaudevillian, when asked "What's the best cure for morning sickness?" might say "Don't get up till the afternoon!" For most of us, this is not a practical solution. The key is to try to eat something before the symptoms of morning sickness set in. Failing that, go for small, dry items such as plain bagels, toast, matzos, or grainy muffins. As always, try to avoid foods that are laden with salt. Take a look at the recipe for Vitamin B₆ Breakfast on page 122. Before having this with cereal, sample a couple of spoonfuls alone. If it goes down nicely, try it with cereal. If it doesn't work with cereal, stick to Vitamin B₆ Breakfast by itself. If this particular recipe doesn't work for you, skip to other foods in this book. Read all about morning sickness on page 50.

Your goal for morning eating is to replace many of the nutrients that were depleted while you slept. If you can eat only a little when you wake up and you have to go out for the day, put some snack foods in your bag such as muffins, fruit or crudités (see page 136). These should be available to you in addition to whatever food you plan to have for lunch. If the sight and smell of food is completely repugnant to you in the morning, then it would be wise to pack your snack and lunch before you go to bed and store them in the refrigerator.

What should you eat for breakfast? The answer to this question is really very simple. You may eat anything that appeals to you, if you follow the guidelines of this book and observe three easy rules:

1. *Avoid foods with caffeine, added sugar or salt.* These include many frozen meals or meals in a can, certain cubes and powders that dissolve, plus dressings and toppings (read the labels).

2. *Avoid all "industrial" foods.* Those that are so overprocessed that they bear little relation to the original, such as strange whips, dips, "whizzes," and cereals with names like Wacky, Smacky, Puff, or Loop. Industrial foods are usually loaded with colorings, preservatives, emulsifiers, stabilizers, and gums, which you don't want or need, nor does your baby.

3. *If your doctor says you have special nutritional needs or that there are foods you should avoid, listen carefully.* Your doctor knows more about your particular pregnancy than anyone else, and if she or he instructs you to follow a special regime, you should do so.

These caveats aside, you should feel free to eat what you want at breakfast, even if it is not a normal breakfast food. If you crave a piece of that leftover chicken or fish, have it. If you want a bowl of fresh fruit, that is all right if you do not have to be overly careful about your intake of natural sugars. If two of those muffins that you baked would really hit the spot, so be it (see the Oat Bran Muffins, page 253.) What follow are suggestions for breakfast in some of the traditional categories.

DAIRY PRODUCTS

Milk: Use skim or whole, although you should lean toward the former. You may enhance skim milk by stirring in a teaspoon of milk solids.

Shakes: Take milk, ice, milk solids, and the noncitrus fruit of your choice (bananas, strawberries, and/or peaches, for example) and blend. This is rich, delicious, and nutritious. If you are taking something like brewer's yeast or some other nutrient powder, it might taste better in a shake.

Yogurt: Plain, lemon, or vanilla yogurt is fine. Instead of sugary fruited yogurt that often has stabilizers and artificial sweeteners, put one of these three yogurts over fresh fruit.

Cheese: A nice chunk of unprocessed cheese (no whiz or spread or easy melt or single-wrapped slices) may be just what you need. This can be accompanied by an apple, a few grapes, a pear, or the fruit of your choice. Parmesan is a great choice, because it is dry and nutty and will less likely turn stomachs afflicted with morning sickness.

BREADS AND CEREALS

Breads and cereals are often the best friends of the morning sickness sufferer. Have bran or other unsweetened cereal, especially if constipation is a problem. You may have cereal with or without milk, as you wish. Put fruit on cereal, if that is your preference. Typically, 1 ounce of healthful cold cereal (when served with ½ cup of low-fat milk) will give you about 180 calories, 7 g protein, 2 g fat, and 31 g carbohydrates.

Hot cereals: Oatmeal, farina, cream of wheat, and grits are perfect for breakfast, and you can enjoy them to your heart's content. Have some variety by adding fruit, fruit sauces, milk, or yogurt or, in some cases (not oatmeal), some freshly grated cheddar cheese. As an example, 1 cup of cooked oatmeal provides 150 calories, 10 g protein (RDA: 60 to 65 g), 24 g carbohydrates, and no fat.

Toast: Toast is also a good response to an upset stomach. Although we generally discourage you from eating commercial white bread, it does seem effective, when toasted, in alleviating morning sickness. Otherwise, for better nutrition, stick to dark breads and the occasional piece of raisin bread, if you fancy it. Put a little jam or preserve on top if it has no added sugar, or some

Carrot Peanut Butter (page 142). And don't forget breadsticks.

French toast: See the recipe for Panettone French Toast on page 123. If you do not have panettone, substitute raisin bread, challah, or whole wheat. Instead of commercial pancake syrup (which has almost no maple syrup in it), try a little jam or the Apricot Sauce (page 131) or Berry Sauce (page 132). Once in a while, treat yourself to 100% real maple syrup, although it does not have the nutrients to be found in apricot or berry sauce.

Muffins and loaves: This book has good recipes for healthy muffins and loaves that will give you nutrition along with taste (see pages 251-254).

FRUIT

Some fruits (such as watermelon, dates, and any fruit packed in syrup) are a little high in sugar, so you should not overdo it. But if your doctor does not say otherwise, you may have three portions of fruit each day. Select only fresh fruit at the peak of ripeness for maximum flavor and appeal. That frozen banana or a bag of frozen grapes may be just right. Slather a little Carrot Peanut Butter (page 142) on the banana if that sounds good. Combine fruit with a cheese, as suggested on page 255. Broil a half grapefruit or have it cold. Or have a glass of fruit juice of any kind, if that appeals to you. A little fruit with a muffin or piece of loaf, plus a dairy product, makes a wonderful breakfast. And don't forget prunes and prune juice. If citrus juice bothers you at breakfast, opt for a noncitrus nectar such as pear, apricot, or peach.

PROTEIN

You need it, you want it; but some of the foods that deliver protein just are not calling out to you right now. So expand your focus. If there is any leftover meat or fish from last night that would taste great, eat it. Are there leftover beans that might be just the perfect consistency in your mouth? Eat them. How about that portion of casserole in the fridge? Go for it.

Among the traditional proteins on the morning horizon there are the dairy products (mentioned on page 117), which are your best choice for protein in the morning, and those old standbys eggs, bacon, ham, and sausage. They all taste great, but they are high in fat and many of the meats are loaded with chemicals.

It is fine to have the occasional egg, whether soft-boiled, hard-boiled, poached, scrambled, or even fried. Eggs are loaded with nutrients, inexpensive, and easy to make. Four eggs a week are probably acceptable, unless your doctor says otherwise. In calculating your egg consumption, don't forget that eggs appear in French toast and in baking. Eggs are fine for any meal, and a hard-boiled egg makes a good snack. It will keep nicely for about 1 hour outside the refrigerator. As for the pork products mentioned above, if you must have some, do it sparingly and enjoy them. Be sure that they are cooked thoroughly and eat the real thing: Don't have imitation bacon bits or ham spread from a can. Fresh, lean ham is delicious and can be enjoyed if it is well made. Salami, bologna, liverwurst, and luncheon meats are no-nos. Canned baked beans, if they appeal to you, have a decent amount of protein.

BEVERAGES You know that it is essential that you have a constant intake of fluids. Water is the best choice, and drinking lots of water should be second nature to you. Seltzer (which is salt free) or club soda are great if you would prefer a palate-cleansing fizz. Soda and soft drinks (regular or diet) are not permitted at any time. They should be avoided even when you are not pregnant.

Coffee or tea: Caffeine drinks also are discouraged because the caffeine just is not the best thing for a pregnant woman and her fetus. Try herbal teas, fruit teas, and infusions instead. Mint teas are perfect if you have an upset stomach. There are even herbal teas that approximate the taste of coffee if you really want it.

Fruit juices: Juices are great, but be sure to read about fruit on page 119 if you need to watch your sugars. Beware of fruit drinks that are not 100% juice. These often have added sugars and syrups that make them highly caloric, unnutritious, and especially problematic for gestational diabetics.

Dairy drinks: Drinks such as milk, buttermilk, and yogurt shakes are fine at any time. Read more about beverages on page 261 and try the recipes for beverages beginning on page 265.

As you know, alcohol is considered by doctors in the United States and in most other countries to be extremely harmful to the fetus when a pregnant mother has a drink. In some countries (such as France and Italy), wine drinking is part of the traditional diet and most mothers deliver healthy babies. But these mothers usually have superb diets and excellent prenatal care. If you can do without alcohol, though, you have one less thing to worry about. So no bloody Marys, mimosas, and screwdrivers at breakfast or brunch. Have a spritzer or alcohol-free sangria (page 267) when you are having a social brunch. If you have any questions about alcohol and pregnancy in your particular case, be sure to talk to your doctor.

Vitamin B₆ Breakfast

1 SERVING

*It is no secret that when you are experiencing the effects of morning sick-
ness, the last thing you want to do is eat. Yet the need for good nutrition
is essential throughout your pregnancy, as you know from reading
Chapter 2 about the nine months of pregnancy. Some research has indicated
that vitamin B₆ may help counteract morning sickness. Although it does not
work for everyone, if you benefit from a vitamin B₆ breakfast, make the
most of it. Bananas, walnuts, wheat germ, and whole wheat are particularly rich in this vitamin, as are milk and orange juice. If either of these beverages nauseates you, replace it with 2 or 3 tablespoons of hot water.*

1 portion hot cereal (oat bran, cream of wheat, farina, or
    whatever you prefer)
1 frozen banana
1 handful walnuts, unsalted
¼ cup orange juice or milk (or hot water)
1 teaspoon honey (optional)

Cook the cereal according to the directions on the package.

While the cereal is cooking, put the banana, walnuts, juice or
milk, and if you wish, honey in a blender. Blend the ingredients
until you have a thick cream but not a watery liquid.

When the cereal is ready to eat, pour the banana-walnut cream
on top. You may eat this as a separate layer before reaching the hot
cereal (thus coating your stomach with this soothing blend) or you
may stir the cereal and the vitamin B₆ cream together to make
something quite delicious.

If you choose, you can consume this cream as a breakfast or
snack all by itself if you find hot cereal unappealing. You can even
spread some on toast.

$\mathscr{P}$anettone French Toast

1 SERVING

Around the Christmas holidays, many stores sell panettone, the fragrant, airy, slightly sweet yeast bread from Milan, Italy. Most people eat it after an evening meal with some sparkling wine, but it also makes sensational French toast. Make this for yourself or for a brunch with family and friends. Note that you should use 1 egg for 1 serving, 2 eggs for 2 or 3 servings, 3 eggs for 4 or 5 servings. All other ingredients should be multiplied by the number of persons you are serving.

If you are unable to locate panettone, your next best choice is challah, which is available from Jewish bakeries and many good supermarkets. The next choice would be a brioche or any airy yeast bread.

1 vertical slice panettone, about 2 inches thick

1 large egg

2 teaspoons vanilla extract

½ teaspoon ground cinnamon

¼ teaspoon ground nutmeg

1 tablespoon unsalted butter or margarine

Cut the slice of panettone crosswise into 3 pieces.

Beat the egg in a large, flat bowl and then add the vanilla, cinnamon and nutmeg and beat until combined.

Melt the butter over medium-high heat in a 10-inch skillet (don't let the butter brown). While the butter is melting, place the panettone pieces into the egg mixture and flip them with a fork so that all sides of each piece are coated with egg. The idea is to thoroughly coat the panettone slices rather than have the egg be absorbed.

Put the coated panettone pieces into the skillet. Cook over medium-high heat, turning the pieces continuously until both sides become crispy without burning (about 30 to 40 seconds per side).

Serve with a little bit of real maple syrup (not commercial pancake syrup) or Apricot Sauce (page 131) or Berry Sauce (page 132). If you don't have these on hand, try a little honey or apricot, strawberry, or raspberry preserve.

DOCTOR'S NOTE

Calories: 316 per slice

This dish will provide 26 g carbohydrates, 13 g fat (more than 10% of the RDA) and 10 g protein (10% to 15% of the RDA).

Enjoy it for breakfast whenever you want a delicious burst of energy.

DRESSINGS AND SAUCES

This section includes recipes for easily made but beguiling dressings and sauces that add flavor, color, character, and moisture to a whole range of dishes. We start with two vinaigrette sauces to be used on salads, followed by an unusually healthy example of ranch dressing. You may refrigerate dressings in tightly sealed jars or cruets for up to 24 hours. Rosemary Olive Oil may be used as a topping for vegetables or as a great ingredient for many recipes that call for olive oil in cooking. Tomato sauce and pesto are classics that are traditionally associated with pasta, but they are now used in many dishes. We have a low-fat version of hollandaise sauce that will not make you pine for the cholesterol-rich type served at most brunches. Then read the recipe for Salsa Verde, which is really delicious when spread over simply cooked meat or fish or boiled potatoes. It is not the sort of salsa that burns the roof of your mouth. Finally, there are three fruit sauces. Use these where you might have used maple syrup or spoon them over frozen yogurt to make a stellar sundae. Although apple sauce (page 244) is not included in this chapter, it too makes a pleasing dressing or condiment with the right food.

Remember that many good dishes are ruined when they are covered in dressings and sauces. All of these recipes are rich and flavorful and should be used in moderation. An overdressed salad overpowers the delicacy of the greens. Similarly, many of us use much too much sauce on pasta. Start with 1 or 2 tablespoons for 3 ounces of pasta and toss before adding more sauce.

If sauce or dressing is left in a bowl and you don't want to waste it, take some good bread and scoop it up. In some cultures this is thought to be gauche, but food lovers know that it is more gauche to set up forbidding rules based on outmoded ideas. So scoop away!

Classic Vinaigrette

2 TO 3 SERVINGS

Certain recipes are so basic and important, yet they are so often misinterpreted and misrepresented. Here is a recipe for a delicious, simple salad dressing that is sure to please. It should dress 2 to 3 cups of greens. Suggested variations follow.

2 tablespoons good red wine vinegar (*not* balsamic vinegar)

1 to 2 teaspoons Dijon mustard

Freshly ground black or white pepper (to taste)

6 tablespoons extra-virgin olive oil

Pour the vinegar into a jar or cruet that can be tightly closed. Add the mustard and pepper. Close tightly and shake vigorously until the ingredients have blended completely.

Add the oil, close again and shake until everything has blended completely.

Pour over the salad of your choice, toss well, and serve immediately. Do not overdress the salad. The leaves should be lightly coated and the bottom of the bowl should not have a pool of leftover dressing. Salad should never be dressed until the moment it is to be served.

VARIATIONS

Garlic: Cut a clove of garlic in half and rub the salad bowl with the two halves to impart the garlic flavor. If you would prefer to bite into the garlic as you eat the salad, mince 1 garlic clove and add it to the jar along with the mustard. Do not use a garlic press; it produces some garlic juice but does not bring the best of the garlic flavor to your salad.

Herbs: Use ½ teaspoon minced fresh herbs (such as basil) that please you. Add them along with the mustard, but plan to use only one herb. Otherwise there will be too many conflicting flavors. Dried tarragon also is a good choice.

Lemon juice: If vinegar does not appeal to you, substitute fresh lemon juice.

DOCTOR'S NOTE

Calories: 243 per serving

The caloric count for this recipe is based on one serving, but you may enjoy more or less, according to your taste. Olive oil is the clear favorite for the dressings (and most other recipes) recommended in this book. It is the healthiest of all oils, with canola oil a close second. Oils and fats contain about 120 cals per tablespoon and 13 g fat.

Vinaigrette aux Fines Herbes

3 SERVINGS (ENOUGH FOR 2 TO 3 CUPS OF GREENS)

DOCTOR'S NOTE

Calories: 253 per serving

This recipe has been calculated on the basis of three servings. Most oils are very similar in their caloric and fat content (approximately 120 cals and 13 g of fat per tablespoon), with virtually no carbohydrates or proteins.

Fines herbes *is a classic combination of herbs that is popular in southern France. You can often purchase imported jars labeled "Fines Herbes de Provence" or you may make them fresh by combining ingredients you purchase or pick from your garden. While it is generally preferable to use fresh herbs, the dried herbs that come in these jars—superbly fragrant with the smells of the hillsides we've seen in so many impressionist paintings—are just fine. One warning: try not to buy packaged fines herbes that include salt (sel in French), as you do not need the extra sodium.*

2 tablespoons wine vinegar

1 tablespoon plus one teaspoon fines herbes de Provence (or one teaspoon minced fresh parsely, 1 teaspoon minced fresh chives, ½ teaspoon dried thyme, ½ teaspoon dried chervil, and ½ teaspoon tarragon)

6 tablespoons extra-virgin olive oil

Combine the vinegar and herbs in a jar or cruet that can be tightly closed. Close and shake well.

Add the olive oil, cover the jar and shake vigorously.

Serve immediately. Do not overdress your food with this vinaigrette; a little bit goes a long way.

Tofu Ranch Dressing

4 SERVINGS (APPROXIMATELY I CUP)

Tofu *may not be everyone's favorite food, but it does have many admirers. It is very rich in protein, a virtue that cannot be easily ignored. Tofu can be found in almost any Asian market and in the fresh vegetable section of better supermarkets. Here is a recipe for those who don't love tofu but are willing to be pleasantly surprised.*

1 8- to 10-ounce cake of tofu

1 garlic clove, peeled and cut in half

2 tablespoons oil (corn, safflower, or canola)

2 teaspoons white wine vinegar or clear cider vinegar

Freshly ground black pepper to taste

Fresh dill or chopped chives to taste (optional)

Put the tofu, garlic, oil, vinegar, and pepper in a blender. Cover and blend until the mixture is creamy.

You may want to stir in dill or chopped chives or some other herb that catches your fancy.

Serve this dressing cold on a crunchy salad.

DOCTOR'S NOTE

Calories: 85 per serving

This dressing is full of extra nutritional benefits. One serving of this dressing will deliver 2.5 g protein, 7.7 g fat, and no carbohydrates. It also provides 50 mg potassium (about 25% of the RDA). Very good for a humble dressing!

Rosemary Olive Oil

1 Quart

Although the title of this recipe may sound to you like the name of a cartoon character, it is actually a magical perfumed elixir that imparts flavor to anything it touches. You know that olive oil is an essential component in a good diet. With the addition of fresh rosemary, the oil becomes the creative cook's best friend. It is delicious when drizzled over tepid or cold boiled potatoes or used as the oil in a salad dressing. If you are making a scrambled egg, use a teaspoon of this oil instead of butter and you will be surprised by the subtle flavor. In fact, instead of buttering your French or Italian bread, pour a little rosemary olive oil on top. Used for sautéeing chicken breasts, the rosemary gives a special taste to the dish that will once and for all silence those who exclaim, "Not chicken again!" By the way, if you are partial to fresh tarragon, it makes an excellent alternative to rosemary.

2 long sprigs bright green fresh rosemary

1 quart (or liter) extra-virgin olive oil

Do not wash the rosemary. Instead, place each sprig on a paper towel and wipe carefully. Do not be afraid to rub the rosemary— →

DOCTOR'S NOTE

Calories: 120 per tablespoon

The fat count for olive oil is 13 g per tablespoon. It is devoid of carbohydrates or protein.

this friction will bring out the perfume. Gather any needles that fall away, but discard those that are not bright green.

Put the rosemary into the bottle of oil, close tightly and store for at least 1 week before use.

Remember that any bottle of olive oil should be tightly capped and stored in a dark, cool place to prevent rancidity. When you have used up the oil, discard the rosemary and make a fresh batch with new oil and rosemary.

The World's Easiest Tomato Sauce

8 SERVINGS

DOCTOR'S NOTE

Calories: 37 per 3-table-spoon serving

This sauce is much lower in calories and salt (and is preservative free) than its store-bought cousins. It is also very low in fat (1.2 g per serv-ing) and carbohydrates, making it a delicious and balanced accompani-ment to carbohydrate-rich pastas.

This sauce is as delicious as it is easy to make. Use it sparingly over al dente spaghetti, macaroni, rigatoni, or penne. Use it to flavor recipes in this book that call for tomato sauce or for dishes of your own creation.

1 tablespoon olive oil

Slivered garlic to taste

28-ounce can crushed tomatoes, preferably from Italy

Freshly ground pepper to taste

4 or 5 fresh basil leaves (optional)

Heat the olive oil in a 2-quart saucepan over medium heat. Add the garlic slivers and sauté them until they are dark blond in color—do not let them burn.

Add the crushed tomatoes and pepper, stir well and simmer over low heat for 8 minutes.

If you are using basil, do not wash the leaves. Wipe them care-fully with paper towels and tear (not cut) them into small pieces. Stir them into the pot 2 minutes before the sauce is done.

Pesto Presto

2 SERVINGS (4 TABLESPOONS)

The word pesto *implies something that has been ground in a mortar with a pestle. Traditionally, what we call pesto comes from Genoa, Italy, and is made with fresh basil. You are too busy to spend time making a pesto by hand, so it's all right to sacrifice some authenticity and use a blender. Pregnant women in Genoa would probably do the same. Pesto should be served with long, thin, flat pasta such as linguine that is cooked al dente. Pesto should never be heated, but simply tossed with hot pasta and served immediately.*

Although many pasta eaters do not like cold leftover pasta that has been sauced, linguine al pesto is an exception that makes a good snack when served cold the following day. You may use pesto to experiment with other dishes, such as chicken salad with a pesto dressing that has been cut with a bit of yogurt or grilled fish over which you have spread the pesto.

20 leaves fresh basil

1 ounce pinoli (pine nuts) or, as a second choice, unsalted
   walnut pieces

2 tablespoons extra-virgin olive oil

1 to 2 garlic cloves, according to your taste

1 tablespoon freshly grated Romano cheese or, as a second
   choice, Parmesan

Wipe the basil leaves carefully with paper towels and remove the stems.

Put all of the ingredients in a blender or food processor. Cover and blend for about 1 minute, or until you have a smooth sauce of well-combined ingredients.

Store in a tightly closed jar in the refrigerator with a little bit of olive oil on top. This sauce will keep for about 1 week.

DOCTOR'S NOTE

Calories: 220 per serving

This sauce actually adds nutritional value to your pasta dishes. The 10 leaves of fresh basil called for in each serving (1 ounce) will provide more than 2250 IU vitamin A (50% of the RDA) and 32 mg vitamin C (about 45% of the RDA). Pine nuts are devoid of salt and high in thiamine, a B vitamin.

Faux Hollandaise Sauce
2 Servings (½ cup)

Hollandaise sauce is rich, creamy, full of eggs, and sinfully loaded with cholesterol. It really should be consumed sparingly and enjoyed to the fullest when it is eaten. In its place, dear reader, because you are a health-conscious individual, we propose faux (false) hollandaise, which will not erase the memory of the real thing, but it will taste good with many dishes that call for hollandaise sauce. If you use lemon yogurt, the sauce will have extra tang.

4 tablespoons lemon (or plain) yogurt

½ teaspoon Dijon mustard

A pinch of freshly ground white or black pepper (optional)

Combine all the ingredients in a bowl, stirring until they are thoroughly blended. Do not overstir or the sauce will become too runny. It is best when it is when it is richly creamy and tangy. Adjust to your own taste by using more or less mustard.

Do not serve ice cold. You may choose to *gently* heat the sauce in a saucepan but make certain it does not get too hot, in which case it might curdle.

Serve this sauce as you would regular hollandaise: over cooked broccoli or asparagus; over salmon loaf or with poached salmon or other fish; or with a version of eggs Benedict that includes an English muffin, a poached egg and a slice of Canadian bacon, ham, or some nicely steamed spinach.

Salsa Verde
4 Servings (1 cup)

This is not a spicy salsa of the Tex-Mex variety, but salsa verde adds flavor to simple, good food such as boiled beef or poached fish. You may increase, decrease, or eliminate any ingredient (except the parsley) to suit your taste and needs.

1 handful fresh parsley, stems and all, washed

1 to 2 garlic cloves, peeled

4 tablespoons extra-virgin olive oil

½ teaspoon capers, drained

2 hard-boiled eggs

3 gherkins (very small pickles)

1 tablespoon Dijon mustard

Put all of the ingredients in a blender or food processor. Cover and blend or process until the ingredients are well combined but not puréed. The salsa verde should be thick and rich, not runny or liquidy.

Serve with the meat or fish of your choice or as a dip for crudités (page 136). The sauce keeps for 3 days in the refrigerator.

Apricot Sauce
20 SERVINGS (1¼ CUP)

U se this delicious sauce on Panettone French Toast (page 123); as a topping for frozen yogurt in a Sundae or Banana Split (page 257); or over baked sweet potatoes, yams, or parboiled carrots.

1 cup dried apricots

1 to 1½ tablespoons freshly squeezed lemon juice

Place the apricots in a medium saucepan with enough cold water so that the fruit is just covered.

Cook over medium heat 10 to 15 minutes until the fruit is plump and resembles fresh apricots.

Then lift the apricots out of the pan with a slotted spoon and reserve the liquid.

Put the apricots and lemon juice in a blender or food processor and blend for 2 or 3 seconds. If you want a thinner sauce, add some of the stewing liquid. (This liquid tastes nice on its own as a juice or poured into fruit salad.)

Serve the apricot sauce warm or cold. →

Mixed Fruit Sauce: Before blending, add other stewed fruits, such as prunes, or try a sliced banana or a little orange juice.

Berry Sauce

16 SERVINGS (1 CUP)

DOCTOR'S NOTE

Calories: 8 per 1-tablespoon serving of strawberry sauce

Almost all berries are similarly low in calories if bought fresh, but we chose strawberries as an example for our calorie count. A serving of this sauce contains 13 mg vitamin C (about 20% of the RDA), no fat, and less than 2 g carbohydrate. If you choose to use frozen berries, the calorie content of the sauce will increase, because berries are usually sweetened with syrup before freezing.

Use this sauce on Panettone French Toast (page 123), as the syrup for the Banana Split (page 257), stirred into yogurt, or for whatever inspiration you might have. Use strawberries, blueberries, blackberries, raspberries, or any combination of these.

1 pint fresh, ripe berries, washed (strawberries must be hulled) or 1 12-ounce package of frozen berries, thawed

1 teaspoon freshly squeezed lemon juice

½ teaspoon confectioner's sugar (optional)

Put all the ingredients in a blender. Cover and blend about 5 seconds or until nearly smooth.

Serve at room temperature or warm.

APPETIZERS

The very sound of the word *appetizer* should immediately tell you what this course of a meal is all about: It should stimulate your appetite. Appetizers tend to be highly flavorful, pleasing to the eye, and not particularly filling. In many homes, the appetizer is the first course of a meal, the course that is quickly prepared while the main course is cooking. In a formal meal, the appetizer might be served with cocktails (see page 261 for nonalcoholic drinks you can enjoy at cocktail hour), to be followed by a soup or pasta, a main course with cooked vegetables, then a salad, then dessert. In meals this size it is common to have some palate-cleansing lemon sorbet.

Although you will not be at formal meals every day, you should still view appetizers in a special way when you are expecting a baby. An appetizer for the pregnant gourmet might be used to stimulate a sluggish appetite, to stave off hunger while waiting for the main course, or as an intriguing snack. Many leftovers make good appetizers (such as Salmon Loaf, page 193). The recipes in this section are familiar appetizers (all of which you should think of as snacks at any time of the day), yet there are many other recipes in this book which, when served in smaller portions, make wonderful appetizers, too. There isn't a better or more appetizing first course than a half portion of pasta (see pages 171-180). In terms of what these deliver nutritionally, consider an appetizer to be half the size of a main course. In some of the recipes on the following pages, we list nutritional content for the dish as a main course and as an appetizer.

Hummus

12 SERVINGS (3 CUPS)

Hummus can be a fundamental food to have ready whenever you want to snack or satisfy hunger. Put some hummus in a pita pocket with chopped vegetables as a brown bag lunch or serve it with healthy wheat crackers (without hydrogenated or tropical oils) or as a dip for crudités. Tahini, one of the essential ingredients of hummus, is available in many supermarkets as well as health food stores, gourmet markets, and Middle Eastern groceries. Hummus kept refrigerated in a sealed container will last 4 or 5 days.

2 cups dried (or 2 16-ounce cans, drained) chick-peas

8 tablespoons freshly squeezed lemon juice (from approximately
    2 to 3 lemons)

5 garlic cloves, minced

½ cup tahini (sesame seed paste)

3 tablespoons extra virgin olive oil

3 tablespoons cooking liquid from the chick-peas or water

¼ teaspoon ground cayenne or paprika

Freshly ground pepper to taste

Chopped fresh parsley for garnish

If you are using dried chick-peas, put them in a medium size broad-bottomed pot. Cover the peas with cold water and cook over low heat until tender, 30 to 40 minutes. (Consult the package directions for guidance.) Drain, reserving the liquid.

Put the cooked or canned chick-peas in the blender or food processor. Add the lemon juice, garlic, tahini, olive oil, and cooking liquid (or water). Cover and blend or process until you have a thick, rich sauce.

Transfer the hummus to a dish and add cayenne and black pepper to taste. Top with parsley and serve.

Cook's note: Taste varies and you should follow your own preferences in making hummus. To make a creamier version, add more lemon juice, oil, and cooking liquid. If you prefer less garlic flavor, add more lemon juice, oil, and liquid or reduce the amount of garlic.

Guacamole

6 SERVINGS (3 CUPS)

You may not want the typical guacamole laced with fiery-hot red and green chili peppers, but this version—although you would never find it in Acapulco—will go down fine. Eat this guacamole on a bed of coarsely chopped lettuce or in a lunchtime sandwich: Spread guacamole on whole wheat bread or in a pita pocket and add thinly sliced turkey or chicken breast (not chicken roll), tomato slices, and chopped lettuce. In selecting avocados, avoid the huge tasteless green ones and opt instead for the smaller, dark pebble-skinned ones. They are ripe when they yield slightly to the touch but are not mushy.

3 avocados

2 tablespoons freshly squeezed lime juice

1 large tomato, diced and seeded

½ medium sweet onion, minced

Freshly ground pepper to taste

Peel, then mash the avocados in a bowl and immediately add the lime juice.

Add the tomato, onion, and pepper. Mix and set aside, covered, for 1 hour before serving.

If you do not plan to eat the guacamole right away, store it in the refrigerator, where it will keep for 2 days.

DOCTOR'S NOTE

Calories: 130 per serving

Guacamole is great for almost any time in your pregnancy. Because of its texture, it might not appeal to you if you are feeling queasy. Rely on your feelings. However, if you are suffering from a bout of constipation, its naturally high fat content might prove helpful, especially when combined with high-fiber crackers. Among foods of vegetable origin, the avocado is the highest in fat content (even more than olives). In addition, it contains a good dose of thiamine and riboflavin. Thiamine (also called vitamin B_1) is one of the B-complex vitamins and forms part of an enzyme that is essential in the conversion of glucose to energy in the body. You cannot store it, however, so it must be provided daily in the diet. Thiamine needs increase during times of stress such as pregnancy or heavy involvement in sports. Read more about thiamine on page 14.

Crudités

4 SERVINGS

Everyone knows how healthy and full of vitamins and roughage raw vegetables are. In addition, they are low in calories and serve multiple purposes: snack, appetizer, or finger food.

A serving of crudités provides 6750 IU vitamin A (more than 100% of the RDA), and 25 g vitamin C (about 33% of your RDA).

The vitamin content of raw, cut vegetables diminishes with storage, especially if you let them stand in water for long periods. Try to prepare them no more than half an hour before eating.

Yes, crudités have become fashionable—even cliché—but they are perfect for snacking, dunking in a yogurt dip, or serving as an appetizer with olives that contain as little salt as possible. The key to good crudités is keeping the vegetables crunchy and fresh.

3 medium carrots, scraped

5 stalks of celery, washed, with the ends cut off

1 red or yellow bell pepper, seeded and washed

1 green bell pepper, seeded and washed

12 cherry tomatoes, stems removed, washed

1 small head of cauliflower or broccoli, washed

Fill a large bowl with cold water and ice cubes.

Cut the carrots and celery into equal-size pieces, about 3 inches in length. Put them into the iced water.

Cut the peppers into 3-inch strips, and add them to the water along with the tomatoes.

Cut the cauliflower or broccoli into bite-size florets. Do not leave on too much stalk. Immerse the florets in the water as well.

When you are ready to serve the crudités (preferably within 30 minutes), drain the vegetables and dry them well. Arrange prettily on a platter and serve.

Marinated Mushrooms and Peppers

8 HALF CUP SERVINGS

An excellent appetizer, snack, or filler for a pita pocket with cheese cubes.

2 green bell peppers, seeded and sliced

2 red bell peppers, seeded and sliced

4 garlic cloves, minced

1 tablespoon extra-virgin olive oil

1 pound fresh mushrooms, cleaned and thinly sliced

4 tablespoons freshly squeezed lemon juice

Freshly ground black pepper to taste

16 Gaeta or other oil-cured, small black olives (optional)

Preheat oven to 375° F.

Toss the peppers, garlic, and oil in a shallow baking pan. Bake for 20 to 25 minutes, until the peppers are tender. Let the vegetables cool.

In a large bowl combine the mushrooms, lemon juice, and peppers. Season with pepper.

Cover the bowl and marinate for at least 30 minutes or up to 6 hours. If you plan to marinate for more than 2 hours, place the bowl in the refrigerator.

Add additional lemon juice, if that suits your taste. Serve with the olives, if desired.

DOCTOR'S NOTE

Calories: 42 per serving

This tasty dish is low in calories and high in essential vitamins. Mushrooms are a very rich source of amino acids. In addition, this dish has a high fiber content, making it good for those days when you need extra help in your fight against constipation. An added advantage is that mushrooms and green and red peppers are available throughout the year in most supermarkets; thus it's a good choice for the winter months when fresh vitamin sources are not readily available.

LUNCH AND BRUNCH

The key word here is *leftovers*. Most of the recipes created for you in this book are designed so that there can be leftover food. Almost every salad (if it is not already dressed), meat, fish, soup, stew, casserole, cooked vegetable, raw or cooked fruit, fruit salad, appetizer, and baked good you can make will keep overnight and perhaps for a couple of days. The only major item that does not keep well is cooked pasta that has been sauced. The exception to this is pasta with pesto sauce (page 129), which does taste pretty good cold.

For most recipes, we let you know how well or poorly a particular food lasts in storage. As a general rule, leftovers should be stored in the refrigerator in a bowl or dish that has been tightly sealed with plastic wrap. Sauces and gravies from meat will tend to gel in the cold. Take the opportunity to skim the fat off them before reheating with the meat.

For most of us, the idea of lunch is a sandwich or salad. You may put any cooked food from your refrigerator between two pieces of whole wheat bread or in a pita pocket and have a fine sandwich. Stuff a pita pocket with vegetables and cheese for another good selection. If you are taking your sandwich with you for the day, wrap it well in aluminum foil and try to keep it in a refrigerator or a cool place until you are ready to eat it. Most foods keep safely out of the fridge for up to 1 hour. Unless you can be sure that you will put your sandwich in the refrigerator, don't slather any mayonnaise (or the more desirable cholesterol-free mayonnaise) on your bread. The same applies to sandwiches in which you have put yogurt. Use the best mustard available to give real character to your sandwich. Ketchup may be used in small amounts, but it is very high in unnecessary salt. Choose low-sodium ketchup instead.

To carry green salads, fruit salads, or fresh vegetables, buy a couple of good-quality plastic containers that seal tightly. (Supermarket containers do not seal well enough for long term use and reuse.) These containers should be washed as soon as they have been used, rather than carrying them home dirty. Again, try to store salads in a cool place until you are ready to eat them.

If you are having lunch at home, choose widely and imaginatively. Aside from your usual repertoire of omelets, quiches, sandwiches, and so forth, select more unusual foods that you normally wouldn't consider for lunch. A bowl of pasta is great. Anything that was last night's main course will be great for lunch, either reheated or used in another way. For example, cold salmon loaf makes a great sandwich or spread. Take a leftover chicken supreme and cover it with torn lettuce or arugula, pour on a little vinaigrette and eat. Be sure there are both chicken and lettuce in every forkful. Roast or boiled chicken becomes good chicken salad when you add a yogurt dressing, raisins, and nuts. Use your imagination and follow some of the suggestions you see in the recipes.

But, whatever you do, don't skip lunch. You need the nutrition and so does your baby. If you don't feel like eating, have a little snack of leftover food or a bit of fruit salad, a spoonful of cottage cheese with a pineapple slice, or melted cheese on a piece of bread or select whatever healthful food calls out to you right now.

Remember to stay away from all commercial luncheon meats such as salami, bologna, liverwurst, turkey or chicken *roll* (which you should not confuse with breast meat), cured ham, pastrami, corned beef, tongue, and so forth. These are filled with salt, nitrites, preservatives, and colorings and are simply not good for you.

$\mathcal{P}$*ita, Pita, Pita*

1 SERVING

W*e do not know if Bette Davis ever uttered the famous "Peter, Peter, Peter," but even that demanding lady would have enjoyed this delicious, simple lunch treat. You can vary the protein (cubed chicken, turkey, ham, leftover roast beef or any other meat or cheese that appeals to you) and can vary the vegetables according to what appeals to you or what you have on hand.*

½ cup cooked chicken, ham, or other protein, chopped or
cubed

⅔ cup diced crunchy vegetables (carrots, peppers, celery,
scallions, or even apples)

1 whole wheat pita bread, toasted

2 tablespoons plain (or lemon) low-fat yogurt

½ teaspoon freshly squeezed lemon juice (optional)

¼ teaspoon honey (optional)

⅛ teaspoon curry (optional)

1 tablespoon raisins

Freshly ground pepper to taste

¼ cup bean sprouts

Prepare the meat and vegetables. Start toasting the pita.

While the bread is warming, make a dressing of yogurt and the optional agreements. Add the meat, diced vegetables, raisins, and pepper and combine.

Put the mixture in the pita pocket, add the sprouts, and enjoy.

DOCTOR'S NOTE

Calories: 386 per serving

We analyzed the nutritive value of this recipe using ½ cup of cooked chicken as the protein source. It will deliver 23 g of protein (approximately 33% of the RDA), 3.5 g fat, 190 mg phosphorus (17% of the RDA), and 8.5 mg niacin (50% of the RDA).

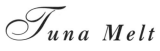

Tuna Melt

2 SERVINGS

You would be amazed how often tuna melt, an essentially simple dish, is poorly prepared. This is usually because restaurants use cold tuna salad that is laden with mayonnaise. The result is a cold, runny sandwich with melted cheese on top. You should only make a tuna melt if you start with tuna that is at room temperature. So keep a couple cans in the pantry if you are a tuna melt lover. To give the tuna salad additional taste, you may add optional ingredients such as minced onion, minced celery, grated carrot, or capers. This recipe will make a filling lunch for one hungry person or a nice lunch for two if it's accompanied by, perhaps, a cup of soup.

½ teaspoon plain or lemon low-fat yogurt

¼ teaspoon Dijon mustard (optional)

1 6½- to 7-ounce can tuna, packed in water

Minced onion to taste (optional)

Minced celery to taste (optional)

Grated carrot to taste (optional)

¼ teaspoon capers (optional)

2 slices of whole wheat bread

2 slices of tomato (optional)

2 slices low-fat Swiss, Munster, or Monterrey Jack cheese or

   2 tablespoons freshly grated Cheddar cheese

Preheat broiler to medium or moderate.

Put the yogurt in a medium bowl and add the mustard if you are using it.

Drain the tuna well and then add it to the bowl. Add any or all of the optional onion, celery, carrot, or capers. Combine the ingredients well using a fork or spoon.

Toast the bread and then place it in an ovenproof dish.

Spoon the tuna salad equally on the two slices of bread. If you wish, put a tomato slice on top of the tuna. Then top with the cheese. →

DOCTOR'S NOTE

Calories: **283** per serving

Each serving of this recipe will provide you with 35 g protein (28 g from the tuna and 7 g from the cheese). In addition, the cheese will add 250 mg calcium (almost 25% of the RDA) and 4 g fat. The bread will provide you with 10 g of carbohydrates.

This recipe is an excellent source of protein, and if you have been diagnosed with gestational diabetes, it can be just what the doctor ordered.

Put the dish under the broiler, and broil only until the cheese melts, about 2 to 3 minutes.
Eat immediately.

Cook's note: If you are in the later stages of pregnancy or at any time have difficulty bending, this recipe can be made in a toaster oven with a broiler setting if your oven's broiler is too low for you to reach comfortably.

Carrot Peanut Butter

8 SERVINGS (2 CUPS)

An ideal brown bag lunch is a sandwich of carrot peanut butter and sliced banana on whole wheat bread. You can also use this peanut butter for snacking by spreading some on a stalk of celery or stirring some into plain or lemon yogurt. Store it in a tightly sealed jar in the refrigerator.

5 medium carrots, washed, scraped, cut into small chunks

1 cup peanut butter, chunky or smooth, without additives

4 tablespoons water

Steam the carrots for about 7 minutes or until soft. Drain the carrots.

Place warm carrots in a blender along with the peanut butter and the water. Blend until smooth or, if you prefer, only until the mixture becomes a chunky paste. If you want the spread to be thinner, add more water, a bit at a time, blending until the desired consistency is achieved.

DOCTOR'S NOTE

Calories: 171 per serving

This delicious concoction will provide you with 8 g protein, 16.2 g fat and 6 g carbohydrate per serving. In addition, it will provide 2035 IU vitamin A (50% of the RDA), 195 g sodium, and a good dose of potassium. Peanut butter is the quintessential energy food because of its high protein content . Keep in mind, however, that peanut butter is also very high in fat. If your doctor has advised you to slow down on your weight gain, you are better off eliminating nuts and nut butters from your diet.

Florentine Omelet

1 SERVING

This dish is perfect for the person who wants to load up on iron, because both spinach and eggs are rich in iron. Eggs are inexpensive, quick to prepare if you are very hungry, and are loaded with protein and iron. By the way, this omelet should more accurately be called a frittata, *which is the Italian term for eggs cooked in olive oil. Any dish that contains spinach is usually called* Florentine, *for this leafy green vegetable is a great favorite in Florence.*

1 pound fresh spinach or 1 10-ounce package of frozen
chopped spinach

2 fresh eggs, large or extra large

1 teaspoon extra-virgin olive oil

1 teaspoon minced onion (optional)

If you are using fresh spinach, tear off any tough stems and wash the leaves carefully to get rid of all the sand. Tear the leaves into bite-size pieces. Steam the spinach in the water that clings to the leaves, adding a little more water to the pot if needed. (see page 231 for details on cooking fresh spinach.) If you are using frozen spinach, cook according to the directions on the package. When the spinach is cooked, use a fork or spoon to press all the liquid from the leaves. Remember to reserve this mineral-rich liquid for use in soups and sauces.

In a mixing bowl, beat the eggs lightly with a fork, combining them with about one-quarter to one-third of the cooked spinach. (Refrigerate the rest of the spinach and serve it ice cold with a squeeze of fresh lemon juice as a perfect vegetable accompaniment to many main courses.)

In an omelet pan or small skillet, heat the olive oil over medium heat. There should be enough oil to coat the pan. Add more oil if you are using a slightly bigger pan. The oil should be hot but should not smoke. →

DOCTOR'S NOTE

Calories: 388 per serving

Eggs contain only 82 calories per egg (slightly higher if you cook in oil), only 0.5 g carbohydrate, and a good dose of vitamin B_6. Eggs are among the leanest and least fattening foods one can choose. Much has been said about eggs and cholesterol, which is concentrated in the yolk (250 mg), and which prompted the American Heart Association to recommend limiting egg consumption to only three or four a week. However, during pregnancy the increased amount of estrogen your body produces has a protective effect against cholesterol deposition in arteries. The mechanism is not yet entirely understood, but it is certain that pregnant women, even the ones who have high cholesterol levels while not pregnant, are not at increased cardiac risk during pregnancy. Spinach provides an impressive array of nutrients. The portion of fresh cooked spinach called for in this recipe has 32 mg vitamin C (33% of your RDA), 9185 IU vitamin A, 105 mg calcium, and 368 mg potassium. A few words of caution on spinach: Its vitamin C content diminishes considerably with preservation. Freezing will maintain most of its vitamin C and calcium, but the soggy, canned variety has almost no vitamin C and is very high in salt.

The total amount of carbohydrates in this dish is 1 g. There are 13 g protein and 16.5 mg iron (more than 50% of the RDA).

This dish is an excellent choice if you are a gestational diabetic watching your carbohydrates and still concerned with your iron and vitamin intake. If you are gaining too much weight too fast and would like to limit your fat intake without sacrificing protein this dish is for you as well.

If you are using the onion, sauté it for a few seconds in the hot oil. Then add the spinach-egg combination and vigorously stir the eggs with a fork for a few seconds with one hand while holding the handle of the pan with the other. Then put the pan over the heat for a few seconds, until the omelet develops a slight skin or crust on the bottom. Check by using your fork.

At this point you can fold the omelet in half, using the fork or a spatula or, as the Italians do, flip the omelet over with the spatula or by sliding the omelet onto a plate and then flipping it back into the pan. This is all much easier than it sounds, and when you've done it once, you'll be a master. Cook the other side for a few seconds and then slide the frittata onto the plate.

A good sliced tomato makes a nice accompaniment to a Florentine omelette. If you are cooking for more than one person, make each omelet individually.

SOUP

This book contains some good and unusual soup recipes, plus that all-important recipe for chicken stock that will form the basis of so many other soups and dishes you will prepare. But you should also experiment by combining foods you like. They will probably please you in soups because you already like how they taste.

Keep a large jar of vegetable liquid in the refrigerator: Every time you steam spinach or other greens, cauliflower, broccoli, asparagus, and other vegetables, there is some flavorful and nutritious liquid at the bottom of the pot. Store this liquid in one jar that you keep tightly shut in the fridge. When you are asked to use water in any soup recipe, substitute the vegetable liquid and you are ahead of the game. But stay away from cabbage liquid, which often has a funny taste or smell.

Your blender is a great friend: We didn't encourage you to buy many new utensils in preparation for your pregnancy because you have enough chores and expenses to think about. But, if you don't already own one, we urge you to purchase a blender. It is amazingly useful and well worth the cost. It can make wonderful shakes and drinks (see page 263) and can make certain cooking tasks easier. But its greatest worth comes in soup making. After partially boiling any vegetables you have around (everything from Brussels sprouts and greens to carrots and potatoes), you can put the vegetables in the blender (reserving the liquid as suggested above) and blend them into a rich creamy soup. These soups may be served hot or cold, with fresh herbs stirred in. You may adjust the thickness of soups by adding cooking liquid or a little olive oil or by running them in the blender a little longer.

SOUP-MAKING
STRATEGIES

Soup Recipes

Chicken Stock

12 Servings (12 cups)

This is the essential ingredient in so many recipes. Make a large amount of chicken stock for storage. Store it in containers of different sizes, because the stock should not be refrozen once it has thawed. Ice cube trays also are good for storing stock for use when you only need a small amount in cooking. (After the stock cubes are frozen, transfer them to zipper-type plastic bags for better storage.) Use the stock as a base for chicken soup or for other soups; use it as a cooking liquid in recipes that call for water, stock, or white wine; or drink it steaming hot from a mug when you need to warm up on an icy winter afternoon.

A good, nutritious soup can be made with piping hot chicken stock and pieces of cooked spinach (see page 231); grate some real Parmigiano-Reggiano cheese on top just before eating.

4 to 5 pounds chicken wings, well-washed and patted dry (you may also use backs, necks, or other scraps in combination with the wings)

10 garlic cloves, peeled and split

6 scallions, washed and cut in half

1 large onion, peeled and coarsely chopped

4 medium carrots, cleaned, scraped, and chopped

2 medium stalks of celery, washed, trimmed, and chopped

1 bay leaf

6 peppercorns

18 cups cold water

In a large stockpot, put the chicken, garlic, scallion, onion, carrots, celery, bay leaf, and peppercorns. Add the water and stir with a wooden spoon to combine the ingredients.

Bring to a boil over high heat. Then reduce the heat and simmer, partially covered, for 2½ hours.

When the stock is ready, strain it through a colander into a large bowl. It might be a good idea to have someone help you with this step, as the pot may be a little heavy. (Old-fashioned stockpots have spigots, but these are difficult to find nowadays.)

When the stock cools, pour or ladle it into clean jars, containers, and ice trays. Refrigerate (up to 3 days) or freeze (up to 6 weeks), as your needs dictate, but always skim the fat off the stock before heating it. The leftover ingredients will be overcooked and not good for other recipes, so they should be discarded.

Orange Chicken Broth

3 SERVINGS (3 CUPS)

We might as well call this "cup of vitamins and minerals." The chicken broth offers a bevy of nutrients, and the oranges bring vitamin C and calcium. It also tastes good.

 2 cups of clear chicken stock (see page 146), skimmed

 1 cup orange juice, strained of pulp

 2 teaspoons minced scallions or chives (optional)

Combine the chicken stock and orange juice in a saucepan and slowly heat the liquid on low until it begins to simmer. If you are using scallions or chives, add them now. Simmer for 2 to 3 minutes.

Serve piping hot in a bowl or mug. As a garnish, add a thin orange slice to the bowl; you can poke it with your spoon to squeeze out additional shots of fresh juice.

VARIATION
You can use lemon juice with chicken broth, a combination popular in Greece, if you don't find it too bitter.

DOCTOR'S NOTE

Calories: 94 per serving

This is a nutritious way to add vitamin C (63 mg, almost 100% of the RDA) to chicken broth. It is especially recommended for the first trimester, when you may want to eat only something light, yet your vitamin needs are high. Orange juice, because of its acidity, is discouraged during the morning sickness times, although in this case the acid is tempered by the chicken broth, so that you might be able to stomach it. In the cooking process, the juice retains most of its vitamin content.

Endive Soup

4 SERVINGS (4 CUPS)

DOCTOR'S NOTE

Calories: 70.5 per serving

This soup is good whenever you need a quick pick-me-up and especially if you feel queasy. Per serving, it will provide 8.2 g carbohydrates, 13.7 g fat, and approximately 2 g protein.

The delicacy of this soup will be welcome if you are feeling rather delicate yourself. If you do not have home-made stock available, you might use a very good low-salt canned version (such as Health Valley), although even the best canned stock never measures up to home-made.

5 tablespoons unsalted butter or margarine

1 pound endive (its base trimmed and discarded), cut into lengthwise strips

½ pound small potatoes, cut in pieces

3 cups hot chicken stock (page 146), skimmed

Freshly ground pepper to taste

Minced parsley

In a large stock pot, melt 3 tablespoons of the butter and gently sauté the endive strips. Add a pinch of salt (if you are eating salt) and the potatoes. Stir briefly and add 2 cups of the hot stock.

Cover and simmer for 30 minutes.

Then pour the ingredients into a blender or food processor and purée only until the soup has a creamy, consistent look.

Return the soup to the pot, add the remaining 1 cup of hot stock and bring to a boil.

Remove from the heat, stir in the remaining 2 tablespoons of butter, and serve topped with freshly ground pepper and minced parsley.

Emerald Soup

6 SERVINGS (6 CUPS)

Loaded with minerals and vitamins and very easy to make. Use greens of your choice. This is a good soup to make if you have various greens that have been in the refrigerator for a few days and seem ready to spoil. The more variety you have, the more interesting the flavor of the soup will be. You should use between 4 and 5 cups of loosely packed greens.

1 bunch watercress

1 bunch scallions

A few celery leaves

1 bunch parsley

1 bunch arugula

A few leaves escarole or other lettuce

A few leaves spinach

Any other greens you might fancy

4 cups boiling water

½ teaspoon freshly ground pepper

½ teaspoon salt (optional)

1 garlic clove (optional)

1 tablespoon extra-virgin olive oil

Wash all of the greens, trimming tough or bitter stems and discolored leaves.

Place the greens in a large stockpot and add the boiling water. If you use a lot of vegetables, use more water. Add pepper, salt, and garlic and simmer for 15 minutes.

Stir in the olive oil and simmer 5 minutes more. Serve as is.

Cook's note: If you choose, top the soup with some freshly grated Parmesan or Romano cheese. You also may purée all or part of the soup in a blender, returning it briefly to the pot to reheat before serving. The purée also makes a good cold soup, garnished with some minced chives or a lemon slice.

DOCTOR'S NOTE

Calories: 40 per serving

Vitamins A and C are always in demand for the pregnant gourmet. Find them in abundance in this delicious soup. Loaded with these and other vitamins, almost calorie-free, completely devoid of fat, but with a light and subtle taste, emerald soup is a dieter's dream come true. Try this soup when you are slightly queasy and are searching for vitamins that come without the acid of fruit and juices. Try it when your weight is going up faster than it should or after your baby's birth when you are looking for ways to lose weight. The ingredients in this soup are left to your imagination and to what looks good in the market. To give you an idea of what this soup delivers, here's an example: If you use 3½ ounces each of escarole and watercress as main ingredients you will get 230 mg calcium (38 mg per serving), 8200 IU vitamin A, and about 100 mg vitamin C (17 mg per serving).

Minestrone Con Fagioli
Florentine Bean Soup
6 SERVINGS (6 CUPS)

*T*aking the shortcut of using canned beans will not seriously detract from the nutritional punch delivered by this protein-laden soup. Buy a good brand of beans such as Progresso or Goya. In making this soup, variety is encouraged. You might consider a can of red kidney beans, a can of chick-peas, a can of lentils, and a can of white beans. Or choose any beans of your liking. This hearty soup can be eaten as a main course with good bread, followed by a dessert of fresh fruit. A cup of this soup makes a fine first course in a larger meal. For something delicious and different on a hot summer's day, eat Minestrone con Fagioli *chilled.*

4 19-ounce cans high-quality beans, drained

6 tablespoons extra-virgin olive oil

1 garlic clove, minced

2 stalks of celery, chopped

2 carrots, washed, scraped, and chopped

1 small onion, peeled and coarsely chopped

4 tomatoes (fresh or canned), chopped and seeded

1 small head leafy vegetable (radicchio, endive, or savoy cabbage), washed and cut in strips

3 tablespoons chopped fresh parsley

A few leaves fresh basil, if available, wiped clean

3 quarts cold water

Freshly ground pepper to taste

½ pound imported Italian macaroni (such as penne, ditali, shells, or maccheroni)

Mix the beans well in a large bowl.

Purée half of the beans in a blender and pour the bean purée back into the bowl.

In a large stockpot, gently heat the olive oil and add the garlic, celery, carrots, and onion. Sauté these ingredients for a few minutes until they soften, taking care that none of them burn.

Add the tomatoes, leafy vegetable, parsley, basil, beans and bean pureé, water, and pepper. Stir well to combine. Cover and simmer over low heat for about 45 minutes, stirring occasionally.

Add the macaroni and cook until the pasta is al dente (check the directions on the pasta box for an approximate cooking time).

Serve, or cool before refrigerating.

Cook's note: People in Italy often eat this with a spoonful of extra-virgin olive oil stirred in. You might try this with Rosemary Olive Oil (page 127).

you may want to skip this recipe if you are prone to gassiness. Try Minestrone con Fagioli during your second and early third trimester, because gassiness is temporary and diminishes considerably after the first trimester.

Rice Soup
4 SERVINGS (4 CUPS)

DOCTOR'S NOTE

Calories: 380 per serving

This comforting soup brings with it a load of calcium (290 mg per serving; 25% of the RDA), 51 g carbohydrate, and only 9 g fat and protein each. It is a good choice if you have trouble keeping things down and are searching for maximum nutrition per ounce. However, if you are a gestational diabetic, skip this soup, because rice is high in carbohydrates. A gestational diabetic should fulfill the calcium requirement primarily by drinking milk and eating dairy products.

A soothing soup for the queasy and the nonqueasy alike. This is a popular dish in northern Italy, where it is given to babies, children, and mothers-to-be. It also tastes good to people who do not fit into one of these groups. It is very important that you use regular long-cooking rice rather than the instant product that promises to be ready in minutes. If at all possible, use Italian rice such as Arborio, although any medium-grain rice is preferable to instant rice.

4 cups whole milk

1 cup uncooked medium-grain rice

Pinch salt (optional)

1 teaspoon unsalted butter

Pinch ground cinnamon (optional)

In a 4 quart pot, gently bring 2 cups of the milk to near boiling. Be careful not to heat it so rapidly that it starts to form a skin. If this happens, simply skim it from the milk. Add the rice gradually while stirring.

In another pot, heat the rest of the milk to near boiling. As the rice starts to get tender, add the hot milk, a little at a time to the first pot.

Then add the salt, butter, and cinnamon to the rice mixture.

Let the soup cook, uncovered, over low heat for about 20 minutes. The result should be a creamy, thick, and delicious soup.

Turkey Rice Soup

16 SERVINGS (16 CUPS)

After Thanksgiving or another family event, too many cooks toss out a valuable source of protein and good eating. Turkey bones help make the foundation of a good broth. If you have any leftover turkey meat, cut it in cubes and add it to the broth just as you are adding the rice.

Bones of leftover turkey

1 onion, sliced

3 carrots, scraped and cut in chunks

2 celery stalks, sliced, and leaves shredded

1 leek, sliced

6 sprigs of parsley

4 peppercorns

¾ cup cooked brown rice

Cubes of leftover turkey (optional)

Put the bones in a large stockpot and cover with cold water (about 2 quarts). Add the onion, carrots, celery and celery leaves, leek, parsley, and peppercorns. Simmer over low heat, partially covered, for about 1 hour.

While the soup cooks, make the brown rice according to the instructions on the package.

When soup is done, remove the vegetables, which you may mash or purée to use as a base for a vegetable soup. Strain the broth and discard the turkey bones.

Return the broth to the pot, add the turkey cubes and rice, and simmer for 2 minutes. Serve hot.

DOCTOR'S NOTE

Calories: 157 per serving

A serving of Turkey Rice Soup will give you approximately 5000 IU vitamin A (100% of the RDA) and 3.5 g protein as well as 60 mg of calcium (5% of the RDA). We recommend this as a healthy alternative to canned soup, which is very high in sodium and has preservatives.

$\mathscr{S}$cotch Broth

6 SERVINGS

$\mathscr{S}$*cotland, more than many places, evokes images that one actually sees during a visit to that beautiful country. There really are men in kilts, highlands dotted with grazing sheep, and stunning castles perched on cliffs above the North Sea. The food of Scotland is often maligned, but there are many hearty, delicious dishes that help take off the chill when there is frost on the heather.*

½ cup large barley

3 quarts warm water

3 pounds flank of lamb, cut in bite-size pieces

1 tablespoon unsalted butter (or margarine)

¾ cup diced carrots

¾ cup diced celery

½ cup minced onions

½ cup diced turnips

2 teaspoons salt

2 teaspoons freshly ground pepper

Minced fresh parsley for garnish

Soak the barley in warm water for 2 hours. Drain, reserving the water.

Place the water and pieces of lamb in a large pot. Bring to a boil and add the barley. Cover the pot and simmer over low heat for 1½ hours.

After 80 minutes, melt the butter in a medium skillet and sauté over medium heat the carrots, celery, onions, and turnips for 10 minutes, stirring frequently. Add the vegetables to the soup along with the salt and pepper.

Cover and continue cooking the soup for 1 hour more.

Skim off the excess fat and serve topped with the parsley.

SALAD DAYS

It is an unfortunate fact that, to many people, a salad usually means a bowl of crunchy, flavorless iceberg lettuce with a few pieces of mealy tomato that has traveled thousands of miles, all topped with a gummy store-bought dressing. This need not be the case. No matter what time of year it is, there are always delicious, nutrient-rich leafy greens in the market that will enliven your salad. You should pay attention to what seems fresh and what is grown locally. In most cases, these greens will have more flavor and nutritional value.

Salads should be thought of in two categories: leafy green salads and those that feature other ingredients. Leafy green salads are perfect as the vegetable course in a meal or as a meal in itself. They should be topped with freshly prepared dressings, such as the vinaigrettes and ranch dressing in this book. Avoid store-bought dressings! They are full of gums, preservatives, flavor enhancers, salt, and fat. Sometimes lemon juice is all that is necessary to make a salad sing.

Salad greens should be eaten within a couple of days of purchase to get all of the goodness out of them. Any green that is older or wilted may be steamed and served hot or used in soups (see Emerald Soup, page 149). But don't waste them unless they have completely spoiled. Wash greens carefully, removing all dirt and sand, and then dry them thoroughly. Shake them in a colander and then pat them with paper towels. This method is effective for drying greens if you do not have a salad spinner, which is ideal. Greens should be eaten once they have been washed. They should be served cool or slightly chilled in a large, clean bowl. Do not dress the salad until it is time to eat it and use less dressing than you think you need. Below are some choices to use in making a special green salad.

Lettuces and greens are among the least caloric of foods, so that most anyone can eat them to her heart's content. For example, one *head* of Boston or bibb lettuce has only 23 calories. The same head will contain about 1600 IU vitamin A (about 33% of the RDA) and 18 mg of vitamin C (about 25% of the RDA). A head of iceberg lettuce has 70 calories, 1800 IU of vitamin A, and 32 mg vitamin C.

Lettuces that are darker green, such as romaine, contain some iron. As they age, though, the iron supply diminishes so you should always eat greens when they are as fresh as possible.

COMBINING GREENS

Arugula: This mustard-flavored green is also called rocket. It has a pronounced flavor that marries well with milder greens and creamy dressings.

Bibb or Boston Lettuce: These small, buttery lettuces are delicious alone or as the base of a salad to which you add more assertive-tasting greens.

Cabbage: Unless you think of cole slaw as a product of cabbage, there are many people who forget that cabbage is delicious raw. In addition to the well-known green cabbage, there is flavorful, eye-catching red cabbage. Sometimes it is almost purple in color. Use some for variety of taste and aesthetics. Chinese cabbage, sometimes called Napa cabbage, is light green and shaped like romaine; it has delicate flavor. So does savoy cabbage, which has curly leaves and is yellow green. Cabbage is an outstanding source of fiber and vitamins A and C.

Chicory: These curly greens have a distinctly pungent taste that is pleasant in small quantities in a salad of mixed greens.

Collard Greens: Also strong in flavor, these are often preferable when cooked slowly rather than used raw. You also can cook them in some chicken broth for a nice soup.

Dandelion Greens: Where do you think dandelion wine comes from? This green sounds exotic, but it has been consumed in many countries for years and is now experiencing a boom of popularity in the United States. They are tangy in flavor and you will be pleasantly surprised the first time you try some.

Endive: Whether you pronounce it "*n*-dive" or "awn-*deeve*," this chic Belgian vegetable with leaves shaped like long petals is a salad star. At times creamy, at times tart in flavor, endive lends elegance and character to your salad. A delicious, if slightly pricey, salad to serve as a course after meat is one composed of equal parts endive and radicchio, with some unsalted walnut pieces and a few leaves of arugula or parsley sprigs thrown in. Toss with a classic vinaigrette.

Escarole: An Italian favorite that is wonderful as a key player in any salad. Also good when steamed slightly and then sautéed with garlic and olive oil.

Iceberg Lettuce: This is a standby in salad bars because it retains its shape and crunch, but it is lacking in the flavor and personality of other greens. If you want to use iceberg, try to serve it in combination with other greens or steam it to put in a soup (to which it gives some body and delicacy).

Kale: This green has bluish tinges and is as versatile as lettuce and cabbage. Very young, tender kale is great in salads. Larger heads may be used for soups or steamed and then baked with cheese

Limestone Lettuce: Supposedly named for the fact that its special flavor and high calcium content derives from its being grown in soil rich in limestone. It is popular in central Kentucky, where the limestone-rich water helped build the bones of generations of racehorses. It is available in most of the country and should be tried for its delicate, buttery flavor.

Mâche: This is also called lamb's lettuce, so you would imagine that it would be gentle and delicate—and it is. Mâche has a slightly nutty taste, which makes it a welcome addition to salads that are combinations of tart and mild greens.

Mustard Greens: Only use tender young mustard greens to give your salads an extra bite. More mature mustard greens need to be cooked for their flavor to be appreciated.

Radicchio: This fashionable, pink- to red-leafed lettuce is from Treviso, Italy, near Venice, but is now a worldwide feature in luscious salads. It is relatively expensive, so it should be used as an accent rather than as the basis of a salad. But it is a wonderful addition, and is especially good when combined with endive.

Spinach: You can read more about spinach on page 231, but don't forget that it makes a wonderful addition to salad or can star as the only green in a salad that includes slivered mushrooms. Spinach can be sandy and must be carefully washed.

Swiss Chard: This is popular in Italy as a stuffing for ravioli. It also makes a nice addition to salads, with its long red or white stems and crisp green leaves. The stems (or ribs) must be firm for Swiss chard to be worth eating raw.

Watercress: The beloved green of the British, who serve it in buttered sandwiches at afternoon tea. Watercress has a peppery taste and may be used instead of arugula. It is quite perishable and should be used immediately.

Combine any or all of these greens in a manner that appeals to you and enjoy them to your heart's content. They are perfect foods for you and your baby.

GREEN SALADS WITH OTHER VEGETABLES PLUS NUTS, FRUITS, AND PROTEIN

If you wish to make a salad using other elements in combination with greens, the range of possibilities is almost limitless. Tomatoes are usually the popular choice. They should be vine ripened to be worth having. Industrially produced tomatoes (that is, those that are grown to travel well rather than to taste good) should be avoided. Other ingredients may be chosen based on your mood, your pocketbook, what looks good in the store, or what you have at home. Select from the foods listed here and make combinations that appeal to you.

Vegetables: Try kidney beans, chick-peas, string beans, mushrooms, peppers, carrots, celery, sprouts, low-salt olives, freshly steamed or low-salt canned artichokes, corn, cold potatoes, onions, cucumbers, and so forth. Vegetables offer roughage, plus vitamins A, C, and D as well as riboflavin, thiamine, and folate. Beans also contain some protein.

Unsalted Nuts: If you are not allergic to nuts, add them to your salad. They add crunch to a salad of leafy greens, of fruit, and of certain vegetables. Try almonds, cashews, pecans, peanuts, walnuts, Brazil nuts, macadamia nuts, and hazelnuts. Nuts provide calories as well as some protein and fat.

Fruit: Orange, tangerine, and grapefruit segments are wonderful in salads made of mild-flavored greens and nuts, dressed with olive oil and a little balsamic vinegar. Apples and pears are also great, especially in salads containing cheese, but they must be spritzed with lemon juice as soon as they are cut to prevent oxidation. Grapes, raisins, currants, cranberries, figs, and dates are but a few more suggestions. Fruit will provide sweetness, roughage, and vitamin C.

Proteins: In this wide-ranging category, you should first think of your leftovers. Is there any chicken, turkey, cold steak, ham, roast beef, or roast pork that needs to be finished off before it spoils? How about chunks of Swiss, Cheddar, or other cheeses? A hard-boiled egg maybe? Any or all of these are wonderful in a salad, particularly when combined with some of the vegetables, nuts, and fruits mentioned above. You may also used canned fish such as salmon, tuna, mackeral, or sardines, but try to use fish packed in water and without salt. Oil-packed fish is all right if you drain the oil carefully. The oil holds a lot of fish flavor and you might find the intensity a bit of a turnoff. Don't automatically assume that tuna and other protein requires mayonnaise to taste good. Try it plain or with a squeeze of fresh lemon juice.

There are two other high-powered additions that you can make to salads that will provide you with nutrients you might not be getting enough of. First, note that 1 ounce of wheat germ (which goes nicely on a salad of greens and fresh fruit) will provide 100 calories, 9 g protein (14% of the RDA), and 3 g polyunsaturated fat (as you read on page 7, storage of fat, for use in breastfeeding and in transporting fat-soluble vitamins, is essential during pregnancy). This ounce of wheat germ also will give you 30% of your RDA for thiamine and zinc, 20% of your daily needs for all-important folate (see page 16) and magnesium, and 10% of your required riboflavin and vitamin B_6.

WHEAT GERM AND SESAME SEEDS

Second, 1 ounce of sesame seeds are useful for women whose doctors insist they healthfully gain weight. This ounce has 220 calories (about 10% of the RDA), 8 g protein (12% of the RDA), 41 mg calcium (3% of the RDA), and 230 mg potassium (around 10% of the RDA). You may either sprinkle sesame seeds onto a mixed salad or put them in your salad dressing.

These are but a few salad suggestions. Remember to use fresh ingredients at their peak, to wash greens and vegetables carefully, and not to dress a salad until you are about to eat it. Aside from what we have suggested above (although you could go for 9 months sampling different salad combinations every day!), there are a few more salad recipes that follow. These should give you inspiration to create salads of your own.

Caspian Cucumbers

2 SERVINGS (1 CUP)

DOCTOR'S NOTE

Calories: 40 per serving

This tasty snack will provide you with 75 mg calcium (6% of the RDA) and 10 mg vitamin C (14% of the RDA). During the first trimester, when it seems hard to get these much-needed nutrients, be sure to try this salad.

This cooling concoction may serve as a side dish or as an appetizer. If eaten with some dry toast, it makes for a light, easy-to-eat snack when you feel you just can't eat much at all. This is also the perfect accompaniment to a summer entrée such as cold Poached Salmon (see page 192). The ingredients in this dish—cucumbers, yogurt, dill and mint—are commonly used in Russia, the Ukraine, and other republics in the southern part of the former Soviet Union. To make this a fancy appetizer or snack, squeeze a little lemon juice into the yogurt and dot it with a few pearls of good caviar, such as that produced in the Caspian Sea. If you use caviar, your herb of choice should be ½ teaspoon fresh dill.

1 small cucumber

½ cup low-fat plain yogurt

1 teaspoon fresh minced mint or ½ teaspoon fresh chopped dill

1 teaspoon fresh lemon juice (optional)

1 teaspoon caviar (optional)

Carefully wash and peel the cucumber. Slice it into paper-thin slices and arrange them prettily on a plate or a shallow bowl.

Stir the mint or dill into the yogurt, then spread this mixture over the cucumber slices and eat.

If you are having caviar, stir the lemon juice into the yogurt first and then stir in the dill. Top the cucumber slices with the yogurt and then scatter the caviar on top.

Mushrooms and Sprouts

2 SERVINGS (1 CUP)

Tasty, easily digested, convenient, and absolutely loaded with potassium and vitamin C, this combination makes a good side dish or something to stuff in a sandwich for extra flavor and nutrition. Use either bean or alfalfa sprouts, or try a combination of the two.

½ cup sliced fresh mushrooms

½ cup sprouts

1 teaspoon olive or vegetable oil

½ teaspoon freshly squeezed lemon juice

⅛ teaspoon prepared mustard (optional)

Carefully wash, trim, and slice the mushrooms and place them in a serving bowl. Add the sprouts.

In a small bowl or jar, combine the oil, lemon juice, and mustard (if you're using it) and then pour the dressing over the mushrooms and sprouts.

Toss well and serve. This salad should be consumed soon after it is prepared—it does not improve with age.

VARIATION

To make this simpler, omit the oil and mustard, letting the fresh lemon juice give zing to the vegetables.

DOCTOR'S NOTE

Calories: 50 per serving

Each serving will give a good load of roughage and small amounts of vitamins C, E, and K as well as minerals and trace elements. It has only 2 g of fat and is virtually free of carbohydrates and protein and, therefore, can be enjoyed at any time by all pregnant women, even if they are placed on special diets by their doctors.

$\mathcal{S}$*prouts Salad*

4 SERVINGS (2 CUPS)

DOCTOR'S NOTE

Calories: 141 per serving

This low-calorie dish is packed with vitamins and fiber (roughage). In addition, it is low in carbohydrates and protein, although not in fat (each serving will have approximately 12 g fat, contributed by the olive oil). The fat content and fiber will help if you experience problems with constipation, but keep in mind that sprouts may be gas producing.

It is probably inaccurate to refer to this dish as simply a salad, but in its most basic form it is indeed a salad. However, it also is the starting point for more creative dishes that suit your mood. You can augment this salad by adding leftover pieces of cold meat (chicken, turkey, beef, or ham) or cheese. You can eat this from the bowl or stuffed in pita bread. This salad, once dressed, can take on a different character if you stir-fry it quickly in a skillet, with or without the added meat. The stir-frying is not recommended with cheese, but would work with tofu.

2 peppers, green, red, or yellow, or in combination

3 mature tomatoes, with or without the peel

2 cucumbers, peeled

½ pound bean, alfalfa, or soy sprouts

1 tablespoon minced fresh parsley or mint

3 tablespoons freshly squeezed lemon juice

Freshly ground pepper to taste

3 tablespoons extra-virgin olive oil

Clean the peppers and tomatoes, removing as many seeds as possible. Dice the vegetables and put in a bowl. Dice the cucumbers as well and add them to the bowl along with the sprouts and parsley or mint. Toss lightly to combine the ingredients. If you are using meat, cheese or tofu, add them now.

Put the lemon juice, pepper, and oil in a jar or cruet, shake well, and dress the salad. Serve immediately.

Orange-Shrimp Salad

1 SERVING

Easy, fresh tasting, and eye catching, this salad works at all kinds of occasions: dinner parties as an appetizer, lunch for one or more, as a snack or as a bag lunch if it is kept cold. You may vary the nuts or fruit to your own taste. Multiply the ingredients you use by the number of portions you plan to serve. The recipe below serves one person as a lunch or two persons as an appetizer.

Romaine or spinach leaves, washed, dried

¼ pound boiled baby or medium shrimp, chilled

½ 11-ounce can mandarin orange segments (drained) or 1

orange, tangelo, or tangerine, or 2 clementines, peeled,

pitted, and with the segments removed from their casings

¼ cup cut-up celery (cut in lengthwise strips)

1 teaspoon chopped scallions or chives

2 tablespoons unsalted cashews

½ lemon or lime

Place the romaine leaves on a dish.

Combine the shrimp, orange segments, celery, scallions, and cashews and place on the bed of romaine. Squeeze the lemon or lime over the shrimp mixture and serve.

VARIATION

Steam the romaine or spinach and serve hot or cold, with the salad on top.

DOCTOR'S NOTE

Calories: 262 per serving

This dish is definitely a dieter's delight. While you do not need to diet when you are pregnant, you may use it when you have exceeded your weight gain allotment or after the baby has arrived. It provides 27 g protein (approximately 25% to 33% of the RDA) and almost no fat or carbohydrates. You'll get lots of phosphorus (1193 mg, more than 50% of the RDA), which is important for nerve conduction, and almost 100% of the RDA for vitamin C.

Waldorf Salad

2 SERVINGS

DOCTOR'S NOTE

Calories: 230 per serving

This light salad pro-
vides 20 mg (25% of the
RDA) of vitamin C and
can be enjoyed by every
expectant mother as it
is low in carbohydrates
and salt.

The classic version of this salad, which to many eaters seems like an artifact from another era, used heaps of mayonnaise. For our purposes, low-fat lemon yogurt is a friendly alternative. Waldorf salad makes a nice appetizer or a cool, refreshing main course at lunch.

2 medium-size eating apples

1½ tablespoons freshly squeezed lemon juice

¾ cup diced celery

¼ cup unsalted walnuts

½ cup low-fat lemon yogurt

Lettuce leaves

Wash, core, and dice the apples. If you are using unsprayed apples, you need not pare them. Immediately douse the apple pieces with lemon juice to prevent oxidation.

Combine the apples, celery, nuts, and yogurt. Toss lightly and serve atop the lettuce leaves.

Insalata Caprese

1 SERVING (MAIN COURSE); 2 TO 3 SERVINGS (APPETIZER)

This salad of Capri is now immensely popular in North America. The essential fact about this salad is that to succeed its three main ingredients—tomatoes, mozzarella cheese, and basil—must be of highest quality and freshness. You should use only fresh mozzarella purchased at the cheese counter or from a specialty shop. The cheese you find wrapped in plastic in the dairy case is a poor substitute that is only acceptable for cooking (and even then, the fresh cheese is far superior). Store fresh mozzarella in a bowlful of cold water that is tightly sealed with plastic wrap.

¼ to ⅓ pound fresh unsalted mozzarella, sliced thin

5 to 6 unblemished basil leaves, wiped with paper towels

1 ripe beefsteak tomato or 2 ripe plum tomatoes, sliced thin

Extra-virgin olive oil

A few Gaeta or other oil-cured olives (optional)

Freshly ground pepper (optional)

Place the slices of mozzarella on a pretty plate that is slightly chilled. Make sure the cheese slices do not overlap. Place a leaf of basil on top of each slice and then place a tomato slice on top of the basil. Drizzle a little olive oil on top and serve immediately. You may also add a few olives, if you wish, and some pepper. Have some good crusty bread at hand to soak up some of the oil.

Cook's note: Many cooks serve Insalata Caprese with the basil leaf on top of the tomato. This may look pretty, but the basil tastes more glorious when it is sandwiched between the distinct flavors of the mozzarella and the tomato. Also, the tomato incorporates the flavor of the olive oil that is poured over it more naturally than the perfumed basil leaf does.

DOCTOR'S NOTE

Calories: 455 per serving

For a main dish serving of this salad we used 4 ounces of part-skim fresh mozzarella cheese. It is a valuable meal indeed because it offers 732 mg calcium (more than 50% of the RDA). It also contains 23 g fat (25% of the RDA). Fresh, no-salt mozzarella is naturally low in sodium and carbohydrates (only 2.4 g for ¼ pound mozzarella).

Insalata Petroniana

1 SERVING

DOCTOR'S NOTE

Calories: 440 per serving

This dish provides 36 g protein (50% of the RDA), 16.3 g fat and 13 g carbohydrates. If you use about 1.7 ounces of Parmesan cheese (enough to give you a layer of fine shavings) you will also get approximately 200 calories, 18 g protein, and only 13 g of fat and the highest load of calcium of any cheese (approximately 570 mg, 50% of the RDA). You'll also get a healthy dose of vitamin A. If you have been advised to keep your salt intake to a minimum, you may want to select a different recipe; Parmesan cheese is very high in salt: 367 mg per 1.7-ounce serving. So use it with caution if you have been diagnosed with high blood pressure or preeclampsia.
The mushrooms in this recipe provide copper (see page 21) and potassium, a crucial nutrient that ensures a

In Italy, anything called petroniana *refers to St. Petronius, the patron of the wonderful city of Bologna. This dish takes ingredients popular in Bologna and uses them in a fashion employed in Milan for serving carpaccio. The key to Insalata Petroniana is that you use ingredients of the highest quality, because you will need to taste the flavors of each. The dish takes only a few minutes to prepare, but you should take time to arrange the ingredients prettily on your plate. If you are serving more than one person, multiply the ingredients by the number of eaters and create a separate plate for each person. Regular store-bought mushrooms are called for here. However, if you have access to fresh funghi porcini from Italy, they would make a wonderful substitute.*

¼ **pound smoked or baked turkey breast (preferably nitrite-free), sliced paper thin**

1 **cup shredded escarole, chicory, or bibb lettuce, washed and dried carefully, torn into shreds**

Pinch coarse salt (optional)

½ **pinch dried sage (optional)**

1 **plum tomato, cut in very thin slices**

1 **chunk imported Italian Parmesan or grana cheese**

1 **ounce mushrooms, cleaned and slivered**

Freshly ground pepper to taste

½ **lemon**

Extra-virgin olive oil

Take a dinner plate that you have chilled in the refrigerator and arrange the turkey slices so that the plate is entirely covered.

Mix the lettuce well with the salt and sage (if these are two items you can eat; the dish will not suffer significantly in their absence). Then distribute the lettuce evenly over the turkey. Arrange the tomato slices randomly over the lettuce.

Using either a truffle shaver or a potato peeler, shave paper-thin slices of cheese onto the salad until the plate is nearly covered with what might look like a light dusting of snow.

Finally, sprinkle the mushroom slivers all over the cheese. Grind on a little fresh pepper if you want it, then squeeze on the juice of the lemon half. Drizzle some olive oil over all and eat.

You do not need to toss this salad. It's more fun to plunge the tines of your fork deep into the dish and eat what you come up with. You may also cut through with a knife and fork, giving you everything from turkey to mushroom in one bite. *Buon appetito!*

strong, steady fetal heart-beat. You should try this dish if you are suffering from a bout of nausea and want to avoid strong aromas and strenuous cooking.

The caloric count for this recipe is based on one serving, but you may enjoy more or less, according to your taste. Olive oil is the clear favorite for the dressings (and most other recipes) recommended in this book. It is the healthiest of all oils, with canola oil a close second. Oils and fats contain about 120 cals per tablespoon and 13 g fat.

$\mathcal{T}$*una–String Bean Salad*

1 SERVING

DOCTOR'S NOTE

Calories: 457 per serving

This protein-filled dish delivers a large amount of roughage and vitamin A. It is a very good choice if you have been diagnosed with gestational diabetes because it delivers 48 g protein (more than 66% of the RDA) and little fat (only 14 g). It provides only 27 g of carbohydrates, which come exclusively from the fresh string beans. In addition, the tuna and the string beans together provide 3000 IU vitamin A (more than 50% of the RDA) and 66 mg vitamin C (almost 100% of the RDA).

Because Tuna–String Bean Salad is a roughage-filled meal, you should not accompany it with your vitamin supplement or a beverage that contains valuable vitamins. If vitamins and roughage are taken together, the vitamins will be carried along and will not be fully absorbed into your system.

A simple preparation that rises and falls on the quality of the ingredients and the care given to cooking the string beans. This is an easy, refreshing summertime meal. You should cook the string beans at least 2 hours before you plan to eat them. You can cook more string beans than you need and save some for salads, for snacking, or for use as a cold side dish.

½ pound fresh string beans, washed and trimmed

1 lemon, halved

1 6½ ounce can tuna, packed in water, drained

8 to 10 rings of sweet onion, such as red or Vidalia (optional)

Extra-virgin olive oil

1 plum tomato, cut in thin slices (optional)

½ 15 ounce can of cannellini (white beans) (optional)

In a large pot, bring at least 4 quarts of water to boil. When it reaches a full boil, squeeze the juice of one-half of the lemon into the water. When it returns to a boil, add the string beans and cook slightly. Taste one after 1 minute of cooking and then every 10 to 15 seconds thereafter until you decide they are cooked. They should be crunchy, not raw, when it is time to drain them.

When the string beans are done, pour the contents of the pot into a colander you have placed in an empty sink. Drain thoroughly and then transfer to beans to a large glass or metal bowl. Place the bowl in the refrigerator, and leave there until the beans are cold.

When you are ready to eat, drain the tuna and flake it over the cooled string beans. Add the onion, if you want, and squeeze the other half lemon over the bowl. Then drizzle some olive oil over it all. Add the tomato and cannellini now, if you are using them. Toss well and serve.

Accompanied by some whole wheat bread, this salad makes a perfectly balanced meal.

Rice Salad

4 SERVINGS (6 CUPS)

The idea here is a tasty dish that you can prepare and then keep for a couple of days if it is not consumed by you and your guests in one sitting. Rice salad is great for snacking when you get hungry between meals. Also, you can easily pack it in a container for a brown-bag lunch or nibble away from home. You will get the best result if you use arborio rice from Italy, but any good quality medium- or long-grain rice makes an acceptable substitute. You should feel free to experiment with rice salads, adding ingredients that most appeal to you at a particular time. This is the perfect meal for the pregnant woman, because she can use only the ingredients she likes and leave out anything she has an aversion to. Whatever the vegetable, cold meat, or fish it is that you crave, the rice will likely be a perfect foil for it. One warning: do not use vinegar to dress the salad. It will seep into the rice and become chokingly overpowering.

1 pound rice, cooked according to the package's directions and chilled

1 pound fresh asparagus, cleaned, with tough ends chopped off, cooked and chilled (any appealing green vegetable can be substituted)

½ pound Gruyère, Swiss, Emmenthal, or Jarlsberg cheese, cubed

1 red or yellow bell pepper, washed and diced

1 cup grated carrots

A few Gaeta olives (optional)

4 tablespoons minced fresh parsley

6 tablespoons extra-virgin olive oil

3 tablespoons freshly squeezed lemon juice

Freshly ground pepper to taste

Place the rice in a glass or metal bowl.
Boil the asparagus ever so briefly in abundant, lightly salted →

DOCTOR'S NOTE

Calories: 557 per serving

In addition to low calories for a main course, a serving of this salad will give you 15 g protein, 16 g fat, 525 mg calcium (almost 50% of the RDA), and 400 mg of sodium. In this recipe, the rice provides most of the carbohydrates you need and almost no fat. It is well supplemented by the cheese, which is an excellent source of fat and protein. Swiss cheese and Gruyère, two of the cheeses recommended in this recipe, are relatively low in calories and high in protein (24 g per serving), calcium, and fat (12 g per serving).

The fat count for olive oil is 13 g per tablespoon. It is devoid of carbohydrates or protein.

boiling water. It should retain its bright green color and still be firm when bitten. Drain the contents of the pot into a large colander placed in an empty sink. Once the hot water has drained away, refresh the asparagus with some cold water and give the colander a couple of firm shakes so that all the water trickles away. Put the asparagus in a bowl, cover tightly, and chill.

When you are ready to make the salad, cut the asparagus into 1-inch pieces. Combine the chilled rice, chilled asparagus pieces, cheese, diced bell pepper, grated carrots, olives, and parsley.

Just before you plan to eat the salad, combine the oil, lemon juice, and pepper in a bowl. Blend with a whisk or fork, and pour the dressing over the rice. Toss thoroughly and serve.

The dressed salad will keep well in the refrigerator for a couple of days.

VARIATION

If you are substituting zucchini, cut them into ¼-inch thick disks, sauté the disks in olive oil with garlic and, if available, some rosemary. You can use Rosemary Olive Oil (page 127) for this purpose. Chill the zucchini as you would the asparagus.

PASTA

There are so many pasta shapes and sauces that one could write a cookbook devoted just to them. You can revel in this variety for months without ever getting bored. Pasta is very easy to cook and quite inexpensive. It provides carbohydrates and energy and is really only as fattening as the sauce you put on it. So enjoy pasta as often as you wish for a perfect lunch or dinner. There is a great deal of debate about how to cook and sauce pasta. Here is how:

Even if you are only making one portion of pasta, you need to use a large pot so that the pasta can roll freely in boiling water. Take a clean pot and fill it two-thirds with cold water. Bring the water to a boil. It is traditional to add a pinch of salt to the boiling water (not the cold water), but if you can do without the salt, so much the better. It adds some flavor, but this is not crucial. Once the water reaches an active boil, add the pasta and stir it with a long fork or wooden spoon so that all the pieces are separated as they cook. If you are cooking fresh noodles, they will be done in about 2 minutes. Test one at that point, and if they are al dente (slightly chewy to the bite) they are done.

Overcooked pasta, the norm in many bad restaurants, is dreadful. You should concentrate on making pasta al dente. If, as most people do, you are cooking dried, packaged pasta such as spaghetti or penne, read the package directions. If the package says, for example, that the pasta will be done in 7 minutes, test one after five. Keep testing every minute until it reaches al dente. A piece of pasta is correctly cooked when, after being bitten or cut, there is no dry white area visible in the pasta's cross-section. It should have a uniform golden white color through and through.

While the pasta is cooking, you should put a colander in an empty sink. When the pasta is done, lift the pot and pour the contents into the colander. The water will drain through, and the pasta will be left in the colander. Give the colander a couple of good shakes to get rid of excess water. Absolutely do not rinse the noodles! This is a common mistake that only serves to make them cold and wet. If you are in your later months and have trouble lifting, you have three choices. The first is to have someone else do it. If that is not possible, use a spaghetti fork, a skimmer, or a slotted spoon (for gnocchi or short pasta) to fish the pasta out of the pot. This is not as hard as it seems once you have the knack. The third choice is to use a smaller pot, make less pasta and use short pasta such as penne that you can stir actively to prevent it from sticking. Pasta is especially important in the days before delivery, because it will provide carbohydrates that will convert to much-welcome energy during the great event.

SAUCING PASTA
Another problem with American pasta cooks is that they over-sauce. Note that 1 or 2 tablespoons of sauce per serving of pasta (2 to 3 ounces of dry pasta) is correct. Certain shapes, such as rigatoni, may require a little more sauce, but you should start with a little sauce and add more only as needed. Put cooked pasta in a large bowl or individual serving bowls, add the right amount of sauce, toss, and serve immediately. Remember that you can always add more sauce, but you can't take it out once it is in the bowl. So use less than you are used to. Sauce should coat and flavor pasta and there should be very little at the bottom of the bowl once you have eaten the pasta.

CHEESE ON PASTA
After making a wonderfully delicate sauce and perfectly cooked pasta, don't mess it all up by smothering it in sandy "grated" Italian-style cheese that comes out of a can found on your supermarket shelf. If you can find fresh Parmesan or Romano cheese from Italy, buy a wedge. Store the cheese in the refrigerator, tightly wrapped in aluminum foil, and grate it fresh over pasta using a hand grater. *Then* you will dine royally. The flavor is unmistakable. Again, use less cheese than you might think. Even good cheese will dry out a sauce, so use it sparingly. You can always add more.

Try to get flavorings such as salt and pepper into the sauce rather than on top of the whole dish. Salt, as mentioned above, should be minimal, and fresh pepper may be too assertive if put on top of some sauces.

ABOUT COLD PASTA
Pasta tends not to keep well or taste good cold, despite the trend of cold pasta salads. But if these appeal to you, then cook the pasta and store it without dressing in the refrigerator. You should sepa-

rate the noodles before storing them. Then dress the cold noodles as you wish. Cold pasta tends to absorb bitter flavors such as vinegar and lemon juice, so use these sparingly. You may wish to make a frittata (omelet) using some leftover noodles. This dish is a great favorite of someone dear to the authors.

This section has several good ideas for making pasta. You should also check out the recipes for The World's Easiest Tomato Sauce (page 128) and for Pesto Presto (page 129). They are each originally pasta sauces, but they appear in the section on sauces because they have become so universal. *Buon appetito!*

Note that ¼ pound of pasta, cooked al dente, provides 420 cals, 14 g protein (22% of the RDA), 1.5 g fat, and 85 g carbohydrates. Pasta is ideal for people who need to limit their fat intake (but watch the fat content of certain sauces) and who want to build up their energy supplies with carbohydrates. Gestational diabetics must consult with their doctor before making pasta part of their diets.

$\mathcal{S}$*paghetti con Pomodoro Crudo*

1 SERVING

DOCTOR'S NOTE

Calories: 544 per serving

This recipe is perfect for those days when you need a carbohydrate load: before delivery or anytime you are gearing up for a physically demanding day. The ¼ pound of spaghetti provides 420 cals, 14 g protein, 1.5 g fat and 85 g carbohydrates (20% of the RDA). The sauce will add 9 g fat, for a total of 10.5 g, and 29 mg vitamin C (40% of the RDA). Use this recipe if carbohydrates are not a problem (as they are in gestational diabetes).

T*his dish is so fast and easy to prepare that you will likely make it a frequent star at your table. It is delicious as lunch or dinner for one or will please family and guests as well. Simply multiply the ingredients by the number of eaters. It is perfect on a steamy summer's day when you don't want hot, heavy food.*

2 ripe plum tomatoes or 1 medium-size ripe beefsteak tomato

2 teaspoons extra-virgin olive oil

A few leaves of basil (carefully wiped and torn) or a sprig of parsley, minced

1 garlic clove, minced or slivered (optional)

Freshly ground pepper to taste (optional)

3 to 4 ounces imported Italian spaghetti (you may also use short pasta such as penne or rigatoni)

Freshly grated Romano cheese (optional)

Bring a large pot of cold water to boil.

While the water is getting hot, coarsely chop the tomatoes and place in a large serving bowl. Then add the oil and either the basil or parsley. If you are using garlic and black pepper, add them as well. Stir the contents gently so that they are all combined.

When the water reaches an active boil, add the pasta and cook until al dente (follow the package's directions but check periodically). Drain the pasta in a colander and immediately transfer it to the serving bowl.

Toss the ingredients well and serve. Add a little grated Romano cheese if you wish, but be sparing. The cheese will dry out the sauce and make the dish heavier.

$\mathcal{P}$.O.P. (*Pasta–Olive Oil–Parmesan*)

1 SERVING

This dish won't win any gastronomic awards, but it is fast and simple to prepare, light and delicious, and good for you. See if it tastes good when you don't particularly feel like eating. If your baby's pop should choose to make a bowlful for you, so much the better. He should use a thick, medium-length pasta such as fusilli, penne, rigatoni, or large macaroni. As for the Parmesan, the pregrated stuff from the grocery shelf is a poor substitute for the real thing. Buy a small piece of cheese from the dairy case or a cheese store and take a moment to grate it fresh as you use it. Keep Parmesan cheese in the refrigerator, tightly wrapped in aluminum foil.

Pinch of salt (optional)

3 to 4 ounces imported Italian pasta

2 tablespoons extra-virgin olive oil

1 tablespoon freshly grated Parmesan cheese

Freshly ground black pepper to taste (optional)

In a large pot, bring about 4 quarts of cold water to boil. When it reaches a rolling boil, toss in a tiny pinch of salt (only if salt is in your diet). When the water returns to a full boil, add the pasta and cook until al dente (follow the package's directions but check periodically). When it is cooked, drain the pasta in a colander and immediately transfer it to a bowl or plate.

Add the oil and cheese. Use spoons to toss thoroughly. Add some fresh pepper, if that is your taste.

DOCTOR'S NOTE

Calories: 574 per serving

This dish can be your best ally during the first months when you are feeling queasy. The relatively high caloric content provides almost 25% of the RDA during your first trimester. There are about 50 g carbohydrates per serving, so that P.O.P. will give you quick energy without weighing you down. Its bland texture will help keep it down if you are plagued with morning sickness. Although this recipe will not fully meet your need for protein and certain vitamins and minerals, it has an interesting surprise in its main ingredient. Among cheeses, which are characteristically rich in calcium, Parmesan cheese is richest by far, 68 mg of calcium per ounce of cheese. In fact, Parmesan cheese is a winner among cheeses in all respects: It delivers the highest amount of protein (2 g per ounce) and is relatively low in fat.

$\mathscr{S}$*paghetti with Olive Purée*

2 SERVINGS

This dish can be prepared in 10 minutes and is delectable. Olive puree is a great source of olive oil, which is wonderful for hair, skin, and digestion. Olive oil also tastes great if you use a high-quality oil (see page 277). This puree can be used as a pasta sauce, served on toasted bread as an appetizer or spread on grilled, baked, broiled, or poached chicken or fish. Use only high-quality black olives such as Gaeta, which are oil-cured and relatively low in salt.

8 ounces imported Italian spaghetti

Pinch of salt

Peel of 1 lemon, well-cleaned and grated (see note below)

8 tablespoons extra-virgin olive oil

8 ounces oil-cured black olives, pitted

1 garlic clove

Bring a large pot of cold water, about 4 quarts, to boil. When it reaches a boil, toss in a pinch of salt. When the pot again comes to a boil, add the spaghetti and cook until al dente. Taste one strand 1 minute before the suggested time of doneness on the pasta package to gauge how much more the spaghetti should be cooked.

While the spaghetti cooks, make the purée. Put the lemon peel, olive oil, olives, and garlic in a blender or food processor and blend until you have a coarse paste.

When the pasta is cooked, drain it in a colander. Transfer it immediately to a serving bowl.

Add the olive purée, toss well and serve immediately.

Note: To grate a lemon peel: Wash a lemon thoroughly, then peel it using a potato peeler. If your blender or food processor can blend the peel to a fine pulp, use it. Otherwise, you will need to use a small hand grater (such as one for Parmesan cheese) and grate the peel and zest (the white part) into a small bowl. This is not difficult as long as you make sure not to scrape your knuckles.

Fettuccine with Walnut Sauce

2 SERVINGS

This dish is elegant, easy to make, and particularly indicated if you are feeling a little queasy. If you buy or make fresh fettuccine, it cooks very quickly—often as fast as 1 minute. Dried pasta takes longer but, as with any pasta, it should be sampled periodically during its cooking process to be sure that it is not overdone. All pasta should be al dente, that is, chewy and firm.

4 ounces unsalted walnuts

1 ounce pine nuts

1½ tablespoons plain bread crumbs

1 garlic clove, minced

3 tablespoons extra-virgin olive oil

1½ tablespoons freshly grated Parmesan cheese

1 pinch marjoram

¾ cup whole milk

Pinch salt

8 ounces fresh fettuccine or 4 ounces dried imported
   Italian fettuccine

Bring 4 quarts of cold water to a boil in a large pot.

In the meantime, put the walnuts, pine nuts, bread crumbs, garlic, and oil in a blender. Cover and blend until a fine paste is formed.

Pour the paste into a large serving bowl and fold in the cheese and the marjoram. Add just enough milk to produce a semithick sauce (see note next page).

When the pot of water reaches a rolling boil, add a pinch of salt (if you eat salt). When the water returns to a boil, add the fettuccine and cook until al dente. Remember that fresh fettuccine will be done very quickly (perhaps within 1 minute), while for dried fettuccine you should use the instructions on the package as →

DOCTOR'S NOTE

Calories: 1191 per serving

Pasta products are virtually fat free. Walnuts, on the other hand, are a high-calorie, high-fat food. The 2 ounces of walnuts necessary for each serving will provide 360 cals and 32 g fat. The total fat content of a serving of this dish is 33.5 g, its carbohydrate content 93.4 g, and its protein content 25.6 g. If you use skim instead of whole milk, there will be 31.8 g of fat and 976 calories per serving. Therefore, this is a perfect recipe to use if your weight gain leaves something to be desired and a recipe to avoid if you are putting on too much weight.

an approximate guide. Sample one noodle a minute before the package says they will be cooked and you will have an idea of how much longer it needs to cook. When the pasta is done, drain it in a colander (or fish the noodles out with a pasta fork if the pot is too heavy), add it immediately to the sauce.

Toss well and serve.

Note: Although this recipe calls for ¾ cup milk, you should follow your own instinct and taste. An alternative is to use skim milk in place of the whole milk, adding it to the sauce until you achieve the desired texture.

$\mathcal{S}$*paghetti alla Pescatora*
2 SERVINGS

DOCTOR'S NOTE

Calories: 834 per serving

For this recipe we used equal amounts of cod and whitefish, so the nutritional content may vary slightly if you choose a different type of fish. One serving will deliver 8000 IU vitamin A (almost 200% the RDA) and 33 g fat as well as a load of carbohydrates.
This is an ideal dish for any woman who needs to gain weight in a healthy way. This could be the morning sickness sufferer who doesn't mind the taste of fish or

The healthy properties of fish are well documented: it is a food loaded with protein, minerals, and flavor. If the taste of fish appeals to you, here is an excellent dish for you to indulge yourself with. This is a good dish to serve to company: Simply double the amounts for four persons, triple the amounts for six, and so on. In choosing fish to use for this dish, your first priority is freshness. You should use fresh fillets from a reliable source. Using fillets will save you preparation time and will spare you from having to handle the fish too much, which is a turnoff to some pregnant women. The important thing is that the fish you choose be fresh and have a hearty flavor and texture; you should use several types. Good choices include scrod, monkfish, catfish, skate, grouper, and whitefish.

¾ **pound mixed fish fillets**

1 **carrot, scraped and cut into large pieces**

1 **stalk celery, cut in large pieces**

1 **medium onion, coarsely chopped**

A little sprinkling salt, preferably coarse

1 **stingy pinch sage**

⅓ **cup dry white wine**

Juice of 1 lemon

6 ounces tepid water

Pinch salt

3 tablespoons extra-virgin olive oil

1 garlic clove, minced

10 parsley sprigs

1 tablespoon tomato paste

¼ pound boiled baby shrimp

6 to 8 ounces Italian spaghetti

Freshly ground pepper

the woman late in pregnancy who still needs to gain weight but doesn't want heavy food. The carbohydrate content is ideal for a near-term woman preparing for delivery. As with all pasta dishes, gestational diabetics need to pay attention to their carbohydrate intake.

Preheat oven to 350° F.

Wash the fish fillets, pat them dry and lay them flat in a large baking dish. Distribute the carrot, celery and half the chopped onion over the fish. Add the salt and sage.

In a small bowl, combine the wine, lemon juice, and water. Pour the liquid into the baking dish, making sure it practically covers the fillets. If necessary, add more water.

Bake the fish fillets until they flake when touched with a fork; plan to cook the fish about 10 minutes for every 1 inch of thickness.

While the fish is cooking, bring a large pot of cold water to boil. When it reaches a boil, toss in a pinch of salt.

Also while the fish is cooking, pour enough olive oil into a large saucepan (at least 3 quarts) so that the bottom is barely covered. Heat the oil over medium heat and add the garlic, parsley, and the remaining chopped onion. Sauté gently (don't burn).

As soon as the fish is cooked, remove it from the oven and set aside.

Add 3 or 4 tablespoons of the fish's cooking liquid to the saucepan. Then add the tomato paste to the sauce, stir thoroughly and turn the heat down to a simmer.

Remove the fish from the pan and chop into bite-size pieces. Cut the carrot and celery into bits.

As the sauce lowers to a simmer add the fish, carrot, celery, cooked onions (from the baking dish), and baby shrimp to the saucepan. Simmer gently, stirring every so often. The sauce should be rather concentrated. Check the sauce after 5 minutes. If you feel you need a little more liquid, sparingly add some cooking liquid from the fish's baking dish.→

While you are making the tomato sauce, you should cook the spaghetti. Add it to the boiling, salted water and stir occasionally with a spaghetti fork. Cook to al dente, around 7 minutes.

When you are almost ready to drain the spaghetti, grind a healthy amount of pepper into the tomato mixture.

When the spaghetti is cooked, drain it well in a colander. Immediately add the spaghetti to the sauce pan and toss for a few seconds until the pasta is completely combined with the sauce. Serve immediately.

Note: Never top Spaghetti alla Pescatora with grated cheese. The delicate flavors of this dish would be overpowered by the cheese and the sauce would be unnecessarily thickened.

MAIN COURSES

On your first shopping expedition you bought frozen fish fillets. They were probably cod, perch, haddock, sole, or flounder from the north Atlantic Ocean. The day will come when it is raining, you are too tired to shop, the fish market is already closed, or some other reason why that frozen fish will suddenly become the perfect solution to the old question "What should I have for dinner?" It is also possible to buy salmon steaks from Norway, which are quick-frozen as soon as they are cut and maintain a great deal of their fresh flavor. Little effort is required to thaw the fish and broil it, and you end up with a delicious meal filled with protein (4 ounces of fish contain 50% of the RDA for protein) and vitamin B (in lean fish such as the Atlantic fillets listed above), or vitamin D (in fatty fish such as salmon, mackerel, bluefish, and trout).

To give you more of an idea of the nutritional benefits of fish, let us look at the contents of a ½ pound cod, which is the serving size used in Brandade de Morue (page 186) and Pescado San Sebastian (page 188). This piece of cod gives you 100% of the RDA for protein (65 g), 620 mg of phosphorus (50% of the RDA) and 920 mg of potassium (about 50% of the RDA). Remember that potassium is essential for nerve action in the cells and for the proper functioning of the circulatory system in your body and your baby's. Fish is one of the richest available sources of potassium. But cod is not the only star in the nutritional sea. Note that 6 ounces of most fish (a good portion size) will give you between 200 and 300 cals, at least 66% of the RDA for protein, and almost no fat to speak of (except for mackerel and, to a lesser extent, salmon).

During your pregnancy, we strongly encourage you to use fresh or frozen fish fillets rather than whole fish. This is because you do not want to devote any extra time to standing or working on food preparation when you are tired, have swollen ankles, or any other additional burden that pregnancy may temporarily impose. Also, some cooks find dealing with whole fish a bit of a turnoff. But you should remember that whole fish is delicious and nutritious and should return to your eating agenda after your pregnancy. You should always make an effort to buy good fresh fish, but it is still better to use frozen fish rather than inferior fresh fish. Fresh fish fillets and steaks should be moist and

Fish and Seafood

Fish and Seafood Recipes

translucent and should have been cut as soon as possible before you eat them. They should smell fresh: Any fishy odor is definitely a sign that the fish is past its prime. The flesh should be firm and springy to the touch. Soft fish should be avoided, as should any fish that is discolored.

To prepare fish, always rinse it well under very cold water and pat it dry with paper towels. You should always use fresh fish immediately. If you are going to keep it for a few hours, place it in airtight plastic bags and refrigerate. If you must keep it overnight, marinate the fish in a pan (tightly covered with plastic) in lemon juice and a little oil.

Add fines herbes or other herbs of your choice. Thaw unwrapped frozen fish overnight by placing it in a pan in the refrigerator. Then rinse it in very cold water and dry it before using it. Or, if your choice of using frozen fish is more sudden, it may be thawed by holding it under cool running water until it begins to soften; then switch to colder water.

Note: For the most part we have avoided recipes for seafood (clams, oysters, large shrimp, prawns, lobster, crab, mussels, octopus, squid, cuttlefish, etc.) in this book for three reasons: (1) these foods tend to be expensive, (2) their preparation is too labor intensive and (3) unfortunately, there have been too many bacteria and impurities in our seafood to consider it safe. If you choose to eat these foods, that is your decision but be wise and do not eat them raw. The likelihood of cooked seafood having harmful bacteria is much lower than in raw seafood. Also, avoid sushi during your pregnancy for the same reasons. Now, back to cooking fish fillets:

BROILING FISH FILLETS AND STEAKS

Broiling is one of the fastest, easiest ways to prepare fish. All that is required is a good piece of fish (steak or fillet) and a substance to keep it moist (olive oil, marinade, butter, garlic butter, herb butter, or margarine). Preheat your broiler, and you are on your way.

For thin fillets: After preheating the broiler and cleaning the fillet (which will be ¼ to ½ inch thick), place it in a lightly greased (with oil or butter) pan, then brush or coat the fish lightly with oil, melted butter, or perhaps a little milk or citrus juice. Then place the fillet about 2 inches below the flame or heat element. It is done when the fish flakes at the touch of a fork. This takes anywhere from 3 to 7 minutes, depending on the size, thickness, and temperature of the fish. You do not need to turn the fillet during broiling.

For thicker fish steaks: The concern with thicker fish steaks (between ½ and 1 inch) is that they not dry out during cooking. To avoid this, you should take three special measures: (1) broil the steaks 4 inches from the heat, (2) baste them by adding additional oil or other moisteners during cooking, and (3) turn the steaks halfway through the cooking time. Otherwise, the process is the same as for thin fillets: Preheat the broiler, lightly oil the pan, and lightly oil the fish. Broil 4 inches from flame, turning the steak after a few minutes, and baste again. Serve when steak flakes and (except for salmon) has no pinkness within.

At some point in your pregnancy you will decide that you no longer want to cook fish in your broiler if it means bending over to use it. Of course, if your broiler is above your range, this will not be a problem. Stove-top preparation of fish will become more important to you if you stop broiling, and there are three easy methods to use: sautéeing, steaming, and poaching. The difference among these methods is the amount of liquid in the pan. What about fried fish? Deep-fried fish may taste good, but fried foods should be kept to a minimum in all healthy diets because of their high fat content.

STOVE-TOP PREPARATION OF FISH FILLETS

Sautéeing: After you have washed and dried your fish fillets, dredge them in flour to which you have added some freshly ground pepper to taste. Some cooks like to dip fish fillets in milk before dredging them in flour. This adds a nice flavor and silkiness to the texture of the fillet, but it is not a required step in the cooking process. Shake off the excess flour before sautéeing. For ½ pound fish, melt 1 tablespoon unsalted butter in a medium skillet to which you have added 1 tablespoon of olive oil. You may use flavored butters (such as garlic or herb butter) to make the taste more intriguing, or you might add herbs or minced garlic as you are melting the butter. As the butter melts, grab hold of the handle and twist the pan so that the butter and oil swirl and combine. Now add the fish fillets and sauté over medium heat until they are golden brown. You will need to turn the fillet over during sautéeing, probably after 2 minutes. Do this carefully so that the fillet does not break. When you put the fish into the skillet, you might try some of these additions to make your fish fillet different and special: lemon or lime juice; lemon juice and capers (this would be called fish Grenobloise); almonds (making it

Amandine fish); seedless green grapes (for fish Veronique); grated carrots, a couple of sultanas (golden raisins), and a few pine nuts (this is a variation on a popular way to make cod in Rome); or anything else that sounds good to you. Serve sautéed fish immediately.

Steaming: Steaming is a popular cooking method that is practiced throughout the world, particularly in parts of Asia and in France. It is also a preferred way of preparing fish for persons who cannot have any butter. You need a metal rack or a traditional wood or bamboo steamer from Asia. You can adapt a metal rack or vegetable steamer you already own or, as a last resort, use a metal colander. If you are using metal equipment for steaming, lightly grease the area where the fish will rest with a little oil. Then place the cleaned, dried fish fillet on that spot. Have a medium-size pot with 1 or 2 inches of boiling water ready for you to place the rack or colander over. Water is the easiest and most obvious liquid to use, but you might consider adding other things to the water. Some white wine in the water will impart flavor without alcohol. You also combine water with bottled clam juice for a taste of the ocean. Also consider flavoring the water with peppercorns, herbs, fresh parsley or dill, carrot chunks, celery stalks, onions, or garlic. Reserve any vegetables from the water to purée for use in any soup you might make. After you have placed your rack above the boiling liquid, cover it with the pot's lid or, at least, cover the fish fillet. It is easy to use a traditional steamer. Place it above the boiling liquid and cover it with its own cover. A thin fillet should be thoroughly steamed in about 5 minutes. Flake it with a fork to test for doneness.

Poaching: Poaching fillets is less tricky than steaming even if you don't have the correct equipment (a fish poacher, which is an investment you need make only if you are a poached fish fanatic). Poached fish steaks (salmon, swordfish, and shark) are wonderful, although they take more time than fillets. The beauty of poached fish is that it usually tastes as good cold as it does hot. Prepare extra fillets for poaching so that you will have leftovers. White fish such as cod and perch are good in salads for lunch. Cold Poached Salmon (page 192) is an elegant main course at a dinner party or a wonderful meal for one. For up to 4 servings of fish, put 2 cups of cold water (or 1½ cups of water and ½ cup of white wine or lemon juice) in a flat, good-size pan and simmer. As the liquid simmers, add any other ingredients you might like: an uncut clove of garlic (not with salmon); dill (especially good with salmon); fines herbes; peppercorns; lemon, lime, or orange slices (wash the peel of the fruit before slicing), or other flavors that will enhance the fish without overpowering it. After the liquid and additions have simmered for 5 minutes, gently place the fish into the pan so that the fillets or steaks do not touch one another. The liquid should just cover the fish. Cover and cook over low heat. Doneness depends on the thickness of the fish, but a good rule of thumb is to poach fish for 10 minutes per 1 inch of thickness, measured at the thickest part of the fish. The fish is correctly poached when it flakes at the touch of a fork. You may serve poached fish garnished with lemon and parsley and accompanied by boiled potatoes or rice. You may also top it with a little pesto (page 129), but use it sparingly because the flavor is intense. The same goes for Salsa Verde (page 130). Or use a little Faux Hollandaise Sauce (page 130). Almost any green vegetable may be served with poached fish. Asparagus or peas are especially friendly to poached salmon. In addition to these essential methods of fish preparation, you will find a few special fish recipes on the following pages. You may eat as much fish as you want during your pregnancy. It is wonderful food for you and your fetus.

Brandade de Morue

2 SERVINGS (MAIN COURSE), 4 SERVINGS (APPETIZER)

DOCTOR'S NOTE

Calories: 661 per serving

One serving of Brandade de Morue, made with ½ pound cooked cod, yields 68.3 g protein (more than 100% of the RDA), 41 g carbohydrates (more than 50% of the RDA), and 21 g fat. Because of the high carbohydrate and sodium (1200 mg) load in brandade, the woman diagnosed with gestational diabetes, preeclampsia, or high blood pressure should abstain from this dish. It also should be consumed in moderation by the woman whose weight is moving up too fast.

Here is a variation on a popular dish from southern France. *Brandade is a sort of baked casserole of fish and mashed potatoes that tastes good, goes down well, and is very easy on the pocketbook. This version of brandade differs only in that you will be able to skip several procedures that take place in preparing traditional brandade. But you can devote the time you save to doing other things, such as selecting a name for your baby.*

1 to 1½ pounds fresh codfish or scrod steaks

¼ cup water

¼ cup freshly squeezed lemon juice

3 tablespoons extra-virgin olive oil

1 garlic clove, slivered (if you really don't care for garlic it can be left out)

Freshly ground pepper to taste

3 cups Mashed Potatoes (page 229)

Preheat oven to 400° F.

Put the fish in a lightly oiled baking dish so that the pieces are not touching. Combine the water and lemon juice and pour into the baking dish. Bake for about 5 minutes and then check to see if the fish flakes at the touch of a fork. Check every other minute until the fish flakes. There is some variation in cooking time, based on the thickness of the fish and the type of oven you have. If the liquid dries up, add a little more water. When the fish flakes easily, it is ready to use.

While the fish is cooking, sauté the garlic in the olive oil. If you are not using garlic, skip this step.

When the fish is done, remove it from the pan, let it cool slightly and then shred it into little pieces with a fork. (Keep the oven on.) Combine the fish shreds with the mashed potatoes, pepper, and the garlic and oil. If you are omitting the garlic, add the olive oil to the potato mixture (see note below). Mix the ingredients well.

Divide the mixture into two lightly oiled flat ramekins or an oiled ovenproof baking dish.

Bake for 10 minutes, or until the brandade is golden brown.

Serve with a green salad with vinaigrette and, perhaps, some toast or rusk crackers onto which you can spread the brandade. This recipe may also be used to make one large appetizer to serve to guests. In this case, triangles of toast or rusks are absolutely essential. Bon appetit!

Note: If you are omitting the garlic you might want to use Rosemary Olive Oil (page 127).

Pescado San Sebastian

2 SERVINGS

San Sebastian, in the Basque country that straddles the frontier of Spain and France, is a beautiful seaside town that is home to a famous film festival. The cuisine is geared to the sea but also to the nearby hills and mountains that yield a bounty of good vegetables. This recipe is influenced by some of the flavors of San Sebastian.

1 pound firm fish (cod, scrod, haddock, pollack, or hake), cut in 2 pieces

Flour

2 tablespoons extra virgin olive oil

1 garlic clove, slivered (optional if garlic does not appeal to you right now)

1 small green bell pepper, washed, seeds removed, cut in strips

5 to 6 canned, peeled tomatoes, cut in half

Freshly ground pepper to taste

12 green or black oil-cured olives, pitted and cut in half

1 teaspoon chopped scallions or chives (optional)

Preheat oven to 350° F.

Dredge the fish in flour, shaking off the excess. Heat the olive oil in a large skillet and sauté the fish over medium heat until it is lightly browned on both sides (about 3–4 minutes per side). Put the fish in an ovenproof baking dish large enough to contain it that has been lightly greased with olive oil and set aside.

Place the garlic and green pepper in the skillet and sauté for a couple of minutes. Add the tomatoes and cook for 5 minutes, stirring occasionally. Then grind in some pepper and add the olives. Cook for 2 more minutes.

Spoon the contents of the skillet over the fish, bake for 15 minutes. Serve immediately with a few scallions or chives atop each piece of fish, if desired. This dish goes well with rice or boiled potatoes and also is good served cold as a leftover.

DOCTOR'S NOTE

Calories: 589 per serving

We used cod as the fish of choice for this recipe. One serving will provide you with 65 g protein (100% of the RDA), 37 g fat (33% of the RDA), 620 mg of phosphorus and 920 mg potassium (50% of the RDA for both). Clearly, this is an ideal dish for the new mother (breastfeeding or not) who is in need of protein and is searching for ways to trim off calories. It is also an ideal dish for the gestational diabetic. Its main ingredients are low in carbohydrates, but the dish still provides a full complement of protein and generous amounts of other nutrients.

Flounder Florentine

1 SERVING

Any lean white-fleshed fish (flounder, sole, whitefish, or whiting) is good for this dish, which is jam-packed with iron, calcium, vitamin C, and protein. It also tastes good. Serving cheese and fish together can be risky business taste-wise, but it works here. The hint of Parmesan flavors the spinach but does not overpower the dish.

½ pound fillet white-fleshed fish

Freshly ground pepper to taste

1 tablespoon unsalted butter or ½ tablespoon olive oil

1 lemon, cut in half

¼ pound cooked spinach, warm or room temperature

1 tablespoon freshly grated Parmesan or grana cheese

Preheat the oven to 475° F.

Season the fish fillet with pepper. Melt the butter or heat the oil in a medium pan, add the fish and the juice of ½ lemon and cook gently over low heat until done, 5 to 7 minutes, depending on the thickness of the fish.

Pour the pan liquid in a lightly oiled baking dish and add the fillet. Distribute the spinach evenly over the fillet, top with the cheese, and put in the oven. Bake until the cheese melts. It should not be too long or the fish will dry out (this is why pan liquids were added).

Serve immediately, accompanied by the other lemon half to squeeze, if desired.

DOCTOR'S NOTE

Calories: 353 per serving

This dish is loaded with good nutrition. The flounder fillet is packed with 32 g protein (50% of the RDA), and the spinach adds 9000 IU vitamin A (almost 200% of the RDA). The dish has only 4 carbohydrates. The dish's fat content also is relatively low: 15 g total if you use the olive oil.

We recommend this dish for the gestational diabetic who is on a carbohydrate-restricted diet as well as for those times during pregnancy when you have gained too much weight but need to maintain your protein and vitamin portions. It also is an excellent choice postdelivery: whether you are breastfeeding and need protein for milk production or you are attempting to lose the few extra pounds pregnancy has added to your body.

Grilled Tuna Cancún

2 Servings

Doctor's Note

Calories: 542 per serving

A serving of this recipe will give you a mere 10 g carbohydrates, along with a healthy 50 mg of vitamin C (more than 50% of the RDA) and 2350 IU vitamin A (50% of the RDA). You can use this recipe during your pregnancy when you have gained too much weight but still need to build your baby with protein (very abundant in tuna) or when you have been diagnosed with gestational diabetes and are watching your carbohydrates. If you are a tuna lover, this dish has a special advantage: It is very low in salt, and therefore, it is suitable for women who are at risk for preeclampsia or for whom the doctor has prescribed a moderate or restricted salt intake and a high-protein diet.

Tuna does not just come in a can. American eaters have recently learned something that other peoples have long known: Fresh tuna makes for a great entrée. This particular preparation has a Mexican accent and is an interesting alternative to the tuna preparations usually seen in fancy restaurants. It also is very easy to make.

1 garlic clove, peeled and minced

¼ cup extra-virgin olive oil

2 tablespoons freshly squeezed lime juice

¼ teaspoon salt

½ teaspoon freshly ground pepper

1 pound ripe, flavorful tomatoes, peeled, seeded, chopped (use good canned tomatoes only if fresh ones are unavailable)

⅛ cup chopped fresh cilantro (coriander)

¼ cup minced fresh parsley

1 pound tuna steak, 1¼ inches thick, washed and patted dry

Make a salsa by combining the garlic, olive oil, lime juice, salt, pepper, and tomatoes in a bowl. Stir so that all the elements blend. Set aside for at least 10 minutes.

About 10 minutes before cooking the tuna, preheat the broiler. Also stir the cilantro and parsley into the salsa.

When the broiler is hot, broil the tuna in a lightly oiled pan about 4 inches from the flame. Cook 3 to 4 minutes per side; the fish should be charred on the outside and slightly pink within.

Remove the tuna steak to a serving dish and cut into thick slabs. Top each strip with some of the salsa. Reserve the rest of the sauce in case someone wants more for the fish or wants to sop it up with good bread.

Broiled Monkfish

1 Serving

Monkfish has long been popular in France, where it is called lotte, and in Italy, where it known as rospo . It was much-maligned in the United States until someone referred to it as "poor man's lobster," and then suddenly this forlorn fish took flight. It is indeed a fish and not a crustacean, but its rich meat reminds some people of lobster. Monkfish is often quite reasonable in price and does not require too much work to make it taste good.

4 to 8 ounces monkfish fillet

2 teaspoons olive oil (perhaps Rosemary Olive Oil, page 127)

Pinch oregano, sage, or rosemary (if not using an herb oil)

Freshly ground pepper to taste (optional)

Juice of ½ lemon

Preheat the broiler.

Carefully wash the fish in cold water and pat it dry with paper towels. Place the fillet in a broiling pan.

If you are not using a prepared herb oil, combine the olive oil with an herb of your choice and the pepper. Brush the fillet on both sides with the oil. Top with the lemon juice. Broil the fish until it is firm to the touch and flakes easily with a fork, about 6 minutes per side.

Serve with additional lemon if you want. Broiled monkfish goes well with mashed potatoes laced with garlic and a broiled tomato, or perhaps, rice and a green salad.

DOCTOR'S NOTE

Calories: 300 per serving

This dish provides 10.3 g fat (mostly due to the olive oil added in cooking), and 25 g protein (almost 50% of the RDA). It also is very low in sodium (only 32 mg) and has virtually no carbohydrates, which makes it an ideal lunch or dinner for the gestational diabetic or the women diagnosed with preeclampsia.

Poached Salmon

I TO 4 SERVINGS (I TO 4 FILLETS)

DOCTOR'S NOTE

Calories: 337 per serving

Using a 6-ounce salmon fillet, this dish provides you with 44 g protein (66% of the RDA), 12.5 g fat, and no carbohydrates. It is also low in sodium (200 mg) and high in potassium (756 mg, 37% of the RDA). Salmon is rich in protein but low in carbohydrates and most essential vitamins and minerals. For a balanced meal, we suggest you accompany this low-calorie dish with a salad and a source of carbohydrates such as potatoes, rice, or grain.

Salmon may be the perfect fish. Its rosy color is a delight to the eye, its flavor is distinctive, and its versatility means you will seldom tire of it. It is also a superb source of protein (44 g per 6-ounce portion; 66% of the RDA). Add to all of this the drama of its journey from ocean back to river to spawn, and salmon achieves legendary status. Poached salmon can be eaten hot or cold with various sauces, in salads, spreads, or casseroles. You may make up to four salmon fillets or steaks with this recipe. If you are eating alone or cooking for two, consider making more to have for a later meal or a delicious brown-bag lunch. It is traditional to use white wine in the poaching liquid. You need not worry about the alcohol, because most of it evaporates in the cooking, but if you wish to do without wine, add an additional ½ cup of water.

1 quart cold water

3 tablespoons freshly squeezed lemon juice

½ cup dry white wine

½ medium onion, sliced

6 to 8 peppercorns

1 bay leaf or 1 sprig tarragon

1 to 4 6-ounce salmon fillets or salmon steaks*

Put the water, lemon juice, wine, onion, peppercorns, and bay leaf in a large skillet. Simmer, covered, for 20 minutes.

In the meantime, wash the salmon and pat it dry. Add it to the skillet. The liquid should just cover the fish. If it does not, add more water.

Cover and simmer over low heat. You should allow 10 minutes of cooking time per 1 inch of thickness measured at the thickest part. The salmon is correctly cooked when it flakes easily at the touch of a fork.

Remove each fillet carefully with a broad spatula, preferably slotted, and drain well.

*You may use whatever size fillet or steak you find, but maximum weight of salmon you should use for this recipe is about 2 pounds.

Salmon Loaf

Salmon bones, which are edible, are a superb source of calcium. In making this dish, mash the bones with a fork so that they become part of the loaf. An easy way to make salmon loaf more alluring is to add ½ cup of cooked peas (fresh or frozen). Serve the loaf hot with rice or potatoes and a leafy green vegetable. Cold salmon loaf makes a nice sandwich filler or, when cut in small pieces, a pleasing hors d'oeuvre.

2 cups cooked or canned salmon

1½ cups plain bread crumbs

2 tablespoons minced onion

1 teaspoon freshly ground pepper

1 tablespoon freshly squeezed lemon juice

½ cup peas (optional)

1 egg, slightly beaten

1 cup low-fat milk

1 teaspoon milk solids

2 teaspoons fresh dill

1 tablespoon unsalted butter

Preheat the oven to 400° F.

In a large bowl, mix salmon (bones mashed), bread crumbs, onion, pepper, and lemon juice. Add peas, if you are using them. Mix in all the other ingredients (without overworking the mixture) and form a loaf. If you think the loaf is too dry, add a bit of liquid from the salmon can or some water.

Place the loaf in a lightly buttered 9-inch long loaf pan (or grease the pan with corn oil), dot with little bits of butter (if you wish), and bake for 25 minutes, or until lightly browned.

DOCTOR'S NOTE

Calories: 262 per serving

Assuming that you use canned salmon for this recipe, you also will get 222 g calcium (canned salmon is particularly rich in calcium) and 23 g protein (33% of the RDA). This dish has very little fat and carbohydrates. Salmon Loaf is particularly suitable for the gestational diabetic who is in constant search of dishes that are low in calories and carbohydrates yet high in proteins and minerals.

Poultry

Cooks know that a *supreme* refers not only to Diana Ross, Mary Wilson, Florence Ballard, and Cindy Birdsong but also to a boneless breast of poultry, usually chicken. In fact, a supreme, which is usually about 1 inch thick, is half a chicken breast. Nowadays, many stores also sell what are called chicken or turkey fillets. These are also wonderful and convenient (call them the marvelettes), but chicken fillets are thinner than supremes and cook a little more quickly. In other words, they are more like the Miracles than the Temptations. Turkey fillets are cut thicker and can usually approximate a chicken supreme in most recipes. Chicken fillets are good for someone who really doesn't want to eat much but knows she should have some protein. Any recipe in this book that calls for a supreme may use a fillet, and vice versa, but just take into account that the cooking time is a little longer for a supreme. But not much longer: In the time it takes to listen to a 45 RPM recording of "The Happening" or "Baby Love," you can cook up a chicken or turkey supreme that will make you sing "I Hear a Symphony."

A chicken supreme contains 189 cals, 36 g protein (50% of the RDA), only 4 g fat (13% of the RDA), no carbohydrates, 290 mg phosphorus (25% of the RDA), 466 mg potassium (about 25% of the RDA), and 13 mg calcium.

COOKING THE BASIC SUPREME

After the bone is removed from a chicken breast, the meat that remains is usually shaped like a butterfly. This is cut in half and the result is two supremes. One supreme is usually a good portion for one person. The supreme should be washed and carefully dried with paper towels and any bits of fat should be pulled or cut away. Pound the breast with your fist or with a mallet to flatten it a bit. This will mean a shorter cooking time and juicier meat. You may dredge the supreme in flour (shaking off the excess) before cooking, which will seal in some of the meat's juices if you sauté the supreme, or you may choose to skip the flour. In this case, you should be sure there is a little more liquid in the pan so the chicken or turkey does not dry out. Heat a little olive oil or unsalted butter in a skillet and then add the supreme, cooking quickly over relatively high heat, shaking the pan every so often to prevent the supreme from sticking. After one side is slightly browned, turn the supreme and cook the second side. Test for doneness by poking into the thickest part of the supreme to see if it is white or very faintly pink, which means that it's ready. This is the recipe for an unflavored supreme, but in most cases you will want to add some flavor.

Liquids: An easy way to give the meat flavor is to add liquid. After briefly sautéing the supreme in butter, oil, or nonstick spray, add enough liquid so that there is flavor in the pan and some cooking liquid, but not so much as to overwhelm the meat and make it all wet. In general, there should be just enough liquid to cover the bottom of the pan. If you use chicken stock, you will maintain and enhance the essential chicken flavor. Light and delicious lemon juice is another favorite, because it cuts some of the greasy taste that can occur in frying, which might be a turnoff to you right now. It also is the ideal base for adding herbs, pepper and other spices, onions, garlic, or capers. You may experiment by using other citrus flavors, such as orange juice, lime juice, tangerine juice, or even grapefruit juice. Although most every doctor discourages consumption of alcohol during pregnancy, most cooks believe that alcohol burns off completely during cooking. Others say that some little bit of alcohol remains. This is up to you and your doctor, but use of a little white wine is a nice touch as a cooking liquid for a supreme. Perhaps you should look into some of the alcohol-free wines that are beginning to appear on the market.

Flavorings: In sautéeing your supreme or fillet, your choice is limited only by your imagination. For anyone who particularly desires a certain flavor in her mouth, combining that taste with a supreme is the best way to get it. If a food normally needs a little cooking, such as onions, garlic, green, bell peppers, celery, grated carrots, mushrooms, shallots, or tomatoes, it should be sautéed briefly before putting the supreme in the pan. The vegetable will give off juices that will flavor the supreme. Then cook the meat as usual. Other flavors, such as herbs, unsalted nuts, or capers, should be added after the supreme has already begun to cook. When using these, there must be a liquid in the pan such as lemon juice or chicken stock. Tarragon is an especially suitable herb, as is the combination of oregano and tomatoes. The last-minute addition of

FLAVORING POULTRY
BREASTS AND
FILLETS

freshly minced parsley, scallions, or chives will give the supreme some zing. Almond slivers, unsalted walnuts, unsalted peanuts, unsalted cashews or unsalted pecans all taste good with sautéed supremes. A few raisins with nuts is very pleasing. The combination of capers and lemon juice is called Grenobloise, for the pretty French alpine town of Grenoble, where this preparation is popular. To make supremes Veronique try adding some seedless green grapes at the last moment to supremes that have been cooked with a little wine (alcohol-free if you prefer). The origin of the term *Veronique* is subject to dispute. Some people say it was the girlfriend of the chef who invented the dish. Others say that it was the name of the woman who actually devised it. Still others maintain that it is honor of the town of Verona, which is one of the major centers of the Italian grape-growing and wine-producing industries. Whatever the origin, the dish is light and tasty.

Toppings: After sautéeing the basic supreme, perhaps with the use of chicken stock or lemon juice, you may wish to top it with something delicious and bake it briefly before serving. Using spinach and Parmesan cheese, for example, you need simply preheat an oven to 400° F. Prepare the basic supreme, place it in a lightly oiled oven-proof baking dish, top with some cooked spinach (see page 231) and some freshly grated Parmesan cheese and bake only until the cheese melts or browns. Do not leave it in too long or the chicken will dry out. Also consider using real (not imitation) unsalted mozzarella cheese over the spinach or over a supreme cooked with herbs, vegetables, or pine nuts. You may also use the mozzarella in combination with mushrooms and a thin slice of lean ham or prosciutto, although in this case it tastes a bit funny if the cooking liquid was lemon juice. A preferable liquid is chicken stock, wine, or pan juices from vegetables. The ham should be put atop the chicken, then the mushrooms, then the cheese. You may put a little freshly grated Parmesan between the ham and the mushrooms. Or you might put spinach or a couple of stalks of cooked asparagus (see page 220) instead of the mushrooms, or simply use asparagus and cheese. Using ham and cheese without vegetables is also superb. A delicious idea is to spread a little Pesto Presto (page 129) or sprinkle a few drops of Vinaigrette aux Fines Herbes (page 126) or Rosemary Olive Oil (page 127) on top of a basic supreme.

The supreme is one of the cornerstones of the cooking repertory for any pregnant gourmet. Make more than one basic supreme when you are cooking. They will keep for a couple of days. Cook additional ones using only liquids and flavorings (no toppings) and save them. They will keep well in the refrigerator for a couple of days. They make perfect fillings for lunchtime sandwiches with vegetables or cold toppings such as pesto or vinaigrette. They may also be used for making other meals using the hot toppings described above or cut up in salads with fresh vegetables or fruit.

SUPREME STRATEGY

Turkey Piccata

1 SERVING

Easy, fast, delicious, nutritious. Turkey fillets (boneless slices of breast meat) now appear in most markets and represent an economical and tasty way to make many dishes that call for more expensive meats such as veal cutlets. You also may use chicken fillets in this dish, but turkey somehow tastes meatier and more substantial.

1 turkey fillet

Flour

Freshly ground pepper

1 teaspoon extra-virgin olive oil (or 1 tablespoon sweet butter)

Juice of ½ lemon

Minced fresh parsley

1 teaspoon capers (optional)

Pound the turkey fillet gently so that it is broad and flat.

Dust the fillet on both sides with flour seasoned with the pepper. Shake off the excess flour. Heat a little bit of olive oil (or butter) in a skillet. Add the fillet and cook over medium heat quickly. After you have turned the fillet, squeeze the lemon juice onto the sides of the pan, add the parsley and capers and give the pan a couple of quick shakes over high heat to complete the cooking.

Serve immediately, accompanied by rice or potatoes and a leafy green vegetable or a salad.

Cook's note: Make two turkey fillets at once by doubling this recipe. It will take very little additional time and you can have the second fillet cold the next day in a sandwich for lunch.

Chicken or Turkey Gismonda

1 SERVING

A good dish for company. You need only multiply the indicated amounts by the number of people you plan to serve. The recipe can be made using either chicken or turkey fillets. The sauce is made of asparagus, parsley and a touch of yogurt. Cooking asparagus must be carefully timed. If you happen to overcook asparagus you were preparing for some other reason, use it for this recipe. Read more about asparagus on page 220.

4 to 5 stalks cooked asparagus

6 sprigs of fresh parsley

1 chicken or turkey fillet

Flour

Freshly ground pepper

1 tablespoon extra-virgin olive oil or unsalted butter
  or margarine

Juice of ½ lemon (optional)

½ teaspoon plain yogurt

Put the asparagus and parsley in a blender. Blend until a purée is formed. Pour the purée into a saucepan.

Flatten the fillet. Dredge it in flour seasoned with the pepper and then shake off the excess.

Heat the oil or butter in a skillet and cook the fillet over medium heat thoroughly on both sides. You may squeeze in some lemon juice if you wish as you turn the fillet. This will add flavor, vitamins and freshness.

While the fillet is cooking, add the yogurt to the asparagus purée and heat it gently over low heat, being careful the sauce does not stick or burn.

When the fillet is done, transfer it to a plate and spoon over the asparagus sauce. Serve with rice or potatoes that have been topped with the pan juices. Easy, elegant, and delicious.

DOCTOR'S NOTE

Calories: 341 per serving

In spite of the low calorie content of this elegant dish, it will provide you with 36 g protein (more than 50% of the RDA) and 17 g fat (about 50% of the RDA). It is low in carbohydrates and easy to prepare, making it ideal for both gestational diabetics and for any pregnant woman whose day has been too hectic for her to have had an ideal diet.

Chicken aux Fines Herbes

4 Servings

Read about fines herbes on page 126. They impart wonderful flavor to this easy, inexpensive chicken recipe. This dish is good served hot with a green vegetable and rice or potatoes to catch the sauce. Leftover, this chicken is delicious and flavorful as a lunch or snack or for use in chicken salad.

1 2- to 3-pound fresh chicken, cut in 6 to 8 pieces (by your butcher or supermarket)

2 tablespoons extra-virgin olive oil or unsalted butter

1 cup chicken stock (page 146)

2 tablespoons fines herbes

¼ cup buttermilk, plain yogurt, or heavy cream (optional)

After cleaning the chicken pieces thoroughly and removing the excess fat, sauté them in olive oil or butter in a large pan or skillet. When the chicken has browned, spill off some of the excess fat in the pan.

Add the chicken stock and the fines herbes. Cover and cook gently for 30 minutes, or until done. Remove the chicken to a warm platter and, if you wish, add the buttermilk, yogurt, or cream to the pan. Heat quickly with the pan juices to make a sauce. (Be sure also to scrape up all the delicious bits stuck to the bottom of the pan.) Spoon a little sauce on the chicken pieces and save the rest for the rice or potatoes. If you don't wish to make this sauce, save the pan juices for the rice or potato.

DOCTOR'S NOTE

Calories: 434 per serving

Assuming that this recipe will yield 4 servings, each serving will deliver 44.3 g protein (66% of the RDA), 10.6 g fat, 6 g carbohydrates, and 1167 IU vitamin A (25% of the RDA). Chicken also is high in niacin, a B vitamin that is very important in the synthesis of progesterone and estrogen, the all-important hormones during your pregnancy.

This dish is an excellent choice for lunch (or a light dinner) for the gestational diabetic or for the woman who is putting on weight too fast and needs to trim off her intake of fat and carbohydrates.

Pollo Castelli Romani

Chicken in the Style of the Roman Countryside

2 TO 3 SERVINGS

The Castelli Romani, the hill country east of Rome, contains some of the most beautiful villas in the world, including one belonging to the pope. The area has been a playground since imperial days. The rolling farmland yields intensely flavorful ingredients, such as superb olives and wine grapes that are made into the local Frascati and Marino wines. Read about olives on page 277 and remember that fresh oil-cured olives should never be confused with the salty store-bought types. Shop for good Italian black olives, such as Gaeta olives, in specialty stores. If you happen to be craving olives, there is not a better dish in this book.

In making this dish you might take the trouble to pit the olives, although this step is not required. (Just remember while you're eating if you didn't pit the olives.) If you are apprehensive about using wine (although most of the alcohol does evaporate during cooking), use hot water or chicken stock.

⅓ cup extra-virgin olive oil

2 garlic cloves, slivered

2 sprigs fresh rosemary, separated

1 2- to 2½-pound young chicken, cut in pieces

⅓ cup Frascati, Marino, Castelli Romani, or other light, dry white wine

¼ cup Gaeta or other high quality black olives

Freshly ground pepper to taste

Heat the olive oil over medium heat in a large, heavy frying pan until the oil is hot but does not spatter. Add the garlic, sauté for 15 seconds and then add the rosemary and chicken pieces. Fry the chicken, turning the pieces frequently so they cook evenly. Continue to watch that the oil is not too hot, as you don't want the ingredients to burn. Cook for 5 minutes.

Pour the wine into the pan and cook for a couple of minutes to reduce the alcohol in the wine. Then add the olives and pepper. →

DOCTOR'S NOTE

Calories: 512 per serving

To compute these nutrient values, we used a 2½-pound fryer. Each serving has 44 g protein (66% of the RDA), 32 g fat (very high), and only 8.2 g carbohydrates. In addition, chicken is very high in vitamin A and this serving will provide you 1718 IU (33% of the RDA).

Cover the pan and cook over a low flame for about 40 minutes, or until the braised chicken is tender. You may need to add some hot water while cooking if the pan juices evaporate.

Serve immediately.

Chicken Livers

1 SERVING

*O*unce for ounce, there a few better sources of iron. If you like them, this is a delicious, easy recipe. If you don't like them, try this once and then decide.

1 tablespoon sweet butter or ½ tablespoon olive oil

¼ small onion, cut in thin rings

5 mushrooms, sliced

1 teaspoon freshly minced parsley

¼ pound (about 6 to 8) fresh chicken livers, cleaned, deveined, and halved

Flour

1 tablespoon sweet butter or margarine

½ cup cooked brown or white rice (cooked according to package directions)

Freshly ground pepper to taste (optional)

You need two pans or skillets for this dish. Set them on the stove before you start cooking.

In one pan, heat the butter or oil and then sauté the onions and mushrooms over low heat. After a couple of minutes, add the parsley.

While the vegetables are cooking dredge the livers in flour, shaking off the excess. Melt the butter or margarine over low heat in the other pan and then sauté the livers over medium heat for 1½ to 2 minutes per side. Once the livers are cooked, remove them from the heat.

DOCTOR'S NOTE

Calories: 380 per serving

A serving of this delicious chicken liver recipe will deliver 22 g protein (33% of the RDA), almost no carbohydrates, and only 5 g fat plus 12 mg iron (40% of the RDA) and 1400 IU vitamin A (more than 25% of the RDA). A portion of chicken livers offers a good dose of riboflavin (a B vitamin) and calcium. This is one of the healthiest foods available.

If your doctor has advised you that you are anemic, which is a very common condition during pregnancy, this is the perfect dish for you. Anemia occurs in pregnancy because your blood gets "diluted" with the extra fluid you

Serve with some rice, topped with the onion, mushroom, and parsley mixture. Use fresh pepper if you wish.

VARIATION

While the livers are cooking, add 1 teaspoon good Port wine. Cook, shaking the pan occasionally, until the liquid has reduced as the alcohol burns off. This will add a nice flavor that tempers the chicken livers a bit.

are retaining and, in addition, you are actively passing iron to your baby. Eat chicken livers often, because they are almost as effective as an iron supplement (and they surely taste better). This dish also is recommended if you have diabetes, as it is devoid of carbohydrates, yet full of the very vitamins that are usually found in carbohydrate-rich foods.

Meat

Meat Recipes

Meat has developed a bad reputation in recent years. The meat industry has been hit on all sides by dietitians, consumer groups, animal rights activists, and environmentalists. Many of these groups have had legitimate claims. Until a few years ago, much of the meat on the market was marbled with fat, but this fattiness used to be considered a virtue in that it made the meat juicier and more succulent. When consumers became more conscious about fat in their diet, all-American beef, which used to be the centerpiece for many a meal, became as un-American as mince pie. Similarly, there has been justifiable alarm over additives and growth hormones that have been fed to cattle to "beef" them up.

Animal rights activists correctly called attention to the fact that many animals were being treated inhumanely. Environmentalists have noted that cows emit an extraordinary amount of methane, which contributes to air pollution. It also is apparent that ranchers, particularly in North America and in the Brazilian rain forest, have chopped down trees to create more grazing land for cattle. This deforestation has had and will continue to have devastating environmental effects if we all don't redouble our efforts to stop it.

But, we ask, is all of this the cow's fault? All of the actions described above (except for the expulsion of methane) are the doings of humans. None of this negates the fact that meat is important sustenance for humans. Many vegetarians live contentedly without it, and if that is your preference, that is fine as long as you make sure to acquire all the proteins you need for you and your fetus (see page 9). But most people do well by consuming 3 or 4 ounces of meat several times a week as an important source of protein. Three ounces of beef, veal, lamb, or pork contain approximately 25 g protein (almost 40% of the RDA). Poultry, fish, and seafood also are valuable protein foods and should figure in your diet at least as much as red meats, if not more. Many Americans still eat much too much fat (which should comprise, at most, 30% of one's daily caloric intake). If you routinely eat more fat than you should, make an effort to have foods that are lower in fat content and avoid all fried foods, luncheon meats, and overindulgence in butter and full-fat cheeses, milks, and ice creams.

To be fair, the meat industry has recognized the problems that faced its products and has begun to do a good job of answering some of the important issues. It is quite easy now to find beef, veal, and pork that is much lower in fat than once upon a time. Meat is often cut in smaller pieces by butchers, or can be had in single slices if you make a roast, so that a 1-pound slab of beef hanging over the side of a plate is no longer the only way to eat meat. You can thus have the benefits of eating meat in moderation—protein, iron, B vitamins, and good taste—without overdoing it. When cooking with ground meat, you can measure exactly how much you eat. Read about burgers below and look at the two meat loaf recipes on pages 211 and 213.

Depending on your religion, dietary and personal preferences, you may choose not to eat pork. This meat has made great strides in recent years in terms of standards of cleanliness and fat content. If you have a pork recipe that you enjoy and make sure to cook the meat thoroughly, you may continue to enjoy it, as long as it is not deep-fried. However, if you are not a pork eater and are unfamiliar with how to handle and cook it, perhaps pregnancy is not the best time to start eating pork. All pregnant women should be careful about eating pork in restaurants because you have less control over the thoroughness with which it is cooked. In some cases, undercooked pork and ham may result in trichinosis, a serious and very uncomfortable intestinal disorder.

All pregnant and nursing women should avoid cured meats such as frankfurters, salami, liverwurst, bologna, sausages, most hams, pastrami, and corned beef. Many of these items are loaded with salt and chemicals and are extremely unhealthy.

BURGERS OF ALL KINDS

For the purposes of this book, *burger* will be the operative word to describe patties of ground meat that are grilled, broiled, or pan-cooked. The word *burger* might not seem wholly appropriate to a grammarian or, for that matter, to the food historian who doubts whether the hamburger is indeed from Hamburg, Germany. Nowadays, a burger might contain beef, veal, chicken, turkey, lamb, other meats, and even fish such as salmon.

Hamburgers made of beef used to be evaluated by the fat content in the meat. Most nutritional guidelines advise that a good diet contain no more than 30% fat, and many dietitians encourage consumers to have even less. Most pregnant women do need a certain amount of fat and do not have to be as preoccupied as the general population about fat consumption. There is another truth about fat and burgers: Those that contain some fat usually taste better. Once upon a time, the ideal was 70% meat and 30% fat. In our more fat-conscious times, this proportion has been altered so that some burgers may be as much as 90% meat and 10% fat. Of course, the final product will be less fatty because much of the fat is released during cooking. Many supermarkets now list the fat content of chopped meat on the package.

As a pregnant woman, eating a beef burger using lean ground sirloin or chuck steak twice a week is fine unless your doctor tells you otherwise. You might choose to make two at a time and chill the other to put in a sandwich for lunch. You may also make burgers from other ground meats, such as the ever-more popular ground chicken and turkey, but you may need to put a little bit of butter in the skillet to compensate for the lack of fat in the meat that makes for good burger cookery.

Any type of cooked burger will keep well in the refrigerator for 24 to 36 hours when placed on a plate that is tightly wrapped in plastic. They are delicious cold for lunch or a snack.

Basic Burgers

4 SERVINGS

T*he key to making good burgers is to start out with good-quality meat and handle it as delicately as possible. This recipe is for burgers made entirely of beef or a combination of beef and veal, chicken, or turkey. If you do not wish to cook four burgers all at once, wrap the uncooked patties tightly in aluminum foil and freeze until they are needed. Frozen burgers must be completely thawed before use. In this recipe, we have given directions for stove-top preparation since, for many pregnant women in the later months, the idea of bending to get food out of a broiler is inadvisable.*

1 pound beef (or ½ pound beef and ½ pound

   other ground meat)

½ cup unflavored bread crumbs

1 egg (lightly beaten) or ¼ cup skim milk

Chopped parsley (optional)

Freshly ground pepper (optional)

¼ chopped onion (optional)

Wash your hands with cold water. Put the meat in a bowl and, if you have more than one type of meat, work it just enough so that the different meats combine. Add the bread crumbs and egg or milk, plus the parsley, pepper, and onion, if you're using them. Fold the ingredients together with your fingers just so that everything is combined. Do not overwork the mixture.

Form flat, round patties by shaping the meat. Do not compress the patties in your hands to flatten them. Pull away extra meat instead of compressing. You can make 4 to 6 patties from this mixture.

Take a good, large heavy pan, skillet, or stove-top griddle and put it over medium heat on top of the stove. Let it get warm before throwing a little piece of chopped meat into the pan. When the meat begins to sizzle, you are ready to cook your burgers.

Put the patties in the pan and let them cook. Give the pan an occasional shake or nudge the burgers with the side of the spatula→

DOCTOR'S NOTE

A ¼-pound beef burger prepared with an egg, according to the recipe, will contain about 300 cals, 16 g fat, 28 g protein (almost 50% of the RDA), and 5.4 mg of niacin (35% of the RDA). If it is made half of beef and half of veal, it will contain 264 cals, 12.7 g fat, and 25.5 g protein. An all-veal burger will have only 225 cals (a better choice if you must limit your weight gain), 9.4 g fat, and 23 g protein.

With all of these burgers (and the types listed below) you will get less than 1 g carbohydrate. If you omit the bread crumbs (and, therefore, also skip the egg and use only a little skim milk) you will have no carbohydrates at all. A burger without a bun is a perfect food for a gestational diabetic.

to prevent them from sticking. Do not press down on the burgers with the spatula! Yes, you've seen everyone do it, but it's not the best method. It squeezes juiciness out and dries up the burger. When the burgers have cooked for 3 to 4 minutes, flip them carefully and cook the second side for another 3 to 4 minutes. The time is variable and depends on how hot your pan is and how rare or well-done you like your burger. Make sure the meat is cooked through. Even in the best meat there are harmful bacteria that need to be cooked out.

SAUCING AND DRESSING YOUR BURGER

Many people contend that the only way to eat a burger is absolutely plain. If you think this way, enjoy. Many burger-eaters insist that a naked burger is, well, naked. They will create a comfortable "bed" for the burger in a doughy bun. If you are serving the burger on a bun (preferably made of whole wheat and toasted), you will likely reach for the bottle of ketchup and perhaps some relish. These are both very high in salt and not good for you. If you must have ketchup, opt for low-salt ketchup or, better still, a slice of fresh tomato. Skip the relish. If you like mustard on your burgers, use a good Dijon mustard for extra flavor. Other good toppings, with or without the bun, include grilled or sautéed onions or shallots, sautéed mushrooms, or simply some freshly cracked peppercorns. There is no need for added salt. A little bit of blue cheese such as stilton or gorgonzola smeared on top will make you forget fast-food type cheeseburgers. Eat these moderately, but enjoy them when you do.

Poultry Burgers

4 SERVINGS

Sometimes ground chicken or turkey actually costs more than ground beef. In other cases, the prices are comparable or even lower. What you get with poultry is a different, lighter flavor that is a nice change. These burgers also are low in fat, so you need to put a little butter in the pan before cooking.

Make poultry burgers using the same ingredients as the Basic Burgers above, and consider adding a chopped herb or green such as a little fresh tarragon or minced chive. As an alternative, eliminate the herb or green and sprinkle in a little curry powder. (Curry poultry burgers should be dressed only with lemon juice).

Form the patties.

Melt a little bit of unsalted butter (or heat a drop of Rosemary Olive Oil, page 127) in the pan and cook the poultry burgers according to the instructions for Basic Burgers. Poultry burgers must be cooked until well done.

Mustard goes well on poultry burgers as does a squeeze of fresh lemon juice. Ketchup will drown out the subtle flavors of the meat and herbs.

DOCTOR'S NOTE

Depending on whether you use dark or light meat (or a combination) from turkey or chicken, there is a slight variation in the nutritional values. As an average, using ¼-pound ground poultry meat and the added egg and bread crumbs, a typical poultry burger will contain about 210 cals, only 5 g fat, and 30 g protein (50% of the RDA). It will also provide you with about 33% of the RDA for niacin.

Lamb Burgers

4 SERVINGS

Ground lamb is a staple in cuisines served in the belt that extends from India clear across Asia and Africa to Morocco. It is flavorful and a good departure from what you are used to.

Make lamb burgers as you would Basic Burgers, using bread crumbs, egg or milk, onion, parsley, and pepper. Add a few pine nuts if you have them.

You probably do not need to put butter in the pan before cooking.

Avoid ketchup and use fresh lemon juice to dress your lamb burger.

DOCTOR'S NOTE

A burger made with lean lamb will contain approximately 230 cals, 8.5 g fat, and 22.8 g

Salmon Burgers

4 SERVINGS

DOCTOR'S NOTE

A salmon burger made with canned salmon will give you 196 cals, 7 g fat and 23 g protein (slightly more than 33% of the RDA). You will also receive 222 mg calcium (almost 20% of the RDA).

As this book was being written, commercially prepared frozen salmon burgers were just being introduced in North America. They are made of salmon meat from Norway and are flavorful when sautéed in an herb butter or with lemon and capers. If you do not want to use prepackaged burgers made of salmon or anything else (some people don't), here's what to do.

Take a large can (about 1 pound) of salmon and drain out almost all of the liquid. Put the salmon in a bowl, bones and all. Mash well with a fork to break up the calcium-rich bones. Add ½ cup bread crumbs, 1 egg or a ¼ cup of skim milk, and 1 tablespoon fresh dill.

Form the patties. Put 1 tablespoon of corn, canola, or safflower oil in a large skillet, heat the oil over medium heat and then sauté the salmon burgers until they are nicely browned.

Serve with fresh lemon juice or ¼ cup lemon juice that has been heated with a few capers added.

MEAT LOAF

Too many people shudder at the suggestion of meat loaf because they associate this wonderful, economic standby with bad cafeteria food. There also is the fact that many meat loaves make better doorstops than main courses. The key to good meat loaf is lightness and delicacy. This is accomplished by having other foods in the loaf that lighten things up a bit and by working the ingredients only until they are combined rather than kneading them as you might a bread dough. Meat loaf is a delicious and versatile main course and is the perfect food to put between two slices of whole grain bread for the next day's lunch.

Basic Meat Loaf

6 SERVINGS

T*he basic meat loaf becomes more interesting if you combine meats rather than using all beef. Try beef combined with veal, chicken, and/or turkey. Following this recipe is another one (which includes chicken liver) that is designed for people who need extra iron.*

4 tablespoons tomato sauce (try The World's Easiest
  Tomato Sauce, page 128) or 2 tablespoons low-salt ketchup

1 pound freshly ground meat: beef, veal, chicken, turkey
  (in any combination)

½ cup chopped onion

½ cup unflavored bread crumbs or ⅓ cup bread crumbs
  plus 1 tablespoon wheat germ

2 tablespoons freshly squeezed lemon juice

Freshly ground pepper to taste

3 tablespoons minced fresh parsley

1 egg, lightly beaten

Preheat the oven to 350° F.

Take a standard 9-inch loaf pan and grease very lightly with a little butter or vegetable oil. Spoon either 2 tablespoons of the tomato sauce or 1 tablespoon of the ketchup along the bottom of the pan.

Place the meat in a large bowl. Add the onion, bread crumbs (and wheat germ), lemon juice, pepper, and parsley. Combine the ingredients gently using a metal or durable plastic fork or spoon (do not use a wooden utensil, which can pick up or transmit bacteria). This folding should only take a few moments.

Make a small depression in the middle of the meat mixture and pour in the beaten egg.

Wash your hands with cold water. Then gently fold and work the mixture only until the egg has been incorporated into the meat mixture. →

DOCTOR'S NOTE

Calories: 226 per serving

We computed the nutritional value of this recipe by using ground beef that is 90% lean, and ⅓ cup bread crumbs and 1 tablespoon wheat germ. One serving will give you 20 g protein (33% of the RDA), and only 10 g fat. In addition, the wheat germ is very rich in thiamin, vitamin E, folic acid, and fiber.

Take the mixture with both hands and transfer it to the loaf pan. Using your fingertips, distribute the mixture to the corners of the pan, but make a point of not pressing or flattening it too much. This way the loaf you form will be light and delicate.

Spoon on the rest of the tomato sauce or ketchup and spread across the top of the loaf.

Bake in the oven for about 45 minutes. If the loaf has developed a nice crust and seems cooked inside when you check it with a knife, then remove it from the oven. Otherwise, bake for a little while longer (total cooking time up to 1 hour) so that it is done to your liking. Make sure the top of the loaf does not burn.

Before serving, let the loaf stand for 20 minutes. Meat loaf marries well with most starches and vegetables, but it tastes particularly special when served with Mashed Potatoes (page 229).

VARIATIONS

What you have just prepared is the most basic recipe. It can be altered by varying the proportions of the particular meats until you reach the balance you like. But there are many delicious foods that you can add. The most popular choice is probably ½ cup cooked rice. Also recommended is ½ cup grated carrot, which adds sweetness and light bulk. Cooked or canned peas (¼ cup) also are a nice addition. Some people think the loaf becomes more delicate and flavorful when 2 tablespoons of either tomato sauce or apple sauce (page 244) are added. Try this if it appeals to you. You may add ½ cup well-drained cooked spinach that has been very finely chopped. This will gave color and good flavor to the loaf. At most you should probably add 1 cup of additional ingredients.

Meat Loaf with Chicken Liver

6 SERVINGS

L iver is one of the very best sources of iron, but it is not everyone's favorite food. This loaf, which happens to be delectable, is a way of having your liver without confronting a strong liver taste. If you want to tone it down further, add some variations recommended for Meat Loaf (page 212). Particularly indicated are cooked rice and grated carrot (you may use both). Try spinach, too.

1 cup cold water

½ pound fresh chicken livers, washed and deveined

½ pound ground veal (or beef, chicken or turkey)

½ cup chopped onion

½ cup unflavored bread crumbs or ⅓ cup bread crumbs
   plus 1 tablespoon wheat germ

Freshly ground pepper to taste

3 tablespoons minced parsley

1 egg, lightly beaten

4 tablespoons tomato sauce (try The World's Easiest
   Tomato Sauce, page 128) or 2 tablespoons low-salt ketchup

Preheat oven to 350° F.

Put the water in a medium pan or pot and place on the stove. Heat the water until it starts to simmer.

Add the livers and simmer for 2 minutes. Remove the livers with a slotted spoon and then mince them with a knife or mash them with a fork (see note next page). After mincing the livers, put them in a mixing bowl.

Add all the ingredients except the egg and tomato sauce.

Prepare the loaf as described in the recipe for Basic Meat Loaf (page 211), adding the egg and the tomato sauce at the appropriate times. Put the loaf in the pan and bake according to the instructions for Basic Meat Loaf.

Serve with mashed potatoes or rice, plus a green vegetable. →

DOCTOR'S NOTE

Calories: 125 per serving

This recipe hits a nutritional home run. For the pregnant woman who needs iron, this offers a good combination of low calories, lots of iron and vitamins, and protein. If you use ground veal in combination with chicken livers, a serving will provide you with 17.3 g protein (about 33% of the RDA), only 5 g fat, 4625 IU vitamin A (100% of the RDA), and 7 mg of niacin (about 50% of the RDA).

   One important note: as we explain on page 23, there are two types of iron present in dietary sources: heme iron, which is exclusively found in animal foods, and nonheme iron, which is found in foods of vegetable origin. Even though the mechanism is not yet entirely understood we know that heme iron is better absorbed and more easily transported across the placenta to the baby than the nonheme iron. Chicken livers are one of the richest sources of heme iron.

Note: Reserve the cooking liquid. If you think you need a little liquid to soften the loaf before putting it in the baking pan, use this nutritious liquid. Otherwise, use it within the next 24 hours to fortify a soup such as Scotch Broth (page 154), Emerald Soup (page 149), or any other soup that appeals to you.

La Milanese (Veal)

1 SERVING

When we think of Milan, we think of one of the most sophisticated cities in Europe, home of the La Scala opera house and the fashion elegance of Armani, Versace, and other great designers. It also has a wonderful local cuisine, with cotoletta di vitello alla milanese being one of the stars. In Austria, this same dish is called wienerschnitzel (which is not, as many people assume, a sausage), and in the United States it is called simply a breaded veal cutlet. But in the States this dish is a heavy affair, often buried under overbearing tomato sauce and industrial-tasting melted cheese. No one in Milan would touch that. What follows is a light, delicious version that would go perfectly with some chilled spinach or a leafy green salad. As a variation on the classic, however, you should take the option of using either a veal cutlet or a turkey fillet, which is less expensive and tastes fine. If you are making more than one, you probably will not need an egg for each cutlet. This also depends on the size of the eggs you use. A leftover cutlet may be served cold, buried under some freshly tossed arugula or other greens with a vinaigrette and perhaps a sliced tomato. A cold cutlet also is good in a lunch sandwich with lettuce and/or tomato.

¼ to ⅓ pound veal cutlet or turkey fillet

Unseasoned bread crumbs

Pinch freshly grated Parmesan or grana cheese (optional)

1 egg

Freshly ground pepper (optional)

1 tablespoon unsalted butter

1 wedge lemon

Pound the cutlet as thin as possible without punching a hole in it.

Put the bread crumbs (combined with the cheese) on a plate. Lightly beat the egg (with the pepper) in a flat bowl.

Press the cutlet into the bread crumbs on each side. Shake off the excess. Then dip the cutlet into the egg, letting the extra egg drip off. Put the cutlet back in the bread crumbs, thoroughly coating each side. Let the extra crumbs fall away.

Melt the butter in a medium skillet over moderate heat. Cook the cutlet quickly and carefully on both sides so that it is cooked through but does not burn.

Serve immediately with the lemon wedge so that juice may be squeezed on top, if desired.

The Perfect Veal Chop

1 Serving

Delicious, easy to prepare, and elegant, this is the kind of thing you should make when you want to treat yourself well.

1 tablespoon freshly squeezed lemon juice

1 tablespoon plain or herbed olive oil

1 garlic clove, minced

¼ teaspoon freshly ground pepper

½ pound veal loin chop, trimmed

1 wedge lemon

A few capers (optional)

Make a marinade by combining the lemon juice, oil, garlic, and pepper with a fork or whisk.

Pour most of the mixture on a plate and place the veal chop on top. Pour the rest of the marinade over the veal and leave it at room temperature.

Preheat the broiler.

After 15 minutes turn the veal and leave it for 5 minutes more.

Place the veal chop in a broiling pan, reserving the marinade. →

DOCTOR'S NOTE

Calories: 472 per serving

This simple dish will provide you with 36 g protein (more than 50% of the RDA), 27 g fat, and about 600 mg sodium. Because this sodium count represents the entire RDA, do not have this dish if you have preeclampsia or swelling of the hands and ankles. This makes an excellent choice to fulfill your protein quota. It also is recommended for the gestational diabetic, as it has virtually no carbohydrates. If your iron is low, this veal chop provides 33% of the RDA.

Broil 4 inches from the flame for 4 to 5 minutes per side, or until the chop is browned outside and still a little pink within.

Just before the veal is cooked, heat the marinade to a full boil in a saucepan, then turn off the heat. Add a few capers if desired.

Transfer the cooked chop to a warm plate, pour on the hot marinade, and serve.

Pan-Fried Steak

1 SERVING

Sometimes, when you are ravenously hungry and have a craving for a quick protein fix, a steak seems just right. If you make a large steak and can't eat it all, the meat is delicious cold or used in a sandwich (see Pita, Pita, Pita, page 140).

½ to ¾ pound sirloin steak, lean and trimmed

1 garlic clove, cut in half

Freshly ground pepper to taste

1 teaspoon unsalted butter

1 tablespoon olive oil

Rub the steak on both sides with half the garlic.

Grind some pepper on a plate and press the steak down so that the pepper attaches to the meat.

Gently melt the butter and heat the oil in a good pan large enough to easily contain the steak. Add the remaining garlic and whirl it around until it turns dark blond. Remove the garlic.

Add the steak and sauté over high heat until it reaches a desired state of doneness (about 5 minutes for rare, 7 minutes for medium, depending on the thickness of the steak).

Serve immediately, accompanied by brown rice (over which you might pour the pan juices) and a green vegetable.

As you have read elsewhere in this book, the excess estrogen produced by your body during pregnancy protects you from the effects of cholesterol deposition in your arteries for the duration of your pregnancy, so that the high fat content of this dish is not a real problem now.

DOCTOR'S NOTE

Calories: 696 per serving

Red meat is good for you when you are pregnant. This is because it is rich in iron and protein, very low in salt, and high in calories. One lean sirloin steak (½ pound) will provide you with 73 g protein (more than 100% of the RDA), 41.5 g fat (quite a high load!), and no carbohydrates. It also will give you 700 mg phosphorus (more than 50% of the RDA). As a nice surprise, the whole steak will only have 180 mg sodium, making it ideal for the times when ankle and hand swelling or high blood pressure is a problem. We also recommend this quick protein fix especially for the gestational diabetic, as it is virtually carbohydrate-free.

Moroccan Shepherd's Pie

4 TO 6 SERVINGS

Throughout the world there are recipes that combine chopped meat and mashed potatoes. Greece has moussaka; Scotland has its shepherd's pie; and Argentina has empanadas, a popular meat pie that sometimes combines the two ingredients. This particular dish is distinctly Moroccan because of the combination of spices. It is not spicy in the upset-stomach sense of the word but is fragrant and flavorful. It also reheats nicely if you can't eat the amount that you have prepared.

3 tablespoons olive oil

4 stalks of celery, chopped

2 onions, coarsely chopped

1½ pounds chopped beef or lamb (or a mixture of both)

3 tablespoons minced fresh parsley

1 teaspoon cinnamon

¼ teaspoon saffron (if available)

¼ teaspoon cumin or mace

¼ teaspoon nutmeg

3 tablespoons raisins (optional)

4 cups Mashed Potatoes (page 229)

Preheat the oven to 325° F.

Heat the oil in a large pan over a medium flame. Add the onions and celery and sauté for a few moments before adding the meat, 1 tablespoon of the parsley, ½ teaspoon of the cinnamon, ½ teaspoon of the saffron, the cumin, and the nutmeg. When you add the meat, turn down the heat so the ingredients do not cook too quickly.

When the meat is almost cooked, add the raisins, if you are using them, and continue to cook. The raisins should start to puff up as they cook.

Once the mixture is cooked, drain the fat and set the meat aside.

In the meantime, add the remaining cinnamon, saffron, and →

DOCTOR'S NOTE

Calories: 579 per serving (based on four servings)

This dish will go a long way toward supplying the daily nutrients you absolutely need. It is rich in protein (47 g per serving, well over 50% of the RDA), 27 g carbohydrates (which come almost exclusively from the mashed potatoes and which will supply 50% of the RDA), and only 10 g fat. We have used chopped lamb for the figures above, so if you decide to mix it with beef, these values will change slightly, depending on the quality and fat content of the chopped beef you choose.

Eating Healthy for a Healthy Baby

parsley to the mashed potatoes and whip them until they are frothy.

Lightly grease a flat, broad baking dish (for example, 9 x 13 x 2 inches) with olive oil or perhaps some of the cooking liquid from the pan. Add half of the mashed potatoes, smoothing them to form a nice even layer. Then add the meat mixture, distributing it evenly. Top with the rest of the potatoes and, if you are in an ambitious or decorative mood, smooth the potatoes with the side of a knife to form pretty patterns. Bake for 15 to 20 minutes, or until the surface is golden brown. Serve hot.

Simple Lamb Stew

4 SERVINGS

DOCTOR'S NOTE

Calories: 546 per serving

The amount of lamb per serving supplies about 25% of the RDA for potassium, which, as you may remember, is very important for the baby's nervous system and cardiac muscle functioning. It also contains 32.5 g protein (50% of the RDA). This dish also gives you about 40% of the RDA for phosphorus. If you are on a sodium-restricted diet, purchase a can of no-salt-added tomatoes.

This recipe is very easy to make. You can eat this stew fresh from the pot or store it for future use. Serve with a side dish of peas or a green salad for a fast, delicious lunch or dinner.

4 tablespoons olive oil

1 small onion, chopped

1 garlic clove, slivered

1½ pounds lean lamb meat, cut in large cubes

1 28-ounce can peeled Italian (San Marzano) tomatoes

¾ pound potatoes, peeled, cut in chunks

2 teaspoons rosemary, preferably fresh

Freshly ground pepper to taste

Pinch salt (optional)

In a large casserole or heavy pot, gently heat the oil over low heat. Add the onion and garlic and sauté briefly.

Add the lamb cubes, brown them lightly, then add the tomatoes (reserving the liquid), potatoes, rosemary, pepper, and salt.

Cover, cook gently for about 45 minutes, stirring occasionally to prevent the ingredients from sticking. This stew should not be overly soupy; however, if you want more liquid, add some sparingly from the canned tomatoes.

VEGETABLES

Vegetables are astonishing in their variety of color, flavor, shape, texture, and utility in cooking. They are rich in vitamins, minerals and dietary fiber, usually low in calories and are often very inexpensive.

Beautiful and tasty though they may be, vegetables arouse strong passions among both their admirers and detractors. Some vegetarians take on a special glow as they wax poetic about the earth's bounty. Popeye is hardly the only person to sing the praises of spinach. On the other hand, some unhappy vegetable eaters, from American presidents to finicky children, have not yet seen the light. More often than not, they have been subjected to soggy, overcooked vegetables that bear no resemblance to the ones you will be able to prepare using the recipes in this book.

In fact, we have included an abundance of vegetable recipes in this book so that each reader can find a few that appeal to her. Be sure to look for all-vegetable dishes in the recipe sections for appetizers (page 133), salads (page 155), soups (page 145) and pasta (page 171). If you are a vegetarian, there is enough here to keep you happy, but we must warn you to be sure to get sufficient protein from beans, legumes, and tofu. See page 9 for a fuller discussion about protein and vegetarians.

Although fresh vegetables are always preferable, certain vegetables (spinach, peas, broccoli, baby carrots, and squash) are also acceptable in frozen form as a substitute. However, you should generally steer clear of canned vegetables, which are laden with salt.

Because vegetables, in most cases, are seasonal foods, you should enjoy them when they are at their peak. Whether it is asparagus in March or tomatoes in August, there is something very beautiful about the idea of growing cycles, of generation and rebirth that occurs in nature as the earth selectively yields its bounty at different times throughout the year.

Basic Asparagus

For everything there is a season, and the noble asparagus that usually appears in mid-March is unquestionably a harbinger of spring. This vegetable has been prized since ancient times for its special flavor, its distinct appearance, and its association with the arrival of the fair time of year. Spring is often thought of as the time of birth and renewal in nature as well as religion, literature, and the hearts of young lovers. Cooks prize spring's bounty of young vegetables, tender lamb, and the arrival of fish such as shad and salmon. You may use asparagus as an accompaniment to practically all of the main courses in this book, as an appetizer, eaten cold as a snack, or as a main course. There is one simple rule: Asparagus should never be overcooked. Properly cooked asparagus will be bright green and firm and have a slight crunch when eaten. Mushy, water-logged asparagus is not worth eating. If you do overcook it (it can happen), purée the asparagus in a blender and use it as a base for soup or a sauce such as Gismonda (see page 199).

The amount of asparagus you need depends on your mood and what else you are eating at a particular meal. Whether you select fat or thin asparagus is purely personal choice. Bear in mind that thin asparagus cooks more quickly. Note that there are special asparagus pots you can buy, but you should only make this investment if asparagus is your favorite food and you have lots of room in your kitchen for extra pots and pans.

To cook basic asparagus, set a large pot of cold water to boil. Preferably the pot should be tall enough for the asparagus to stand up.

Wash the asparagus well and chop off the woody white ends. Some cooks say that if you hold an asparagus stalk with one end in each hand and bend the stalk, it will snap in the right place. Try this if you wish, but don't waste too much of the good stalks.

When the water is rapidly boiling, add the asparagus and let it cook. If the asparagus is standing, the stalks and tips should be completely immersed in water. If they are not standing, they should have some room to move about.

If you are using thin asparagus, test one after 1 minute by poking a fork in it. If the fork goes through, the asparagus is probably ready. Test fatter asparagus after about 2 minutes. Remember that

DOCTOR'S NOTE

Asparagus is a very appealing vegetable for the pregnant cook. It is very low in calories (only 30 per ¼ pound of cooked asparagus), has no carbohydrates, and virtually no fat (ideal for gestational diabetics). Per ¼ pound of cooked asparagus you will get 40 mg vitamin C (more than 50% of the RDA). Asparagus also contains some vitamin A and protein and is low in sodium.

a limp asparagus is overcooked. You may choose to taste one after you have done the fork test.

There are two ways to remove the asparagus from the pot. One is to empty the contents of the pot into a colander. If you are well along in your pregnancy and there is no one around to help you lift heavy things, then skim the asparagus out of the pot with a slotted spoon and put it in a colander.

You may eat asparagus hot, warm, or chilled without any sauce and it will be delicious. It might be a good idea to cook up to 2 pounds at a time and save some to eat cold as a snack or appetizer or for use in another recipe.

Asparagus au Faux Hollandaise

Prepare Faux Hollandaise Sauce according to the recipe (page 130). Adjust the seasonings to your taste.

Cook asparagus as for Basic Asparagus.

Serve hot, with some sauce spooned on top.

DOCTOR'S NOTE

This recipe will provide 70 cals for ¼ pound asparagus and 1 tablespoon of sauce.

Asparagus aux Fines Herbes

Prepare Vinaigrette aux Fines Herbes (page 126).

Cook the asparagus as for Basic Asparagus.

Serve hot with some vinaigrette. Or you can chill the asparagus and dress it with this vinaigrette.

This is good as an appetizer, side dish, or main course.

DOCTOR'S NOTE

This recipe provides 155 calories per ¼ pound of asparagus plus 1 tablespoon of vinaigrette.

Asparagus Benedict

DOCTOR'S NOTE

1 serving of this recipe will yield 235 cals and 8 g protein.

Preheat the oven to 325° F.

Cook the asparagus as for Basic Asparagus.

While the asparagus is cooking, make 1 poached egg.

Prepare Faux Hollandaise Sauce (page 130).

Place 3 or 4 asparagus spears in a lightly buttered baking dish or ramekin, put the poached egg on top, then spoon on some Faux Hollandaise Sauce.

Bake for a couple of minutes to heat through.

Serve immediately with a couple of sprigs of fresh parsley. Have the peppermill nearby. This is a nice brunch dish.

Asparagus Bismarck

DOCTOR'S NOTE

This recipe will give you 235 cals and 7 g protein.

Bismarck *is a general term for food topped with a egg fried sunny-side up. These dishes are popular in central Europe, but it is not certain if Herr Bismarck favored this style of cooking or if some chef was trying to pay him an honor. Nonetheless, veal and beef are often served à la Bismarck and so is asparagus.*

Cook 6 asparagus spears as for Basic Asparagus.

Fry 1 egg, sunny-side up and place it atop the cooked aspargus.

Serve. This makes a good brunch dish.

Asparagus Parmesan

DOCTOR'S NOTE

This recipe will provide about 155 cals, 5 g protein, and 68 mg calcium.

Cook asparagus as for Basic Asparagus and immediately transfer it to a warm plate.

Pour a little melted unsalted butter or margarine on top. Then grate fresh imported Parmesan or grana cheese over all.

Serve immediately as an appetizer.

Baked Asparagus Rolls

For every 3 fat or 4 thin asparagus stalks you should have 1 very thin slice prosciutto or good ham.

Preheat the oven to 350° F.

Cook the asparagus as for Basic Asparagus. When cooked, set it aside to cool slightly.

In the meantime, grate some fresh Parmesan or grana cheese.

To assemble, take a piece of ham, sprinkle a little cheese on one side, and then add the asparagus. Wrap the ham around the stalks to form a tight bundle.

Put each bundle in a lightly greased (with unsalted butter) ramekin or ovenproof baking dish. Dot each bundle with a little more butter.

Bake for 10 minutes, or until it seems like the cheese is melted and the ham is hot. Serve 1 bundle as an appetizer or more as a main course.

DOCTOR'S NOTE

Calories: 213 for each roll

Red Cabbage–Green Apples

12 SERVINGS (6 CUPS)

Loaded with vitamin C, this dish is delicious hot and also makes a good cold side dish. Make a lot and keep some in the refrigerator.

3 cups freshly shredded red cabbage

3 cups sliced Granny Smith or other tart green apple

4 tablespoons freshly squeezed lemon juice

3½ cups boiling water

⅛ teaspoon ground cloves (optional)

¼ teaspoon ground nutmeg (optional)

½ cup raisins→

DOCTOR'S NOTE

Calories: 44 per serving

A serving of this salad will provide you with 63 mg vitamin K (100% of the RDA). This combination of ingredients (cabbage, apples, and raisins) provides a load of fiber and is an excellent dish to have if you are constipated. It is also quite low in carbohydrates and calories making it an ideal dish to have if you have been diagnosed with gestational diabetes or are watching your weight gain.

Wash the whole head of cabbage in cold water and place it on a proper cutting board (see page 94). Then cut the cabbage in quarters using a sharp knife. Shred one of the quarters by holding it firmly to the cutting board while cutting downward with the knife in the other hand. If you have a food processor and prefer to shred the cabbage that way, go right ahead. When you have shredded 3 cups of cabbage, wrap the rest of the cabbage in plastic or put it in a plastic container and refrigerate. Put the shredded cabbage in a large saucepan and set aside.

Slice the apples and top them with 1 tablespoon of the lemon juice to prevent oxidation. Put the apples in the saucepan. Add the boiling water, cloves, and nutmeg to the saucepan. Simmer uncovered for 15 minutes. Add the raisins. Simmer 5 minutes more. Add the remaining fresh lemon juice, stir well, and serve.

Lemon Yogurt Slaw

6 SERVINGS (3 CUPS)

For noshing or as a side dish, yogurt slaw delivers the goods: vitamins A and C, calcium, protein, fiber, and taste. See the recipe for Red Cabbage–Green Apples (page 223) for instructions about shredding cabbage.

DOCTOR'S NOTE

Calories: 34 per serving

This refreshing side dish provides more nutrition than many main courses. Each serving delivers 2000 IU vitamin A (50% of the RDA), 41.5 mg vitamin C (more than 50% of the RDA), and some calcium. Remember that cabbage is gas producing, so if you suffer from indigestion or flatulence eat this dish in moderation.

3 cups of carefully shredded green cabbage (or use some red cabbage for color and taste)

1 cup freshly grated carrots

2 teaspoons Dijon mustard

¼ teaspoon freshly ground pepper

1 tablespoon freshly squeezed lemon juice

½ cup lemon yogurt

¼ cup raisins (optional)

After washing and shredding the cabbage and washing and grating the carrots, you are ready to prepare the dressing. Stir the mustard, pepper, and lemon juice into a bowl until the ingredients are thoroughly blended.

Add the yogurt and blend well. Toss the dressing with the cabbage and carrots (and, if you wish, some raisins) until all the elements are combined. Serve cold.

This keeps 24 to 36 hours when stored in a tightly covered container in the refrigerator.

Carrot-Potato Purée

4 TO 6 SERVINGS

D*o not be deceived by the number of servings. This stuff is so good that it is addictive. It also goes down very well when you are feeling queasy and is packed with vitamin A and minerals. The perfect morning sickness food, midafternoon snack, or accompaniment to meat dishes. Carrot-Potato Puree is delicious hot or chilled, when it becomes custardy. Make a lot of purée at one time and save it.*

½ pound potatoes, peeled and cut in chunks

2 pounds carrots, peeled and cut in chunks (or use baby carrots)

2 tablespoons plain yogurt, buttermilk, or unsalted butter

½ teaspoon nutmeg (optional)

In a large pot of boiling water, add the potatoes first. After 5 minutes add the carrots and cook until they are soft enough that they can be poked through by a fork. Drain the vegetables and put them in a bowl.

Mash the vegetables (with a fork, ricer, or potato masher) into a purée, gradually adding either the yogurt, buttermilk, or butter and nutmeg. If you prefer, put the ingredients in a blender and purée them, making sure the mixture does not become too soft.

VARIATION

Cook a couple of parsnips with the carrots and potatoes and purée them all. In this case, eliminate the nutmeg and use a little pepper.

DOCTOR'S NOTE

Calories: 113 per serving

This delicious side dish has many advantages. It is low in calories and carbohydrates (only 16 g, 25% of the RDA), provides 1200 IU vitamin A (25% of the RDA), and virtually no fat. It is a perfect dish for when your doctor says you have been gaining weight too fast or, after delivery, when you are trying to shed a few pounds.

Cauliflower-Pepper Crunch

4 TO 6 SERVINGS

DOCTOR'S NOTE

Calories: 187 per serving

This recipe is yet another winner for the pregnant woman who needs roughage and vitamins but is watching her calorie intake. Assuming that the recipe will provide 6 servings, each serving will yield no carbohydrates or protein, about 13 g fat and 100 mg vitamin C (150% of the RDA). Keep in mind that cauliflower is gas producing, and if this proves to be a problem in early pregnancy, try the recipe later when this discomfort is less common.

The key to Cauliflower-Pepper Crunch is that the cauliflower should be cooked only until it is hot and crunchy and should be eaten right away. You may vary the color of your peppers according to seasonal availability, but you always need 3 of them.

1 tablespoon Dijon mustard

2 tablespoons wine vinegar

Freshly ground pepper to taste

7 tablespoons olive oil

1 head of cauliflower, approximately 1 pound, thoroughly washed and broken into florets

1 garlic clove, mashed (optional)

1 yellow pepper, cut into ½-inch wide strips

1 red pepper, cut into ½-inch wide strips

1 green pepper, cut into ½-inch wide strips

Put the mustard, vinegar and pepper in a jar. Close the lid tight and shake the jar vigorously. Open the jar, add 6 tablespoons of the olive oil. Close the jar again and shake well. Set this dressing aside.

In a large pot of lightly salted boiling water, cook the cauliflower florets until they are just hot and still crunchy.

Meanwhile, heat the remaining oil in a medium-size saucepan over moderate heat and add the garlic (do not burn it). Then add the peppers and sauté them until they are just past the point of crunchiness, but not quite soft.

When the cauliflower florets are cooked, drain them well in a colander and then put them in a large serving bowl. Top them with the cooked peppers and their pan juices. Toss well. Give the jar of dressing a good shake and pour the dressing over the vegetables. Toss well and serve immediately.

The potato, which has long been a staple in most world cuisines, is prized by cooks and gourmets for its versatility, low cost, and nutritional content. Baked, boiled, mashed, or roasted, potatoes go well with most main courses. Also, plain or mashed potatoes are friendly foods when your stomach is upset. They contain no fat and more vitamin C than you might expect (31 mg per potato; the RDA is 70 mg). There are various types of potatoes you can select. The larger, coarser-skinned, more rectangular potato from Maine, Idaho, and many places in between, is preferable for baking. Smaller, rounder, thin-skinned potatoes are better suited for boiling. You should peel these smaller potatoes before boiling them. A small flavorful potato with a red skin, known as the Red Bliss potato, is usually eaten with the skin on. Here are various ways to put potatoes to good use.

About Potatoes

Baked Potato

Preheat the oven to 425° F.

Scrub a baking potato well, dry thoroughly with a paper towel or cloth. Prick the potato in two places on the upper side with a fork.

Bake for 45 to 60 minutes, depending upon the size of the potato. It will be correctly baked when it yields to the press of a finger. If you are using an organically grown potato, eat the skin as well—it is loaded with minerals.

DOCTOR'S NOTE

One baked potato contains 145 cals, 4 g protein, no fat, 33 g carbohydrates (about 50% of the RDA), and 31 mg vitamin C .

Stuffed Potato

Bake a potato as for Baked Potato (above).

Slit the potato lengthwise. Carefully remove the potato with a teaspoon and rice it (cut into little pieces by running the tines of a fork through the potato) in a bowl. Blend with 1 tablespoon low-fat yogurt or cottage cheese or a low-fat melting cheese, such as Cheddar or Jarlsberg. Place the mixture back in the potato skin. →

Reheat briefly, if you wish to warm or melt the ingredients you stuffed the potato with.

DOCTOR'S NOTE

To give you an idea of the nutritional content of a stuffed potato, if you use some broccoli florets and 1 tablespoon low-fat yogurt, you will have 156 cals, 27 g carbohydrates, and 106 mg vitamin C (more than 100% of the RDA).

VARIATIONS

For other versions of stuffed potatoes, use your imagination and follow your taste. Any combination of ingredients, when blended with the riced potato and stuffed back into the potato skin, will make a wonderful lunch. Some suggestions for stuffing potatoes: yogurt and broccoli; sautéed chopped meat, tomato, and Cheddar cheese; boiled baby shrimp and lemon juice; sautéed peppers and onions; sautéed mushrooms; diced ham and cooked peas; apple sauce (see page 244); chopped cooked spinach and 1 tablespoon of low-fat yogurt; sautéed lamb and mint leaves; ratatouille.

Boiled Potatoes

Scrub small or medium potatoes. Peel the skin, unless you are using Red Bliss potatoes.

Place the peeled potatoes in a pot, cover with cold water and boil 20 to 25 minutes, or until one of the potatoes can be split with a fork.

Drain, reserving the liquid for use in soup.

Season the potatoes as you wish. Good seasonings include fresh chopped parsley, freshly ground pepper, paprika, fresh rosemary, and chopped chives.

Cold Potatoes

Make Boiled Potatoes.

Cut the potatoes into large pieces and chill.

Serve as a side dish with good olive oil drizzled on top and, if you wish, some fresh rosemary. Or use Rosemary Olive Oil (page 127).

Potato Salad

Make Cold Potatoes, but do not add oil.

Mix the potatoes with 1 teaspoon prepared mustard (such as Dijon or Dusseldorf) to every 3 teaspoons cholesterol-free mayonnaise or low-fat yogurt.

Add ingredients you enjoy: minced onion or chive, pepper or paprika, chopped celery, shredded carrots, or raisins.

DOCTOR'S NOTE

Per potato, this recipe will give you 186 cals, 43 g carbohydrates, 1 g fat, and 36 mg vitamin C.

Mashed Potatoes

Cook 8 potatoes as directed for Boiled Potatoes.

Mash them in a bowl with a fork or potato masher. Add 1 tablespoon unsalted butter (or margarine), ½ teaspoon salt (optional), 1 teaspoon freshly ground pepper, and ½ cup hot milk.

Beat until fluffy and serve immediately.

DOCTOR'S NOTE

Each serving (about 1 potato) will give you 188 cals, 28 g carbohydrates, and 9 g fat.

Sweet Potatoes

Tasty and very high in vitamin A. Use medium-size moist sweet potatoes.

Preheat the oven to 425° F.

Scrub the potatoes well and then dry thoroughly with a paper towel or a cloth. Prick each potato in two places on top using the tines of a fork.

Bake for 30 to 45 minutes, until soft to the touch.

Slit open immediately and serve (perhaps with Apricot Sauce, page 131).

VARIATIONS

Boil sweet potatoes as you would regular potatoes. They are good as is or mashed.

DOCTOR'S NOTE

Each sweet potato will provide 148 cals, 34 g carbohydrates, 27 mg vitamin C, and 22,000 IU vitamin A (about 500% of the RDA).

Sweet Potatoes and Prunes

Boil sweet potatoes as for Boiled Potatoes. Mash.

Sliver pitted prunes and combine thoroughly with the potatoes. This delicious combination—loaded with vitamins and iron—is perfect with roasted meat or by itself, hot or cold.

Potatoes Provençal

4 GENEROUS SERVINGS

The thought of Provence brings to mind sunny shores with seaside cafés, the paintings of van Gogh, Picasso, and Braque; ancient Roman buildings and herb-scented meals enjoyed at country inns. Herbs such as tarragon, thyme, rosemary, and basil abound in Provence and are ubiquitous in the area's cuisine, which—based as it is on fish, wonderful fruits and vegetables, herbs, and garlic—is extraordinarily healthy. These potatoes will provide friendly accompaniment to many entrées. They are also delicious when lightly mashed and served with a drizzling of good olive oil. Only if you have no access to fresh herbs should you consider using dried herbs in about half the quantity called for with fresh ones. But the glory of this dish is the flavor and fragrance of fresh herbs.

4 tablespoons extra virgin olive oil

2 garlic cloves, peeled and cut into slices

2½ pounds of small, thin-skinned potatoes, skins on, well-scrubbed

4 sprigs fresh rosemary

2 sprigs fresh tarragon

4 sprigs fresh thyme

Salt and freshly ground pepper to taste

Heat the olive oil in a large frying pan over medium heat. Add the garlic slivers a few moments after you start heating the oil.

Make sure not to burn the garlic. When the oil is hot, add the potatoes, herbs, and little bit of salt and some freshly ground pepper.

Cook for 15 to 20 minutes, turning the ingredients often so that they do not stick to the pan. Cut one potato in half and taste to see if it almost done to your liking. Because potatoes vary in size and texture, you will need to use your judgment. You will probably want to cook the potatoes a few more minutes.

Cover the pan, reduce the heat, and cook for 5 more minutes. Taste the other half of the potato you cut, and if necessary, cook for a few more minutes with the pan uncovered.

Serve hot, tepid, cool, or cold—these potatoes are delicious at any temperature.

get a generous 886 mg potassium (43% of the RDA) and only 13 g fat. Serve it with a high-protein entrée and a green vegetable for a perfectly balanced meal.

About Spinach

Popeye is not the only person who ever did well by eating spinach. It is loaded with iron and does taste good if you toss away your prejudices. Raw spinach as part of a salad is nice indeed, and there is something wonderful about a side dish of chilled spinach. It marries well with most fish and poultry dishes and tastes good as a snack. Make a lot of spinach at one time and keep it for use in omelets (see page 143), for stuffing in tomatoes or zucchini, to put in hot chicken broth (see page 146) or lentil soup topped with grated cheese, or to bake on top of chicken (page 194) or fish fillets (page 182). For cooking purposes, frozen leaf spinach is acceptable, but if you plan to eat it raw or chilled, you must use fresh spinach. In cooking fresh spinach, you will discover that a lot of it, when cooked, turns out to be much less. A rule of thumb in cooking is that a 10-ounce package of frozen spinach will yield the same amount as 1 pound fresh. Always save the cooking liquid for use in soups, gravies, or high-powered drinks from the blender.

Chilled Spinach

Wash fresh spinach carefully, getting rid of all the sand. Yank off the tough stems.

Place the spinach in a pot over low heat and, using only the water clinging to the leaves, and perhaps a little more if you think →

DOCTOR'S NOTE

There are 30 calories per ¼ cup of raw spinach or ½

cup of cooked spinach. This same amount of cooked spinach will give you 7300 IU vitamin A (more than 100% of the RDA), 82 mcg folate (about 25% of the RDA), 89 mcg vitamin K (more than 100% of the RDA), plus other good nutrients: 106 mg calcium, 2.4 mg iron, and more than 100% of the RDA for vitamin C.

the leaves are too dry, steam only until the spinach becomes soft or you will cook out all of the nutrients and the spinach may stick to the pan.

Using a slotted spoon to move the spinach to the side of the pot, press out all the liquid for other uses.

Chill the spinach in a well-sealed bowl or container. Serve ice cold with a wedge of lemon and some good olive oil at hand as condiments. Delicious.

Frozen Spinach

Cook according to package directions. Press out all liquid, using a slotted spoon against the side of the pot, to save for other uses. Store spinach until needed.

Creamed Spinach

Cook frozen spinach and press out liquid. Combine spinach with about 2 tablespoons of buttermilk and a pinch of nutmeg.

Heat gently in a pot and serve immediately.

You may also make this with fresh spinach, but it is less time-consuming to use frozen.

About Tomatoes

This is a delicate subject for anyone who really loves tomatoes. Once upon a time, tomatoes came from the garden at the peak of their ripeness and brimmed over with juice and flavor. Nowadays, most so-called fresh tomatoes are bred and grown for durability rather than flavor, so that most of them would be more useful as doorstops or paperweights than as a protagonist in a meal. A good tomato will be a bright red and will have a lovely fragrance. They come in three main types: (1) beefsteak, the big, fat round tomatoes that are the most familiar to us, (2) plum, a smaller, egg-shaped tomato that often has less juice than the beefsteak, but is very flavorful and is good for cooking as well as eating, and (3) cherry, the small juicy tomatoes that appear in salads but are also good for Crudités (see page 136) and for snacking.

How can one best appreciate tomatoes? The first way is to consume them with abandon during their peak season (late summer). Eat them by themselves, as you would most fruit; cut them into salads; slice them to use in sandwiches or as side dishes; stuff them with tuna or salmon; broil them, or bake them. Tomatoes are the star in many spaghetti sauces, and fresh tomatoes should be employed whenever they are available.

Second, because it also is possible to buy good tomatoes in other seasons (although they will be more expensive), you may enjoy them then too. Hothouse or "hydroponically grown" tomatoes come periodically from Israel and Holland, and ripe tomatoes come during the South American summer (the winter months in North America). In addition, Florida and Mexico have good winter crops that are shipped all across the continent. Use them in the same ways you would use local tomatoes in season.

Finally, there are excellent canned tomatoes in supermarkets, most of which come from Italy. Be careful in reading the labels on tomato cans to note whether the tomatoes are actually from Italy. Many brands have Italian names but sell inferior tomatoes from other places. The best of the best Italian tomatoes are San Marzano (this is a type, not a brand), most of which are grown and packed near Naples. They will be marked as such on the label. Most Italian tomatoes are *pelati*, that is, they are peeled. They are ideal for making sauces or for any recipe that calls for peeled tomatoes. Redpack, an American brand, has its admirers and is usually available if you

DOCTOR'S NOTE ABOUT TOMATOES

About ½ pound tomatoes (typically, one large or two medium tomatoes) contains 45 cals, no fat or carbohydrates, 27 mg calcium, 500 mg potassium (about 25% of the RDA), 1860 IU vitamin A (about 40% of the RDA), and 50 mg vitamin C (about 70% of the RDA).

cannot locate Italian tomatoes. Note also that you may buy crushed tomatoes (Italian or American), which are excellent if you need tomato pulp for a recipe. Crushed tomatoes are very useful for making a fast, delicious tomato sauce (see recipe on page 128).

And there is tomato paste. Buy a tube of imported Italian tomato paste and use it stingily. A little drop imparts great flavor and color to many dishes. Store the tube in the refrigerator once you have opened it.

As you can see, you do not have to endure the mealy, orange rocks wrapped in plastic that most markets try to pass off as tomatoes. Where, by the way, do you think the term "tough tomato" came from? Use real tomatoes as described above, and you will enjoy good tomato flavor all year in one form or another.

Baked Tomatoes

Preheat the oven to 375° F.

You will need one beefsteak-type tomato per serving. Wash it well before using.

The simplest way to bake a tomato is to cut it in half horizontally and scoop out a lot of the seeds. Add some chopped fresh herbs (parsley, chives, etc.), some minced garlic, a drop of olive oil or butter, and top with a bit of freshly grated Parmesan cheese and perhaps some bread crumbs.

Bake for 10 to 15 minutes.

Eat this as a snack, an appetizer, or the vegetable course in a meal. If there are other flavors or tastes you want to add or substitute, use your tastebuds and imagination.

Baked Stuffed Tomatoes

Preheat the oven to 350° F.

Use 1 beefsteak-type tomato per serving. Wash it well. Cut the tomato horizontally about one-quarter from the top and save the cap. Scoop out and discard many of the seeds, but try to save some of the liquid. Also scoop out the meat from the center of the tomato and put it in a bowl. Chop or mash the tomato meat coarsely and add whatever tomato liquid you saved.

Now comes time for improvisation.

Combine ingredients that you think go well together in the bowl that contains the tomato meat. Add herbs and freshly ground pepper to taste and stuff the tomato's cavity with the mixture. Cover with the cap if you want to be decorative. This will also prevent the ingredients on top from getting too brown.

Bake in a lightly oiled ovenproof dish for 10 to 15 minutes, just until all the ingredients are hot and any cheese has melted.

A baked stuffed tomato, like Stuffed Potatoes (page 227), is a perfect meal in a container. A mixture of different ingredients (protein, grain, vegetable) stuffed in a tomato will deliver a complete nutrient load.

STUFFING IDEAS

There are so many items that you can bake in a stuffed tomato, that your only limitation is your creativity. Look in your refrigerator for any leftovers that might taste good when baked in a tomato. There are many vegetables and grains that will go well inside a tomato: chopped onions; grated carrots; chopped celery; sliced mushrooms; red, yellow, or green peppers; olives; cooked rice; cooked barley; and cooked bulghur or couscous. A few bread crumbs may be used to bind other ingredients together, but don't overdo it. Raisins, currants, and unsalted nuts also go well with cooked grains and cooked chopped meat. Among the many proteins you may use are cooked chopped meat; diced ham, chicken, or turkey; chopped hard-boiled egg; and melting cheeses such as Cheddar, Gruyère, Appenzeller, Swiss, unsalted mozzarella, grated Parmesan and grated Romano. You may use any flaked fish that is left over after you have cooked fish fillets or canned tuna or salmon. Another favorite is cooked baby shrimp.

VARIATIONS

Here are some interesting combinations: drained tuna, chopped onion, celery and carrot, and cheddar or Swiss cheese (a tuna melt); cooked rice, onions, cooked chopped meat (beef, lamb, turkey, or chicken), raisins, and almonds; cooked rice, chives, cooked baby shrimp, and grated Parmesan; cooked rice, diced meat (ham, chicken, or turkey), and Gruyère, Swiss, or Cheddar cheese; split cherry tomatoes, diced unsalted mozzarella, torn basil leaves, and olives.

Broiled Tomatoes

DOCTOR'S NOTE

If you use 1 pound of tomatoes with 4 tablespoons olive oil and 2 tablespoons vinegar to make 4 servings, 1 serving will contain about 143 cals.

Preheat the broiler.

Take smaller beefsteak-type tomatoes, cut them in half horizontally, scoop out some of the seeds and brush the tomato halves with a little olive oil. Top, if you wish, with some freshly minced parsley and minced garlic (these toppings are optional). Instead of parsley you may use basil or, if you omit the garlic, either oregano, tarragon, or fines herbes.

Put the tomatoes in a lightly oiled pan and broil until they ooze some of their juice. A broiled tomato will look a little flatter than a baked tomato.

It is a perfect accompaniment to grilled meat, a plain chicken supreme or turkey fillet, a plain fish fillet, or an omelet. Broiled tomatoes are also delicious served cold.

Tomatoes Provençal

This is a form of tomato salad that is popular in the south of France.

Take good tomatoes of any kind (beefsteak, plum, or cherry) and chop them into large bite-size pieces. Put them in a bowl or dish, preferably one that has a cover.

Add lots of chopped parsley and minced garlic.

Add excellent olive oil and red wine vinegar in a ratio of 2 parts oil to every 1 part vinegar. How much you add depends on how many tomatoes you use. (Don't worry if you use a lot. If there is leftover liquid in the bowl, you may use the liquid either for more tomatoes or as the base of a salad dressing.)

Combine the ingredients gently so that the tomatoes don't fall apart but are able to mingle with the other ingredients. Cover the bowl (use plastic wrap if your bowl does not have a cover) and let marinate for at least a few hours.

The result will be fragrant and delicious. This combination keeps (and improves) for up to 3 days. Serve the tomatoes with only a little bit of the dressing. Tomatoes Provençal are delicious as the accompaniment to an omelet of Swiss or Gruyère cheese. It is excellent with drained, flaked tuna fish and lettuce in a bowl or in a sandwich. Try some spooned over a sautéed chicken supreme, turkey fillet, fish fillet or La Milanese (Veal) (page 223).

OTHER TOMATO IDEAS

The classic combination of fresh unsalted mozzarella, fresh basil leaves, and fresh tomatoes, called Insalata Caprese, is only as good as the quality of its ingredients. It has become a very chic appetizer or main course at tables all over North America. See the recipe on page 165, among the salads. The Roman dish Spaghetti con Pomodoro Crudo can be made in very little time and with great facility. It uses fresh tomatoes and very little else. See the recipe on page 174.

A few words about sun-dried tomatoes: These expensive little pieces of leather became all the rage a few years ago and most cooks use them incorrectly. They were originally the product of necessity: farmers and cooks in the Liguria region of Italy (the Italian Riviera) would dry tomatoes and put them in oil to conserve them for the seasons when fresh tomatoes were not available. They would then be reconstituted with oil or water and used as tomatoes in cooking. Nouvelle chefs often use them as tough little pieces of intense tomato flavor that appear in all kinds of dishes. Use them if you wish, but they are not recommended from this quarter.

$\mathcal{B}$*aked Zucchini and Onions*

4 SERVINGS

The virtues of this dish are many: It is easily prepared, can be kept for future use, and may be had as a main course, side dish, or snack. It delivers protein, vitamins, and flavor and can be eaten with relative abandon as it is not terribly caloric.

1 cup sweet onions, sliced in thin rings

1 pound zucchini and/or yellow squash, cut in ¼-inch-
thick discs

2 cups grated low-fat Swiss cheese

⅛ teaspoon salt

Freshly ground pepper to taste

Pinch fresh rosemary (optional)

Preheat the oven to 325° F.

Steam the onions and the zucchini for 5 to 10 minutes, depending how firm or tender you want the vegetables to be. This can be done by placing the vegetables in a colander that you can suspend over a pot of boiling water.

Combine the vegetables with 1½ cups of the cheese, and the salt, pepper, and rosemary.

Grease a baking dish with a little olive oil and put in the vegetables. Sprinkle the remaining cheese on top. Bake in oven for 45 minutes (more or less depending to your own taste). Serve hot, warm or even chilled the next day.

FRUIT

The color, beauty, and taste sensations that exist in the great variety of fruit available to us is a never-ending source of pleasure for happy cooks and eaters. Fruits serve as snacks, breakfast foods, as a side dish or on center stage in lunch and dinner, and of course, as desserts. They can be used to flavor meats, they can be blended to make great drinks, or they can be baked into wonderful loaves and crisps.

Devote a few minutes to reading About Fruit Salad. A wise eater always has delicious fresh fruit salad available for breakfasts, snacks, or desserts. You need only use the fruits that most please you.

There are other ideas for using fruit, plus a recipe for that classic staple apple sauce, which is soothing if you are queasy, blends well with mashed potatoes, and makes an excellent side dish for roast meats.

A wonderful, balanced lunch, snack, or dessert is fruit, cheese, and good bread or low-salt crackers such as crispbreads from Norway and Sweden. Grapes, apples, and pears are the most typical fruits for cheese, but others, such as peaches and cherries, also make subtle choices. Select hard cheeses such as aged Parmesan or Cheddar, or creamy cheeses such as Brie, Camembert (a bit fragrant), or Gourmandise. If you are watching your fat intake, there are many delicious low-fat cheeses, such as certain Emmenthals (Swiss), Goudas, and munster. Sheep and goat's milk cheeses are delectable, although some people are allergic to them. Check with your doctor if you are unsure.

ABOUT FRUIT SALAD

Fruit salad is one of the cornerstones in the cooking repertoire of the pregnant gourmet. First of all, you should immediately put out of your head the notion that fruit salad comes in a can or jar, packed in heavy syrup, and has one excessively red cherry for everyone to fight over. Real fruit salad is made of fresh fruit that is at the peak of its ripeness. Canned pineapple packed in juice is really the only canned fruit that can hold its own with its fresh cousins.

You may use any fruit in combination with any other, as long as the flavors, colors, and textures please you. There are only two important rules to remember. First, fruit that oxidizes, such as apples and pears, must be doused with lemon or lime juice as soon as it is cut. Second, bananas should be added at the last minute. They should not be refrigerated in a salad and they should not spend much time in the company of other fruits. If you observe these rules, your fruit salad will be a success.

You may combine two fruits that pair well, such as strawberries and bananas or go all out and put together a large combination of fruits, including citrus, apples or pears, stone fruit (peaches, nectarines, plums, and apricots), seedless grapes, pitted cherries, melons, berries, coconut, guava, mango, and even more exotic tropical fruits.

In preparing fruits for a salad, be sure that they are fresh, ripe, cleaned thoroughly, peeled (if that is indicated), and cut in bite-size pieces. Put the fruit pieces in a large glass or earthenware bowl and douse with some lemon or lime juice (or a little orange or grapefruit juice), even if there are no apples or pears in the salad. Toss gently with a spoon so that the fruit is combined but nothing is smashed.

This may seem like a lot of work, but it is the kind of task you can do seated at a table with the washed fruit placed in front of you. All you need is a good knife, a cutting board, a plate to put the pits and peels, and the bowl that will hold the fruit salad.

Make a lot at one time and this process will not seem so labor-intensive as you enjoy the salad for 3 to 4 days. Fruit contains a wide range of vitamins and nutrients, particularly vitamins A and C.

FRUIT SALAD IDEAS

Breakfast: Fruit salad topped with a dollop of low-fat yogurt or low-salt cottage cheese accompanied, perhaps, by toast, a muffin, or a piece of loaf. Fruit salad, drained of any liquid, may be added to dry cereal. Make a shake of milk, milk solids, fruit salad, and perhaps, ice.

Lunch: A large bowl of fruit salad topped, perhaps, with wheat germ, nuts, seeds, raisins, and cut dried fruit such as prunes, figs, and dates. Serve with a protein such as low-fat yogurt or low-salt cottage cheese. Fruit salad that is packed in a good container and kept cold makes a perfect lunch to be brought to work.

Snack: A small bowl of fruit salad and a fruit salad shake are ideal snacks.

Dinner: If you don't want something heavy, have the fruit

salad as described for lunch. Fruit salad also makes an interesting side dish with certain meats, such as roast pork.

Dessert: There is no dessert more perfect than fruit salad.

Special Combination: In Europe, at the height of berry season, there is nothing more delicious than small fresh berries in combination, topped with a little lemon juice. Use strawberries, blueberries, raspberries, currants, blackberries, elderberries, and boysenberries. These berry combinations make particularly wonderful shakes with milk, milk solids, and ice.

DOCTOR'S NOTE
Calories: 148 per serving

The calorie count we provide for this fruit salad is somewhat arbitrary: For nutritional analysis we made our fruit salad with 1 pound apples, 2 bananas, and 1 pint strawberries and seasoned it with 1 tablespoon lemon juice. This provided 4 servings. Of course, you may vary the fruits for your salad, according to freshness, season, and your imagination, but chances are the caloric count will vary only slightly. At any rate, each serving of fruit salad will provide a low-calorie snack or part of a meal, which is high in vitamin C (this example has 54 mg, 25% of the RDA), and moderate in carbohydrates; it can be enjoyed at any time during your pregnancy. It is especially good for the first trimester when you are searching for light snacks, or later on, if you have gestational diabetes and are craving something sweet but have to watch your glucose intake.

Nutrition Counts for Common Fruits

Fruits	Calories	Vitamins A (IU)	C (mg)	K (mg)	Carbohydrates (g)	Protein (g)
Apple, 1 med, with skin	81	74	8	159	21.1	0.3
Apricots, 3 med	51	2769	11	313	11.8	1.5
Banana, 1 med	105	92	10	451	26.7	1.2
Blueberries, 1 cup	82	145	19	129	20.5	1.0
Cantaloupe, 1 cup pieces	57	5158	68	494	13.4	1.4
Grapes, 1 cup	58	92	4	176	15.8	0.6
Orange, 1 med	65	256	80	250	16.3	1.4
Peach, 1 med	37	465	6	171	9.7	0.6
Pear, 1 med	98	33	7	208	25.1	0.7
Pineapple, 1 cup pieces	77	35	24	175	19.2	0.6
Plum, 1 med	36	213	6	113	8.6	0.5
Strawberries 1 cup whole berries	55	90	88	244	12.5	1.0

NOTE: All fruits are *very* low in fat and most have less than 0.25 g per serving.

Poached Dried Fruit

8 Servings

Good as a dessert; snack; or meal with yogurt, cottage cheese, nuts, and seeds.

3½ cups cold water

1 tablespoon honey (optional)

2 teaspoons anise seed

Zest of 1 lemon, cut in ½-inch strips

½ pound dried apricots

½ pound dried pears

½ pound raisins or dried cherries

In a large pot combine the water, honey, anise seed, and lemon zest (the white lining beneath the peel) and bring to a simmer over low heat.

Add the apricots and pears. If necessary, add more water to cover fruit. Simmer, covered, for 5 minutes.

Add raisins or cherries, cover and simmer for another 5 to 10 minutes, or until the fruit is tender.

Remove zest, if you wish, and serve hot, warm, or cool with some of the liquid spooned over the fruit.

DOCTOR'S NOTE

Calories: 143 per serving

This delicious recipe might prove to be your best ally in the fight against constipation. One low-calorie serving provides a good amount of roughage, 36 g carbohydrates, and 850 IU vitamin A (almost 25% of the RDA).

Apple Sauce

8 Servings (8 cups)

This is a basic recipe, one that will provide you with a food to snack on, to use as a side dish, and to use in baking or in combination with other edibles. For example, apple sauce blended with mashed potatoes (called "Heaven and Earth" in Germany, where it is popular) makes a great side dish for ham, pork, and grilled meats of all types. Try apple sauce combined with puréed raspberries or chunky cranberry sauce. Stirring plain or berry yogurt into apple sauce makes for a special treat. Try to keep down the amount of sugar you use in the apple sauce. Sweetness is an acquired taste; good apples should provide all the flavor you need. Use whatever apples are at their peak (domestic or imported), blending different varieties if you wish.

5 pounds of apples, carefully washed, unpeeled

Lemon juice

¼ cup sugar (better to use none)

1 teaspoon ground cinnamon

Core the apples, cut them in quarters, and remove all seeds. Immediately douse the apple pieces with lemon juice and put them in a large saucepan. Once all the apples are in the pan, add enough cold water to more than cover them so they will have room to move about as they boil.

Bring to a boil, then reduce the heat and simmer until the apples are tender, about 10 minutes.

Discard the water and run the apples briefly in a blender or food processor to make a thick sauce. The softened peels will be blended to form part of the sauce.

Pour the sauce back into the saucepan, add sugar (if desired) and cinnamon and simmer for 3 minutes more.

Serve hot, warm, cool, or cold.

Frozen Bananas

2 SERVINGS (1 BANANA)

If you are in the mood for a great snack that is good for you, welcome to the wonderful world of frozen bananas. There are all sorts of foods that taste good when combined with a frozen banana. Pick the combinations you like. One of these as a midafternoon snack or before-bedtime treat will make you very happy.

For the basic frozen banana, find a ripe, flavorful banana, peel it, and cut it in half across the middle. Insert a straw or stick in each half. Wrap the banana halves in aluminum foil and freeze.

VARIATION

If you want to combine the banana with other flavors, you might start by using this combination.

1 tablespoon peanut butter

2 tablespoons powdered milk

Combine the ingredients until they are creamy.

Roll the banana pieces in this mixture, using the straw or stick for leverage.

You may then wrap them in foil and freeze.

Or use the mixture as an adhesive to hold any one of the following ingredients: crunchy bran cereal, shredded coconut (used in moderation), chopped nuts, strawberry slices, sesame seeds, or anything else that tastes good to you.

DOCTOR'S NOTE

Calories: 125 per serving (Basic Frozen Banana, plus peanut butter and milk solids)

The nutritional power of this recipe comes from the blend of ingredients. It will be a tasty surprise to find out just how many good things are packed in this snack. One half banana contains 50 calories, 13 g carbohydrates, and 225 mg potassium, which is needed for nerve impulse transmission and proper functioning of the heart musculature in both you and baby. Among the added ingredients you might use, 1 ounce of nonfat milk solids will add 100 cals, more than 10 g protein, over 500 mg calcium, lots of phosphorus, and additional potassium. Just 1 tablespoon peanut butter will add about 94 cals, 4 g protein, and about 8 g fat. Choose this snack carefully, conscious of its high caloric composition. When not much else will go down, it is almost a meal in a bite.

Frozen Grapes

DOCTOR'S NOTE

Calories: 107 per serving

While low in calories and ideal for snack food at any time, grapes are high in carbohydrates (28 g per serving), which come from fructose, a natural sugar found in fruit. Thus they should be consumed only in moderation by the gestational diabetic. Grapes contain no fat and plenty of dietary roughage, making them a natural ally against constipation.

A cooling, healthy snack that can be enjoyed when you want something sweet and refreshing.

2 cups mixed red and green seedless grapes

Separate the grapes from their stems and wash them thoroughly in a colander with rapidly running cold water. After they are well-washed (grapes benefit from careful attention during washing), let the remaining water drip through the colander.

Put each cup of grapes in its own plastic bag, letting a few water droplets cling to the grapes. Seal the bags well and freeze.

Strawberries Modena

2 SERVINGS

Modena (accent on the first syllable) is a remarkably prosperous city in northern Italy. If it is not a household name, its products are world famous: fancy sports cars; opera stars such as Luciano Pavarotti and Mirella Freni; filled pastas from the Fini company; and delicious cherries, walnuts, cheese, and ham. Another uniquely Modenese product is balsamic vinegar. Until recently, this ancient condiment was known only to people who knew Modena, but now it is available worldwide. If you have never tasted it, toss away your preconceptions about vinegar and enjoy balsamic's unique flavor. This is a great dessert at the end of an elegant meal.

1 pint fresh, well-chosen strawberries

1 tablespoon balsamic vinegar

Wash the strawberries. Use a small knife to cut away the stems and hulls.

Put the berries in a pretty bowl, top with the balsamic vinegar and toss lightly.

Let the berries marinate for about 1 hour before serving.

VARIATION

If you want to do something a little fancier, take a chilled plate and spoon on the vinegar. Arrange the berries pointing upward so that the essence of the vinegar will float upward into the cavity of the berries. They can then be served as finger food for dessert or as an esoteric hors d'oeuvre.

DOCTOR'S NOTE

Calories: 60 per serving

A 1-cup serving will give you about 14g carbohydrates, no fat, and a healthy load of vitamin C (130 mg, almost 200% of the RDA). Never use frozen strawberries, as they are almost always sweetened (sugar is employed as a preservative).

Because of their low fructose (the type of sugar found in fruit) content, fresh strawberries are a recommended dessert for the gestational diabetic with a sweet tooth.

BAKED GOODS

Baking is unlike any other area of cooking in that, while most recipes allow you to experiment and adjust to your own tastes, making a bread, loaf, muffin, pie, or cake is an exact science. Baking is about measurement of time and ingredients and understanding—through instinct, trial, and error—how much experimenting you can attempt. Because baking also means rolling pins, bending, lifting, and lots of manual labor, your pregnancy is probably not the time you would consider ideal to be up to your elbows in flour.

The recipes in this chapter, therefore, are designed so that work is minimized and taste and nutrition are maximized. The muffins and loaves (or breads) should command most of your attention. They are delicious, low in added sugar and represent good options when you crave a snack that supplies flavor and roughage or you just want to have a few quiet moments with a cup of herb tea or some hot milk. Note that some of the basic recipes include variations, so that the Orange Apricot Nut Loaf (page 251) can be made in three other versions with different ingredients. They also pair well with fruit salad topped with yogurt or cottage cheese. Remember that muffins and loaves freeze nicely and warm up with a little toasting or a few minutes in the oven. Pack a muffin as the ideal snack to keep in your bag when you are at work or out for the day.

Corn Bread

8 SERVINGS (1 LOAF)

This great favorite from the American South is good and plain. Southerners who jealously guard their great culinary traditions would never take the shortcut of using instant mixes and neither should you. This recipe is easy to prepare and there is no reason you should have to eat the preservatives that are put in most packaged mixes. Corn bread is ideal if you are not interested in eating but must eat something.

1 cup low-fat milk

1 teaspoon low-fat dry milk solids

4 tablespoons melted, unsalted butter (or margarine)

1⅔ cups sifted unbleached flour

1 tablespoon baking powder

¾ cup corn meal

¼ teaspoon salt (optional)

Preheat the oven to 425° F.
Combine the milk, milk solids, and butter in a large bowl.
In another bowl, mix the flour, baking powder, corn meal, and salt.
Add the dry ingredients to the liquid and stir together until lightly mixed.
Pour into an 8 x 8 x 2-inch greased (with butter or corn oil) pan. Bake for 30 minutes. Cool for 5 minutes before cutting.

DOCTOR'S NOTE

Calories: 180 per serving

Nobody thinks twice about corn bread, and yet it is surprisingly nutritious. It is also close to the ideal food for your battle with morning sickness, because of its bland texture and acid-absorbing properties. This recipe contains milk and milk powder, giving 49 mg calcium per slice, which is of benefit to those who do not find milk an appealing possibility during their first trimester.

Banana Buttermilk Bread

8 SERVINGS (1 LOAF)

DOCTOR'S NOTE

Calories: 249 per serving

This is a low-sugar treat that will give you some calcium and potassium as well.

A high calcium and potassium treat to have with fruit and yogurt or with herb tea or milk.

½ cup unsalted butter (or margarine)

½ cup packed brown sugar, preferably granulated (optional)

2 eggs, well-beaten

1 teaspoon vanilla extract

1 cup overripe bananas, mashed

2 cups unbleached flour

2 teaspoons baking powder

¼ teaspoon salt (optional)

1 teaspoon baking soda

¼ cup buttermilk

Preheat oven to 350° F.

In a large bowl, cream the butter, gradually adding the sugar. Fold well.

Add the eggs, vanilla, and bananas, and beat well.

Sift the flour, baking powder, and salt together. Dissolve the baking soda in the buttermilk.

Gradually add the flour mixture and the buttermilk, alternately, to the banana mixture. Combine thoroughly.

Pour into a lightly greased (with corn oil or butter) 8 x 8 x 2-inch baking pan.

Bake for 45 minutes. Let cool before removing from pan.

Orange Apricot Nut Loaf

8 SERVINGS (1 LOAF)

L oaded with flavor and vitamin C, a slice of this loaf makes a good accompaniment to a meal of fresh fruit and cottage cheese or yogurt or as a snack with a cup of herb tea or a glass of milk.

1 egg

½ cup sugar

2 tablespoons sweet butter or margarine

2 cups unbleached flour

2 teaspoons baking powder

¼ teaspoon baking soda

¾ teaspoon salt

¼ cup cold water

½ cup orange juice

1 cup chopped pecans or Brazil nuts

½ cup dried apricots, gently washed in warm water, cut in bits

Preheat the oven to 350° F.

Beat the egg slightly in a large bowl. Stir in the sugar and mix well. Add the melted butter and stir.

Sift the flour with the baking powder, baking soda, and salt.

Add the dry ingredients alternately with the water and orange juice to the egg mixture. Then add the nuts and apricot pieces. Mix well.

Pour the mixture into a lightly greased (with corn oil or butter) 9-inch loaf pan. Bake for 1 hour. Cool before removing from the pan.

VARIATIONS

In place of the orange juice, apricots, and suggested nuts, try one of these combinations: lime juice, dried bananas, and pine nuts; grapefruit juice, dried figs, and walnuts; or pineapple juice, dried cherries, and macadamia nuts.

DOCTOR'S NOTE

Calories: 325 per serving

In addition to good nutrition, this loaf offers iron (in the apricots), potassium, vitamin C (in the orange juice), and a good load of protein (15 g) thanks to the egg and walnuts. It is a good substitute for sugary ready-made breakfast fare, especially for the gestational diabetic, as it contains very little sugar.

$\mathcal{N}$ew England Loaf

DOCTOR'S NOTE

Calories: 450 per serving

This loaf is delicious as a substitute to store-bought breakfast pastries and desserts. It contains no salt or artificial preservatives. If you use the fresh cranberries, you will get the extra benefit of fresh vitamin C: 1 cup of fresh, whole cranberries provides 13 mg vitamin C, 67 mg vitamin K and 12 g carbohydrates with no protein or fat. Count approximately one-sixth (16%) of the values for each slice of New England Loaf.

Nothing tastes better for breakfast than something freshly baked. This loaf takes only minutes to prepare, and can be put to good use. Have a slice or two for a snack during the day, perhaps with a glass of milk or a cup of herbal tea. Serve it warm from the oven to your brunch guests, or have a sliver in the guise of dessert.

1 cup fresh cranberries or 1 12-ounce package
    frozen cranberries
2 cups unbleached white flour, sifted
2 teaspoons baking powder
¼ cup sugar (optional)
1 large egg
½ cup canola or corn oil
¾ cup orange juice

Preheat the oven to 350° F.

Carefully wash the fresh cranberries in a large colander, removing stems and small leaves. Let them dry. If you are using frozen cranberries, do not thaw.

Into a large bowl sift the flour and baking powder, add the optional sugar and mix well.

In another bowl add the egg, vegetable oil, and orange juice. Take a whisk and beat well so that the mixture is aerated. Pour this mixture into the dry ingredients and stir only until the mixture is well blended. Do not overwork.

Fold the berries in, using a rubber spatula. Make sure they are evenly distributed, without working the batter too much.

Oil a 9-inch loaf pan and, with the aid of your spatula, pour the batter in.

Bake for 60 minutes or until the outside crust is brown, and a knife inserted in the middle comes out clean. Cool for 10 minutes before removing from pan. Let stand on wire rack for at least 2 minutes before slicing.

If you have any leftovers, do not refrigerate, as this will dry out the bread. Instead, wrap tightly in aluminum foil and store at room temperature for up to 4 days.

VARIATION
You may use fresh or frozen blueberries in place of the cranberries.

Oat Bran Muffins
16 MUFFINS

Here it is. Oat bran has been touted as the greatest thing since sliced bread but, because many commercially made breads are so uninspiring, the comparison is not really a fair one. Oat bran is viewed by many health officials as a sort of culinary white knight that will save people from clogged arteries and digestive problems. Although there is still debate about oat bran's effectiveness against the buildup of cholesterol in the arteries, it is unquestionably good as a source of roughage. These muffins make fine, healthy snacks or can serve as a component in a well-rounded breakfast or brown-bag lunch.

2 cups oat bran

1 cup unbleached whole wheat flour

2 teaspoons baking soda

1 cup buttermilk

1 large egg, beaten

2 teaspoons corn oil

2 tablespoons honey

3 tablespoons puréed pumpkin or squash (available canned or frozen) or mashed banana

½ cup chopped dried fruits of your choice (apricots, pears, peaches, figs, dates, etc. See note next page)

½ cup chopped nuts (walnuts, almonds, or pecans. See note next page)→

DOCTOR'S NOTE

Calories: 109 per muffin

These muffins will remain a nutritional favorite long after the baby is born. They are a good choice for morning sickness sufferers and women who need to lose weight. They are low in calories per individual muffin and high in roughage and carbohydrates: a mini–carbohydrate load. The dried fruit will add iron and potassium. While they will make excellent treats for anyone in need of extra dietary fiber, you should eat them cautiously if you are a gestational diabetic.

Preheat the oven to 425° F. Lightly grease the muffin pans (enough to make 16 muffins) with corn oil on a sheet of paper towel.

In a large bowl, combine the oat bran, flour, and baking soda. Pour in the buttermilk and add the egg, corn oil, honey, and pumpkin (or squash or banana). Blend with a wooden spoon until the ingredients are combined, but avoid overworking the mixture.

Fold in the fruits and nuts. Spoon the mixture into the muffin pans, filling each cup halfway.

Bake for about 15 minutes, or until the muffins no longer cling to the sides of the pan. Serve warm or at room temperature.

If you plan to save some of the muffins after baking them, they will last for two days in the refrigerator wrapped individually in aluminum foil. If you expect to keep them longer than that, store the muffins, wrapped in foil, in the freezer and warm them as necessary.

Note: If you choose not to include *either* the fruit *or* the nuts, increase the amount of the ingredient you *do* use to 1 cup.

DESSERTS

It is unfortunate that the notion of a good dessert is so often tied to guilt. This need not be. A good dessert is like a happy exclamation point at the end of a good meal and there are many healthy ones that fit your needs.

Although the prospect of a fancy or gooey sweet may be enticing, we believe that the best dessert is also the simplest. Nothing can match a piece of fruit at the peak of its ripeness, served at room temperature for maximum flavor. Another perfect choice is a well-prepared fruit salad (page 240). In many countries, a wonderful dessert is had by pairing fruit and cheese. This will provide you with added calcium. Here are but a few choices:

Crisp apples with sharp Cheddar, Jarlsberg, Swiss, or runny Camembert
Juicy pears with walnuts and Stilton or Gorgonzola
Red or black grapes with creamy Brie
Cherries with Appenzeller, Gourmandise, or Italian Fontina
Strawberries dipped in Mascarpone that is softened with a spoon
Ripe peaches with Doux de Montagne
A piece of nutty Parmesan from Italy

Here are the nutrient contents of selected cheeses, per ounce (for fruits, see the chart on page 242):

Blue or Roquefort cheese: 104 cals, 6.1 g protein, 8.6 g fat, 80 mg calcium
Camembert: 85 cals, 5 g protein, 7 g fat, 80 mg calcium
Cheddar: 113 cals, 7 g protein, 9 g fat, 213 mg calcium
Emmenthal or Swiss: 105 cals, 8 g protein, 8 g fat, 262 mg calcium
Parmigiano-Reggiano (imported Parmesan): 111 cals, 10.2 g protein, 7.4 g fat, 323 mg calcium

Parmigiano is your best bet nutritionally. In Italy, it is regularly fed to pregnant women and *bambini*.

Sweet stuff: When had in moderation (say, twice a week), ice cream is acceptable as a special treat, although you should not overindulge. Also, it should be pure, high-quality ice cream without gums, stabilizers, artificial sweeteners, flavorings, and colors. Just 1 cup of vanilla ice cream contains 300 cals, 6 g protein, 30g carbohydrates, and 16 g fat. A better choice if you like this kind of food is an equally pure frozen yogurt or low-sugar sorbet. In 1 cup of frozen low-fat vanilla yogurt you'll find 200 cals, 10 g protein, 34 g carbohydrates, and only 3 g fat. Frozen yogurt is certainly preferable nutritionally to ice cream. Along the same lines is delicious Frozen Banana Puree (page 258). Sprinkle some nutty wheat germ on these frozen desserts for extra flavor and nutrition. In 1 tablespoon of wheat germ you'll get 33 cals, 3 g protein, 4 g carbohydrates, and 1 g fat. It also contains thiamine, zinc, magnesium, and other essential minerals.

If you like baked items, have a slice of loaf or bread (these are sometimes called tea loaves). Try the bread and loaf recipes in this book, and you probably have additional favorites of your own. Remember to go easy on added sugar.

As for out-and-out desserts, we have included two that will be pleasing to crowds and to small dinner parties. Above all, they are easy to make and are good for you, if you don't overindulge (a rule that applies to everyone, of course). The frozen yogurt pie recipe can be used with many combinations of fruit flavors. The fruit crisp also can be adapted to whatever good fruit you are in the mood for. But don't forget, you don't have to serve baked goods to be considered a model gourmet and host. A perfect fruit with some good cheese or a bowl of delectable fruit salad (page 240) are classic desserts that are always welcome.

If you are in the habit of eating "junky" desserts such as packaged cookies and boxed cakes loaded with chemicals and preservatives, now is the time to break the habit. They offer absolutely nothing nutritionally and only serve to fill you up with empty calories. They certainly are not the kind of foods you will serve to your baby in the future so don't do it now! And, if you really think about it, we eat most of these foods out of habit, not because of their taste. So now is the right time to separate guilt from dessert by eating delicious desserts that are good for you.

ABOUT ICE CREAM, SORBETS, AND FROZEN YOGURT

Pregnancy is a time when you can make certain indulgences, but you should still be mindful of a couple of rules. Because you should eat ice cream only as a special treat, you should always select the healthiest one available. You do not need to have ice cream that is overloaded with added sugars, artificial ingredients, artificial sweeteners, and colors. Choose ice creams that are made only of real milk or cream, have real fruit or flavors and use sugar rather than sweeteners.

Plain ice creams such as vanilla, banana, or other fruits are better than those laced with ripples, syrups, and nuts. Better still are low-fat ice creams, frozen yogurt, and sorbets, which are frozen desserts made of real fruit and ice. Lemon sorbet is a fabulous dessert and a good palate cleanser. And *no*, we will not provide you with a recipe for pickles and ice cream!

Sundae

If you want to make something a little fancy, make a sundae of frozen yogurt or vanilla ice cream topped with Berry Sauce (page 132) or Apricot Sauce (page 131) and a few unsalted nuts. Add a few berries too, if you wish.

Banana Split

Cut a ripe banana in half and then cut the halves lengthwise. Place them in a flat bowl.

Add a scoop each of different flavors of frozen yogurt or, once in a while, some ice cream. Sprinkle on some unsalted nuts and top with Berry Sauce (page132) or Apricot Sauce (page 131).

Note to Diabetics: If you are controlling your sugar intake and your doctor advises you to watch what you eat, you must only eat the ice creams, ice milks, sorbet, or frozen yogurts your doctor recommends.

Frozen Banana Purée

1 SERVING

DOCTOR'S NOTE

Calories: 210 calories

This snack will provide you with approximately 53.5 g carbohydrates (almost 10% of the RDA), 2.5 protein, 902 mg vitamin K (about 1300% of the RDA!), and 20 mg vitamin C (just under 33% of the RDA).

This dessert will make you think you are eating ice cream or a wonderful banana custard. It is astonishingly easy to prepare.

2 frozen plain bananas

Unwrap the bananas and cut them into chunks 1 or 2 inches long. Put the chunks in your blender and purée for a few seconds. The result should be like rich, slightly soft ice cream or, if you prefer, a slightly softer cream. Serve immediately.

VARIATION

Add broken, unsalted walnut pieces as you put the bananas in the blender.

Fruit Crisp

6 SERVINGS

This is an all-purpose recipe that can be adapted to your mood and to whatever fruit you have at hand. Peaches, apples, blackberries, and ripe, juicy pears are particularly delicious in a fruit crisp. You will find that most fruits, except perhaps bananas, will work well. You may make this crisp with one type of fruit or by combining fruits that appeal to you. Use your imagination, but note that apples and pears should be peeled, cored and, seeded before slicing. Grapes and berries should be washed and drained; cherries, peaches, apricots, nectarines, and plums should be pitted. The oats in this fruit crisp provide flavor, crunch, and some always-welcome roughage.

4 cups fruit, cleaned and cut as required

2 tablespoons freshly squeezed lemon juice

1¼ cups uncooked quick rolled oats

½ cup unbleached flour

1 teaspoon ground cinnamon

⅓ cup unsalted butter or margarine, cut in bits

Dollop of plain or vanilla yogurt (optional)

Preheat oven to 350° F.

Prepare the fruit as necessary and place it in a 10-inch pan or dish (preferably glass or Pyrex).

Immediately top the fruit with the lemon juice to prevent oxidation. The lemon juice also imparts its own fresh flavor.

In a large bowl, combine the oats, flour, and cinnamon. Then add the butter and mix just until it is incorporated. Avoid overworking the combination. Distribute the mixture evenly over the fruit.

Bake for 30 minutes.

Serve hot or cold, topped, if you wish, with the yogurt.

Cook's note: This fruit crisp is made without added sugar as there should be quite enough sweetness in the fruit. Therefore, sample a bit of the fruit to determine that it is ripe and flavorful before making the fruit crisp.

DOCTOR'S NOTE

Calories: 153 per serving

For this recipe, we used 2 cups strawberries, ¼ pound grapes, 1 cup peaches, and 1 cup plums. The caloric breakdown will vary slightly if other fruits are used. Our combination will yield 77 mg vitamin C (100% of the RDA) as well as a good helping of dietary fiber. Fructose, the sugar found in fruits, is easier to digest than glucose (table sugar) but, as with any other recipes high in carbohydrates, this one should be consumed in moderation by the gestational diabetic.

Frozen Chocolate-Banana Yogurt Pie

10 SERVINGS (1 PIE)

DOCTOR'S NOTE

Calories: 362 per serving

In computing the nutritional value for this pie, we did not include the optional almonds and sugar. This is a low-calorie dessert that is nevertheless loaded with calcium (abundant in the yogurt and cream cheese) and potassium (in the bananas) and will satisfy those inevitable sweet cravings. Like all desserts, it should be consumed in moderation, especially if you have been diagnosed with gestational diabetes.

For the Crust:

30 chocolate wafers

¼ cup almond slivers (optional)

¼ cup sugar (optional)

⅓ cup unsalted butter or margarine

For the Filling:

2 ripe bananas

16 ounces low-fat banana yogurt

16 ounces low-fat cream cheese, softened, cut into bits

Preheat oven to 350° F.

In a blender, food processor, or a large bowl, crumble the wafers. Add the almonds, sugar, and butter or margarine and blend thoroughly. Press this mixture evenly into a 9-inch pie plate, covering the bottom and sides. Bake 8 to 10 minutes. Cool the crust thoroughly before adding the filling. Slice the bananas and line the crust with a single layer of banana pieces.

In a blender or bowl, blend the yogurt and cream cheese until smooth. Pour over the bananas and smooth with a spatula.

Cover the pie with aluminum foil so that the foil is above the yogurt but does not touch it. Freeze for 5 hours. Let stand for 20 minutes before serving.

VARIATIONS

For the crust, try 24 graham cracker squares instead of the chocolate wafers. Bake until lightly browned. For the filling, try one of these combinations: blueberries with vanilla yogurt (use a graham cracker crust); sliced strawberries with strawberry yogurt; sliced apricots, nectarines, or peaches with plain yogurt; or pitted orange or tangerine segments with lemon yogurt.

BEVERAGES

You may very often find yourself thirsty during your pregnancy, but even if you don't, it is essential that you consume fluids in the course of your day. The body needs liquid along with solid foods for complete sustenance. Water is always the perfect choice. It is refreshing, calorie free, and readily available. If you live in an area where the tap water is less than desirable, be sure that you always have bottled water at home and at work. Carbonated waters (without additives) are also excellent choices, if you like the fizz and it doesn't upset your stomach. Most seltzers do not have added salt and most club sodas do. Check the label if you need to limit your added salt intake. And try Lemon-Mint Water (page 265).

Milk is an excellent beverage if you are not allergic to it. You do not need to drink whole milk, which delivers more fat than you require. Skim or low-fat (so-called 99, 1%, or 2%) milk tastes delicious. If you feel these low-fat milks are too thin, take 1 teaspoon of nonfat dry milk solids and dissolve them in the milk. Aside from giving a richer taste, you are helping yourself to an extra dose of much-needed calcium. Many stores have acidopholus-enriched milk and casein-free milk for people who are allergic to regular milk. Use milk to make shakes and smoothees.

Here is the nutritional breakdown for different types of cow's milk (per cup):

Whole milk (3.5% fat) contains 160 cals, 8.5 g protein and fat, 12 g carbohydrates, and 288 mg calcium.

2% milk (which is 2% fat) is similar to 99 milk, except that it has 121 cals per cup and 3 g fat

99 (also called 1% milk because it is 1% fat) contains 100 cals, 8 g protein, 2 g fat, 11 g carbohydrates, and 300 mg calcium

Skim milk (no fat) contains 88 cals, 9 g protein, 12 g carbohydrates, and 300 mg calcium

As you can see, 4 cups a day of any kind of milk will fulfill your RDA for calcium. However, the amount of fat you consume is according to your needs and should be determined by your doctor. As

Beverage Recipes

WATER, MILK, JUICE, AND JUICE COMBINATIONS

you have read in the section about fat (page 7), pregnant women require more daily fat intake than nonpregnant women.

Juices of all kinds are good, if you bear in mind a couple of cautionary thoughts. The first is to be sure the juice is a natural as possible. Fresh juice is always superior to juice made from concentrate in terms of nutritional benefit and usually in terms of taste. If you have a juicer to make fresh fruit and vegetable juices, then you are in the best of all possible worlds, although they are not essential appliances. (A hand-operated citrus squeezer will make delicious orange and grapefruit juice.) Be sure to avoid juices with coloring or preservatives. Read labels carefully to see whether something is 100% juice or a "juice beverage" that contains fruit juice plus water, syrups, and enhancers. The only juice that regularly appears as a beverage or cocktail is cranberry juice, which is really a combination of juice, water, and sometimes syrups. These cocktails tend to be relatively pure, and you may partake of them. When using frozen juice concentrates, the juices will often become frothier and delicious when the concentrate and water are combined in a blender. If you are using concentrated orange, tangerine, or pineapple juice, cut a banana into the blender before blending. This drink is rich, delicious, and nutritious.

The second caution is to avoid juices that are full of salt. As you know, most commercially sold juices contain complete nutritional information on the label. Canned tomato and vegetable juices (including V-8) are loaded with salt unless the label says otherwise. Only drink the low-salt or low-sodium juices and, if you wish to enliven them a bit, squeeze in some fresh lemon or lime juice and grind in a little fresh pepper.

Here is the nutritional breakdown for 1 cup of three of the most popular fruit juices. Note that all three have 0 g fat.

Apple juice has 87 cals, 22 g carbohydrates, 11 mg calcium, and no vitamin C (unless the label on the brand you've purchased indicates that ascorbic acid has been added)
Cranberry juice cocktail has 134 cals, 31 g carbohydrates, 30 mg vitamin C
Orange juice has 112 cals, 25 g carbohydrates, and 125 mg vitamin C

Many juices are delicious when combined with others. Here are a few ideas: apple-grape, apple-cranberry, apple-raspberry, apricot-pear, cranberry-grapefruit, cranberry-orange, orange-pineapple, and pineapple-tangerine.

Spritzers

Fruit juices are often filled with natural sugars. If you need to cut back on sugar or if you simply want a lighter drink, fill a glass halfway with juice and then add some seltzer or club soda. This spritzer will delight you.

Smoothees and Shakes

Smoothees and Shakes are beguiling drinks that are made in the blender. Depending on your mood or appetite, you may make these drinks as thick or thin as you want. The base of a smoothee includes milk, 1 teaspoon milk solids, and usually, ice (which makes the drink cold and cuts the thickness). Many smoothees also include a banana for richness and nutrition. Beyond this, you should add the ingredients (typically fruit) that sound good. Examples include pears, strawberries, a mixture of berries, peaches, and apricots. More acidic fruits such as oranges work less well, although the combination of milk, orange juice, and a banana does have many admirers. If you like it, enjoy it. To make a smoothee, combine the milk, milk solids, ice, banana, and fruit in a blender and blend until the ingredients are thoroughly combined and the ice has been broken up.

Shakes, in the ice cream parlor sense, usually feature milk or ice cream. For the purposes of this book, a shake is a drink made in a blender, combining ice and fruit or vegetable juices. Most vegetable juices (do not confuse these with cooking liquids from vegetables) mix nicely, and some fruits and vegetables (such as apple and carrot) go well together. Use your imagination.

Other Beverages

Broths and consommés may be considered beverages. Another term for these is *stock*, which can be made from poultry, meat, fish, or vegetables. Avoid broths made from cubes; they are usually loaded with salt, monosodium glutamate, and artificial flavorings and color. A bracing cup of broth, rich in nutrients and warming on a chilly day, is a great drink (see Chicken Stock, page 146).

Alcoholic beverages are not in the cards. Although women in

some cultures consume alcohol and deliver healthy babies, the prevailing medical wisdom in the United States is that alcohol can be harmful to a developing fetus. However, other factors (such as poor diet and health of the mother), when combined with alcohol, tend to increase the likelihood of fetal damage. Read all about alcohol and pregnancy on page 77. If your culture or tradition dictates otherwise, you might choose to drink alcoholic beverages. However, you should not ignore the potential consequences. There are substitutes. Alcohol-free wine and beer are now sold in many stores. Or you can try a spritzer or alcohol-free sangria (page 267).

Tea and coffee also are prohibited. Caffeine is not healthy for a developing baby. Interestingly, many women seem to lose the desire to drink coffee during their pregnancies, so perhaps this will happen to you. Even decaffeinated coffee should be avoided, as the beans are often processed with harmful ingredients.

Instead of coffee and regular tea, try the vast range of herbal teas available. They come in many flavors, some with fruit, some derived from plants and herbs. Mint tea is excellent if you have an upset stomach. Many people think chamomile tea is great when they are having trouble falling asleep. There are even herbal teas that approximate the taste of coffee, if that is your wish. See page 274 for more about herbal teas.

Lemon-Mint Water

*L*emon-Mint Water serves two functions: It is especially refreshing and also settles the stomach. It is perfect at cocktail or dinner parties when you can't partake of alcohol. Leftover Lemon-Mint Water may be used for poaching or steaming fish or vegetables.

1 quart still bottled water or good tap water

½ lemon, skin washed, sliced thin

6 sprigs fresh mint, gently wiped with a paper towel

Ice cubes

In a pretty pitcher or jar, add the water, lemon, mint, and ice. Stir briefly.

Keep covered and cold.

Serve strained or with the lemon and mint, whatever you prefer.

Keep for only 1 day.

$\mathscr{P}$*arsley-Pineapple Smoothee*

*I*f you are only accustomed to parsley as a colorful garnish on the fringe of your plate, you have not given this food its due. Parsley is loaded with vitamin C and contains all-important calcium. The pineapple offers vitamin C, roughage, and for many people, helps improve digestion. Have this drink if you feel you cannot take in much food or if you are looking for a cooling, nutritious snack.

8 ounces *fresh* pineapple plus 2 ice cubes or 8 ounces
    unsweetened pineapple juice
1 fistful of curly or flat parsley, washed and dried

In a blender, purée the parsley and pineapple until the ingredients are thoroughly combined. Serve this drink cool.

Sensible Sangria and Scintillating Spritzers

On occasions when you would like to enjoy a festive drink, you do not have to feel left out because you are not drinking alcoholic beverages right now. In fact, these drinks are so appealing that you shouldn't be surprised if other people want to imbibe along with you.

Sangria

12 SERVINGS

1 6-ounce can frozen orange or tangerine juice

1 6-ounce can frozen lemon or lime juice

1 6-ounce can frozen cranberry, cranapple, or
   cranraspberry juice

2 liters or 2 quarts seltzer or club soda

Orange slices

Ice cubes

Mix the juices according to the directions on the can, using the seltzer in place of water. You will have some seltzer left over. Combine all of these juices in a punch bowl, stirring to mix all the flavors well.

Add ice cubes and orange slices and serve.

Spritzers

1 6-ounce can of unsweetened juice concentrate

1 liter or 1 quart seltzer or club soda

Follow your tastebuds and create a drink that appeals to you. Simply substitute seltzer for the water you would normally use to make juice. You will have some seltzer left over. Almost any flavor of juice will do: apple, orange, cranberry, grape, tangerine, lemon and lime, and so forth.

DOCTOR'S NOTE

Calories: 85 per glass of Sangria

One serving delivers 40 mg vitamin C (more than 100% of the RDA). As you may remember from reading the nutrition chapter, it is very important to keep on drinking liquids while you are pregnant. Your blood volume increases to one and a half its before-pregnancy amount due to the development of amniotic fluid and the fetus's circulatory volume.

9

Although particular characteristics of certain foods are addressed in the recipes that use them, you may want to use this section as a special reference for shopping and storing the foods you eat. Beginning on page 97, you will find a list of foods and supplies for your first shopping trip. These are staple items that will serve you throughout your pregnancy to delivery, breastfeeding, and beyond. You will also need to restock your larder with fresh, perishable foods and replace the staples as necessary.

In shopping for food, take time to check dates of expiration on dairy products, baked goods, meat, fish and anything else that might be labeled. If you can choose between two packages of the same item, always pick the one with the later expiration date. This means not only that the item will last longer at home, but that it is fresher. So if you eat it sooner rather than later, you will be eating fresher food that is likely to have more of its nutrients intact.

In storing foods, it is a good idea to rotate them in the pantry and on refrigerator shelves so that the oldest are in closest reach and will be used first. This is easier than you think. Simply line the same items in rows, bringing the row forward and putting the newest item in the back. The theory is the same whether you are dealing with fresh heads of lettuce, frozen fish fillets, or cans of soup.

Place perishable fruits and vegetables in air-tight plastic containers and liquids in jars, preferably those made of dark glass to keep out vitamin-destroying light. Place light-colored masking tape on the container or jar and write on it what is inside and when it was stored. Fruits and vegetables that require further ripening, such as melons, avocados, and tomatoes, should be kept out of the refrigerator until they have ripened. Bananas should never be refrigerated.

The following list of items in the pregnant cook's pantry, while not exhaustive, does touch on many of the ingredients most often called for in this book and will give you good ideas to use every day.

Apples: This most popular fruit is alleged to keep the doctor away. We suggest you eat an apple a day as a dessert or snack and then go visit your doctor regularly. He or she must follow the progress of you and your fetus. If you maintain a good, balanced diet, your doctor will be pleased. A perfect snack is an apple, a piece of cheese, and a piece of whole wheat bread or a Scandinavian crispbread. There are dozens of varieties of apples, from sweet Golden Delicious to tart Granny Smiths. Pick and choose and select your own favorites. There was a scare a while back about alar, a substance that was used on some apples for aesthetic reasons. It also has been customary in some orchards to polish or wax apples (and cucumbers and green peppers, too) to make them look more appealing. If an apple looks like it jumped off the pages of a magazine, wash it carefully with water and consider peeling it before eating it. Apples from farmers' markets may look mottled and bruised, but they are good for you as long as they have not turned brown or mushy. Even an apple that is soft in one part may be wonderful in another. Cut away the bad and eat the good. Don't forget that an apple, once cut, peeled, or bitten, will oxidize (turn brown) when exposed to air. There is nothing wrong with this except that it loses some of its nutrients and may not taste as fresh. If you are cutting apples for a fruit salad, sprinkle lemon juice on the apple pieces to prevent oxidation.

Apricots, dried: You may not already be in the habit of eating dried apricots, but they make an ideal snack. They are rich in vitamin A, iron, and calcium and taste wonderful. They are delicious as is or they may be steamed to produce plump apricots when fresh apricots are unavailable. Dried apricots may be slivered to go into muffins, atop cereal, into fruit salads, or in poultry stuffings. Excellent dried apricots come from Turkey and Australia and the domestic variety, from California, also is very fine. Store them in an air-tight container at room temperature.

Bananas: This is another contender for the title of "The Perfect Food," replete as it is with nutrients, good taste, visual appeal, and portability. Some people contend that bananas do not taste as good as they used to. While, in many cases, this notion is a cliché about the good old days, it happens to be true about bananas. It used to be that bananas were tree-ripened before they were picked and had to be consumed soon after being purchased. Nowadays, many bananas are picked while they are still green and sprayed with a gas on the way to market to promote ripening. What you usually get are either green or brown bananas. The former are very starchy even when they lose their green color. The latter are mushy and have a strong, unpleasant flavor. You should select bananas that are yellow or golden. Store them in a bag outside the refrigerator and check them daily. Golden bananas that start to turn brown are probably delicious as long as you don't let them turn too brown. The way to test for ripeness is to pull at the top of the peel. If it offers resistance, it is not yet ripe. If it gives easily, then the banana is ready to eat. If a recipe calls for a softer banana, let it ripen until the peel is a mixture of brown and gold. Bananas spoil in the refrigerator but are wonderful when frozen (see page 245). As with any stored food, rotate frozen bananas in the freezer so that the oldest one is within the easiest reach.

Brewer's yeast: This powder, available in health food stores and nutrition centers, is an acquired taste, no doubt. But if you find brewer's yeast palatable when mixed with orange juice or with cool or hot water, you are doing yourself a lot of good. The RDA of all-important folate (see page 16) for pregnant women is 400 mcg. Just 1 tablespoon of brewer's yeast contains 313 mcg and 6 ounces of orange juice contains 102 mcg, so you can meet your RDA very easily. Because the next best sources of folate, beef liver (123 mcg for 3 ounces), raw spinach (106 mcg for 1 cup), and romaine lettuce (98 mcg for 1 cup), are not always available or to everyone's liking, the brewer's yeast and OJ combo looks increasingly attractive. Brewer's yeast also contains goodly amounts of vitamin B_1, niacin, and magnesium.

Broth (also called stock): This is a basic component for soups and in the preparation of many dishes. No commercial broth is an acceptable substitute for the homemade variety. Too many cooks take the inadvisable shortcut of making broth from a cube. This is wrong on many counts: The cube is loaded with chemicals, preservatives, colorants, monosodium glutamate, and heaps of salt, all of which are bad for you and your fetus. Equally important, broth from a cube never tastes very good. If you do not want to prepare your own broth (chicken, beef, vegetable, and fish are the most common varieties), then seek a commercial brand in a can or jar that is free of anything artificial and does not list salt among its first three ingredients. One decent canned broth is made by Health Valley and is available in parts of the United States. See page 146 for a chicken stock recipe that you may make in large amounts and store in jars in the refrigerator for imminent usage and in the freezer for later consumption.

Butter: Without question, sweet (unsalted) butter is preferable to salted butter for cooking and eating. Once upon a time, salt was added to butter for purposes of preservation, but nowadays the refrigerator is all you need to keep butter fresh. Salted butter simply does not taste as good as fresh and it delivers unneeded salt. In parts of the United States it is difficult to find sweet butter, even in dairy-producing regions such as upstate New York. If you cannot locate sweet butter in your market, be sure to ask them to stock it on their shelves.

In buying butter, you may choose between stick butter, which is sold in ¼-pound sticks (equivalent to 8 tablespoons) and whipped butter, which is sold in ½-pound tubs. You only need a little bit of whipped butter to get the good flavor of butter, so this should be the preferred butter for eating. Because it is much easier to measure stick butter than whipped butter, you should buy sticks when you need to use specific quantities of butter. However, if only whipped butter is available, here's how to measure it: Let's assume, for example, that you need 3 tablespoons of butter. Put very cold water in a measuring cup until it measures 1 cup. Then, with a measuring spoon, take out 3 tablespoons of water. Now add chunks of butter and watch the level of water rise. When the combined volume of the water and butter equals 1 cup, you will have the amount of butter you need.

One caveat about cooking with butter: If, in melting butter, it turns brown, spill it out, wipe the pan, and melt more butter. Brown butter has undergone a chemical conversion that produces unhealthy by-products. To store butter, keep it tightly wrapped or covered and place it in a cool, dark part of your refiregerator. Many people customarily leave butter out for several hours and then refrigerate it. This is inadvisable because it loses vitamins in contact with air and, if it gets too warm, may turn rancid or pick up bacteria in the air.

Cereals: This most essential breakfast food can also be had at other times of the day, especially if you are afflicted with morning sickness and can only tolerate very few foods. The best breakfast cereals (oatmeal, farina, cream of wheat, raisin bran, granola, and shredded wheat) and side dish dinner cereals (kasha, couscous, bulgur, and cracked wheat) are wonderful sources of B vitamins, minerals, and trace elements. Reading a box of cereal is not unlike reading the products list of a chemical factory. Even the plainest cereal lists various chemicals but, as you know, many of these are actually good for you. Just a quick glance at the chapter on nutrition in pregnancy (page 2) will remind you which of the many exotic-sounding names are essential to your health and that of your fetus. Read the cereal box carefully to see how many nutrients the cereal delivers per portion (usually 1 ounce of cereal plus skim milk). It is likely that you will eat more than the recommended portion, which is perfectly fine. Remember, when reading the cereal box, that the RDAs (and percentage of RDAs) indicated on the box do not apply to pregnant women, but you can still learn how many vitamins and minerals you will receive per portion.

Since new studies are published all the time that make various safety claims about the many ingredients that appear in commercial cereals, we encourage you to err on the side of caution. Do not purchase any cereal that has added sugar (which is safe, but unnecessary); artificial sweeteners such as aspartame or saccharin; preservatives, colorants, and dyes (red, blue, yellow, green); and antioxidants including, but not limited to: BHA, BHT, monosodium glutamate (MSG), and phosphoric acid.

If at all possible, store cereal in air-tight plastic containers or jars in your closet or pantry to maintain freshness and nutrient content. Otherwise, tightly fold down the lining inside cereal boxes and close the boxes completely.

Chicken: This versatile, inexpensive food is a major player in the kitchens of great cooks. In selecting chicken, you should look for meat that is shiny and fresh. If the chicken still has skin on, the skin should be yellow or golden, though not too dark. The skin should have no discoloration that might be a product of age or exposure to air. Never purchase chicken that has blood on either the meat or the skin. In using a whole bird, always clean the cavity thoroughly with lots of fresh cold water, picking away all the excess fat. The same rule applies to chicken parts. Remember that cut chicken will spoil more quickly than a whole bird. Raw chicken that is well-wrapped may be refrigerated, but it should be cooked as soon as possible. You should only refrigerate it until the date of expiration on the wrapper. If you buy a lot of chicken at once, try to gauge how much you will use in the 48 hours after purchase and then freeze the rest. Do not freeze chicken in the package it comes in. Instead, remove it from its package and wrap it tightly in aluminum foil. As with anything else you freeze, label this package with its content and date of being frozen and rotate the items in your freezer so that the older items are used first.

Eggs: Alphabetically, at least, the chicken comes before the egg. We will leave the rest of that debate to scientists and philosophers. Eggs usually come in cartons that have been marked for the last date of sale. Do not plan to keep the eggs more than a few days after the last date of sale. If you buy a half-carton of eggs, be sure to choose a half that is dated, unless you are separating the carton yourself. Always open an egg carton and examine each egg. Lift it to check that it is not broken: Sometimes a broken egg is not immediately apparent, especially when the carton is made of plastic foam. Any egg that has a discolored or blotchy shell should not be purchased. You may happily choose either white or brown eggs. Many people think brown eggs have more flavor; decide for yourself. Eggs come in several sizes, from medium to jumbo. In most recipes, large or extra large eggs are the preferred size. When you crack open an egg, there should be no blood spots on the yolk, the white and yolk should smell fresh and the yolk should be firm unless you have accidentally broken it. Discard any egg that does not meet these standards. There may be nothing wrong with it, but you don't want to take a chance. You should not eat raw eggs or dishes (such as Caesar salad, hollandaise sauce, fresh mayonnaise, or pasta alla carbonara) that use raw eggs. In recent years there have been outbreaks of illnesses caused by bacteria in raw eggs. An egg in perfect condition, when cooked, should not present problems.

Garlic: A wonderful food that is often maligned, misunderstood, and abused. Garlic is delicious and thought to be very healthy. You should use only fresh garlic sold in bulbs. In using garlic, pull away one clove from the bulb, peel away the pinkish skin and cut the clove in half. With the tip of your knife, remove the greenish yellow center that contains the bitter flavor some people associate with garlic. Use these half cloves to rub in salad bowls or cooking pots to impart garlic flavor. Cut the cloves into thin slivers or mince them up if you plan to use the garlic in cooking. Do not waste money on a garlic press and, if you have one, throw it away. Garlic presses extrude semibitter juice from the clove and flatten the sweet flesh of the garlic until it is worthless. Many people think they are chic cooks when they use a garlic press, but this implement is no friend of the garlic clove. Avoid precrushed garlic that is sold in jars or tubes. It is laced with chemicals to preserve some flavor and, in fact, tastes vile compared to the real thing. Similarly, avoid garlic salt. Its taste has nothing on the real thing, and you certainly do not need additional salt. During lactation you may consider eliminating or reducing garlic in your diet. It often passes into breast milk and is not a flavor that pleases most newborns. But what a treat is in store for them when they get a little older!

Herbal teas: These delicious beverages, almost always caffeine-free, are ideal when you want a hot drink at the end of a meal or with a muffin at snacktime. They are very popular in Europe, where they are called *infusions* or *tisanes* . Most herbal teas come in tea bags and are based on herbs, flowers, plants, or fruits. Herbalists (persons who specialize in the study of herbs) assert that many herbal teas have special properties that are beneficial to health. While some of their claims are far-fetched, others seem quite natural and plausible. For example, many people who have trouble falling asleep to find chamomile tea a lovely, safe sedative. We recommend that you seek out the herbal teas that please your taste buds and speak to your doctor if you have any particular medical conditions that need attention. Your doctor may recommend something herbally based, but it is wise that you not self-medicate, whether with herbs or with medications. One special thing you should remember: Do not buy loose herb teas that you would then brew in a teapot. While these are often safe, sometimes they are not handled with enough care and may contain other leaves or ingredients that are harmful. You may feel perfectly safe purchasing leading commercial brands of herbal teas in tea bags, such as Celestial Seasons, Twinings, and the top European imports from France, Italy, Switzerland, Austria, Germany, and the Netherlands.

Herbs: This vast category of wonderful flavorings of vegetable origin (usually in leaf form) represents a great area for experimentation and innovation for the creative cook. Certain cultures ascribe favorable medicinal properties to particular herbs, but that is a subject for another book. Let it simply be said that the perfumes of fresh basil or rosemary, once sensed, can never be forgotten. Most herbs should be as fresh as possible to get the most flavor and nutritional value from them. Certain herbs—such as oregano, thyme and imported fines herbes—are acceptable when used dried, but others (basil, rosemary, sage, and mint) are infinitely better when fresh. Many experienced cooks ruin their fresh herbs by washing and cutting them. If you have a fresh herb, wipe it well with paper towels to remove any dirt and then *tear* the herb to the size you want. The metal of even a clean knife causes changes in the delicate flavors of many herbs. The best herbs are those taken directly from a living plant. To keep store-bought fresh herbs, put them in a cool dark place in loose plastic bags. Dried herbs should be kept in a dark place in tightly closed jars.

Leafy greens: This vast range of vitamin and nutrient-rich vegetables is discussed in more detail beginning on page 155. You should always look for the darkest green vegetables because they contain the most nutrients. If it is a vegetable that has a white base when fresh, such as cabbage and many lettuces, always select the one with the whitest base or is one that is just beginning to go brown. Store them in the refrigerator in air-tight plastic containers and do not wash them until you are ready to eat them. Greens should be washed in abundant cold water so that hidden soot will be eliminated. Invest in an inexpensive salad spinner, which you can use to spin dry leafy greens. Never cut leafy green vegetables, simply tear them into pieces suitable for eating or cooking. You should only bring a blade to greens if you are mincing them (for a pasta filling, for example).

Lemon: This wonderful, versatile fruit stars in many recipes in this book. Its bracing, refreshing flavor is lovely on its own or in combination with meats, vegetables, fruits, beverages, and baked goods. Lemon juice, which should only be gotten from fresh lemons and not the reconstituted store-bought variety, is ideal for preserving cut foods, as the acid in the juice inhibits oxidation. Select lemons that are bright yellow, that have a thick skin and are not bruised.

Lettuce: See leafy greens (page 275) for ideas about selecting and handling lettuce. If you customarily eat iceberg lettuce, try to diversify. Iceberg lettuce is relatively flavorless and low in nutrients compared with other lettuces. Romaine lettuce is a dependable choice that also happens to have a lot of folate. Boston, Bibb, limestone, and other lettuces all have different flavors and textures. Make a composed salad that combines various lettuces (plus other leafy vegetables such as spinach, endive, arugula, mesclun, and radicchio) for a really wonderful salad that will make you glad you came out of the iceberg age.

Liver: In most cookbooks, liver would not figure in a listing of basic ingredients. It is no secret that it has at least as many detractors as it does admirers and many people's childhood memories of liver are distinctly unpleasant. Throw away those memories: Liver is grown-up food that appears on menus elegant and humble. In France, geese are fed prunes to give their livers the most sublime flavor in the world. In Venice, calf's liver cooked in sweet onions is the local specialty that gives gondoliers the energy they need to row their boats. In 3 ounces of cooked beef liver there is more than the RDA for pregnant women of the following nutrients: vitamins A and B_{12}, folate, pantothenic acid, and copper. In addition, that same portion has significant quantities of vitamins B_1, B_2, D, and K and biotin, iron, phosphorus, and zinc. There have been occasional scares about liver containing toxins ingested by the calf or chicken. Animals are carefully fed so that this problem is minimized, and the value of liver in the diet of pregnant women far exceeds the concern she should have about toxins. Liver is high in cholesterol, but this is not a source of concern for most pregnant women. You should only avoid liver if your doctor tells you to cut down on cholesterol. Try beef, calf, or chicken livers in preparations that appeal to you. If you develop a taste for liver, you will be doing yourself and your fetus a lot of good. Liver should be as fresh as possible when you buy it. Do not refrigerate it for more than 24 hours and never freeze it. In preparing liver for cooking, rinse it well in lots of cold water and pull away and discard any fat or connective membrane. Pat it dry with paper towels before dredging in flour or sauteeing.

Milk: For the purposes of the recipes in this book, we are talking about cow's milk (as opposed to milk from goats, sheep, yaks, soybeans, or anything else that provides delicious milk). You are encouraged to drink skim or low-fat milk. The extra fat is unnecessary for you. If skim milk tastes too thin, you may enhance it by adding 1 teaspoon of nonfat dry milk solids, which provide extra calcium along with richer taste. Milk can be combined with bananas or other fruit along with milk solids to make a delicious, nutritious blender shake. If you are lactose intolerant, talk to your doctor about milk alternatives or ways that you can comfortably get some milk into your diet.

Nonfat dry milk solids: This inexpensive powder is a nutritional boon to women who need added calcium. Aside from making skim milk richer, 1 teaspoon of milk solids may be surreptitiously added to loaves, cakes, soups, certain sauces and stews, yogurt, and some beverages to provide calcium. Keep milk solids around at all times.

Olive oil: The preferred cooking fat for many great chefs, this oil is found in kitchens all around the Mediterranean Sea and, increasingly, in many parts of the world. As packaged in Italy, where most of the world's best olive oil is produced, it is labeled either as *extravergine*, *vergine*, or simply as *olive oil* or *olio d'oliva puro*. These denominations have nothing to do with how virtuous the olives were, but rather, how much acid content the oil has. Olive oil, the third type, is occasionally blended with other oils. You should select oil that is either extra virgin or virgin. There is a myth that the greener the oil, the better it is. Green olive oil is often luscious to see and taste, but it is not necessarily superior to a paler extra-virgin oil. The dark or pale color derives from the different varieties of olives that may be used in pressing. Your preference is strictly a matter of taste. Olive oil should only be purchased if it comes in a bottle or jar. Tins impart a metallic flavor that ruins the delicate oil. Store your bottles of oil, tightly sealed, in a cool cabinet or closet. Despite a common misconception, olive oil should not be stored in the refrigerator. Oil properly stored in a closet will last about 6 months.

Olives: Most good supermarkets and stores now sell loose olives that are imported from all over the world. One could safely make the generalization that olives grown in Mediterranean countries are the best, even though there is a great deal of diversity even among these olives. A real olive connoisseur, for example, could probably taste an olive and tell you if it is from Morocco, Spain, France, Italy, or Greece. For the purposes of this book, and for cooking in general, the recommendations are two: *only buy oil-cured olives* rather than salt-cured olives and *don't buy olives sold in cans.* Fresh, loose olives are the best choice, although olives in jars are acceptable as long as they don't have any added salt, colorants, or preservatives. Avoid olives stuffed with pimentos, because they are too salty, and try to choose olives that still have their pits, as they have much more flavor. An excellent, basic black olive that is widely available is the Gaeta olive, which is grown between Rome and Naples.

Onions: The much-maligned onion is often the wonderful flavor at the base of many delicious dishes. If you are using basic yellow onions for cooking, select three small ones instead of a single big onion. The reason for this is that the big onion will lose some of its punch if not used immediately, even if it is well-stored. A small onion may be the amount you need for a recipe and, even if you do not use it all, the part remaining will be less likely to be wasted. You can use the leftover part to give a hint of onion flavor to dishes that would be overwhelmed if more onion were used. Yellow onions—which should be hard and unblemished—should be kept at room temperature until they are used. Once you have cut an onion, store the unused part in a small plastic bag to be kept in the refrigerator. There are other types of onions, such as sweet Vidalia onions, purple onions, and red Spanish onions. All have their distinct flavors that are ambrosia to onion lovers.

To sauté onion slices in olive oil, heat a little oil over medium heat until the oil is hot but not smoky. Add the onions and cook them slowly to avoid burning or frying. To sautée them in sweet butter, melt the butter gently (making sure it does not brown) and then add the onions and sautée until they become translucent and golden. The fragrance will drive you wild with desire.

Many people avoid onions due to fear of crying. There is a secret that works well for some people: Before slicing an onion, stick a piece of bread (preferably white) in your mouth. This bread absorbs many of the fumes that would otherwise reach your nose and eyes, thus minimizing the impact of the onion on your tear ducts. By the way, never use onion salt or minced onion sold in jars. These are bad for the same reasons you read about in the discussion of garlic.

Orange juice: The best juice is still that which is directly squeezed from an orange. The next best is juice in a container that indicates it is *not from concentrate.* This means that the container holds chilled fresh juice (that is probably pasteurized). If this is unavailable, then select juice made from concentrate. This means that water has been added to the orange concentrate to produce the juice you are drinking. Read the container to check that it holds 100% juice. If something is described as an orange beverage or a juice drink, this means that other things have been added which you probably don't want. You should keep a couple of cans of frozen orange concentrate in your freezer for days when you run out of juice in the container. Avoid juice sold in cans or glass bottles. The metal in cans will impart a taste to the juice. Bottled juice is acceptable only if containers are unavailable, as juice exposed to light loses much of its vitamin content.

Some packaged orange juice is fortified with nutrients such as calcium or vitamin D. Although these usually are juices made from concentrate, the addition of these nutrients makes the juice worth purchasing if you need to increase your intake in that particular nutrient.

Parmesan cheese: The full name for genuine parmesan cheese is Parmigiano-Reggiano. This cow's milk cheese is produced in the towns of Parma and Reggio Emilia in north-central Italy. It is made once a day with a combination of milk from the morning and afternoon milkings. Parmigiano-Reggiano always has its name prominently stamped on the rind of the cheese, often with the added design of a king's crown, since this is also known as the "King of Cheeses." Real Parmigiano (as it is more simply called in Italy) has a wonderful nutty flavor that makes it a great eating cheese when served with a ripe pear.

Parmigiano is an especially good food for pregnant women. It is a very rich source of calcium and phosphorus. Just 1 ounce of Parmigiano contains 329 mg of calcium (almost 30% of the RDA) and 193 mg phosphorus (16% of the RDA).

Italy also exports a cheese called Grana, which is very similar to Parmigiano, except that it does not come from the classic region named for the two towns. It is made under larger, more mechanized conditions and therefore is not quite the extraordinary cheese that Parmigiano is. Yet Grana cheese is often an excellent, less expensive substitute for Parmigiano, and you may buy it with confidence if real Parmigiano is not available. Do not waste your money on parmesan-type cheese from the United States, Argentina, or other countries. It simply is not as good. Pre-grated cheese sold in refrigerated jars or green containers has absolutely nothing to do with real Parmigiano.

For purposes of grating, you should buy a wedge or chunk of Parmigiano or Grana and only grate as much as you need at the moment you need it. Store the wedge in the refrigerator, wrapped tightly in two layers of plastic wrap and a layer of aluminum foil.

Do not confuse Parmigiano with Romano cheese. Romano is often called *pecorino* cheese, a sheep's milk cheese popular in Sardinia and central and southern Italy. Pecorino (*pecora* means "sheep" in Italian) is more piquant than nutty and goes very well on pasta dishes with spicy sauces. In Italy, pecorino comes either as a fresh soft cheese or, as is usually seen in the United States, a hard grating cheese with a black or brown rind.

Pepper, black: This spice will enliven whatever you eat it with. As you already know, it is far superior when it is freshly ground. You should invest in a simple pepper mill so that you can always have freshly ground pepper. If you think that a pepper mill is, of necessity, one of those arm-long pretentious monstrosities that are used in snooty restaurants, think again. A perfectly good pepper mill will fit in the palm of your hand and cost only a few dollars. Keep whole peppercorns (which come in black, white, pink and green, each with their own special taste) in tightly sealed jars in your cabinet until you need to put them in your pepper mill.

Prunes: The notion of a black, wrinkly fruit that is typically associated with elderly people has given a great food a bad name. Prunes are sweet and delicious, wonderful in baking or when cooked with pork and other meats, served with yogurt or in fruit salads, or just eaten as a snack. They are excellent for relieving constipation, a problem that faces many pregnant women. Prunes are loaded with iron, which is a nutrient many women are deficient in whether they are pregnant or not. Excellent prunes come from California and are sold with their pits removed. Choose containers with plastic lids rather than thin plastic packages that are difficult to seal once opened. Prunes may be stored tightly sealed in a pantry or in your refrigerator.

Salt: This food is dealt with in many chapters in the book. The basic thing to remember about salt is that pregnant women need salt for their well-being and that of their fetus. However, most women in modern societies consume more salt than they need through consumption of a balanced diet that features foods that naturally contain salt. Therefore, you do not need to add salt to your diet unless you are instructed by your doctor to do so.

In purchasing salt for cooking or for the rare occasion when you add it to food, you have a couple of options. The most typical is salt that comes in tiny grains or crystals. It is referred to as iodized salt if it has the addition of iodine, an essential nutrient. You also may purchase coarse salt, which is sold in larger crystals. This is often packaged as kosher salt or sold in cannisters and called rock salt or sea salt. (Kosher, rock, and sea salt are similar, though not the same.) Coarse salt, unless used for cooking, needs to be ground in a mill. Salt mills are often sold in specialty stores near the more necessary pepper mills.

Spices: Spices should be kept in tightly sealed jars away from direct heat and light. Many people have pretty spice racks near their stoves. This may be decorative, but the heat and light rob the spices of some of their potency. Some people keep spices in their refrigerators, which keeps then fresh, though the chill neutralizes some of the fragrance and flavor of the spice. Wherever possible, buy spices in their whole form and grate or grind them as needed. Pepper, cinnamon, ginger, and nutmeg (the most essential spices for the user of this book) are all examples of spices that may be purchased whole. At the very least, do your tastebuds a favor and grind your peppercorns in a pepper mill as you need them.

Vinegar: This food is usually thought of for salad dressings or as a cleaning substance. Actually, vinegar may be used for cooking and flavoring all sorts of foods. The first vinegar was made from wine (in French, *vin* =wine; *aigre* =sour), but it is now made from apples and other fruits as well. You may use red or white wine vinegar without any concern about alcohol consumption. The alcohol disappears from wine as it converts to vinegar. Wine vinegar is the best choice for classic *vinaigrette* salad dressing. You may also purchase vinegars that are flavored with particular herbs (rosemary and tarragon, for example) or fruits (such as raspberry) for use in salads or in cooking. A popular new dish is boneless duck breast cooked with a little raspberry vinegar. There is a special vinegar called balsamic vinegar or *aceto balsamico*. This wonderful condiment, flavored with herbs and aged for years in different woods, is marvelous when poured over many foods. A little olive oil plus a few drops of balsamic vinegar is a perfect salad dressing. It gives wonderful flavor to strawberries. It is produced in Modena, Italy, and you should accept no imitations. Be sure you see the name Modena on the label. All vinegars should be stored in tightly capped (or corked) bottles or cruets in a cool, dark place in your pantry.

Water: Too many cooks, experienced or not, forget that water is one of the most essential ingredients in any kitchen. Whether you use it for drinking, diluting juice concentrates, making soups or sauces, or moistening many dishes, water is indispensable. Water is also vital for washing food, cleaning hands and dishes, cooling the brow, and satiating a giant thirst.

In recent years, it was a given in most developing countries that water was free, safe, and abundant. This is no longer a given. As the average person consumes more water than ever, supplies are taxed. Pollution in some water supplies, even in the most modern country, means that water must be carefully treated to make it safe for drinking.

The North American reader of this book probably knows if her available drinking water is safe. Readers in other parts of the world should check if their water is safe by calling local health officials if they have any doubts. Women who travel will notice differences in water from one place to the next, even within their own countries. Water contains minerals and, for example, the presence of calcium often gives water a "hard" taste. It is just a matter of getting used to. If you are ever in doubt about water, boil it completely and then cool it before using it. Remember that water is also used for cleaning food. If you suspect your available water is not safe, either use cooled boiled water or eat food (such as oranges and bananas) that does not have to be washed.

Nowadays, most supermarkets stock bottled water for drinking. This is a good alternative for people who live in areas where the tap water tastes funny. In general it tends to be safe, especially the famous brands. But you should watch the news closely to see if there is ever a report of problems, such as occurred a few years ago with Perrier. While that brand is now considered safe again, problems in a few bottles required that it be pulled from shelves for a period of time.

The point of this discussion is to remind you that water is vital, that you should ascertain that the water available to you is good, and that you should drink as many glasses a day as you can of this delicious, precious essential liquid.

Wheat germ: This crunchy cereal is particularly rich in B vitamins and certain minerals. Purchase a jar, which you should store in the refrigerator, on your first shopping trip. Sprinkle 1 or 2 teaspoons of wheat germ over cereal or fruit salad and yogurt. It also adds bulk (valuable fiber) to breads and loaves, meat loaf, and breading that you might use on fish fillets or chicken breasts.

Wine: Although it is generally wise not to drink alcoholic beverages during pregnancy, wine still may be used as a cooking ingredient in many dishes. Select a good, though not necessarily expensive, wine that you can serve as a beverage in a meal that features the same wine in the dish being served. Alcohol evaporates during cooking as a sauce simmers, so you will only get the flavor of the wine without the alcohol. Recipes typically call for a particular wine, such as Bordeaux or Frascati; but when in doubt, use a Chianti (not necessarily Chianti Classico, which is usually more expensive), a Bordeaux *vin du table*, or a simple cabernet, or merlot for a red from California, Australia, or Chile. For a white, select a fresh-tasting, inexpensive Chablis or Vouvray from France; a crisp semillon blanc or pinot blanc from California, Australia, or Chile; or an Italian Vernaccia di San Gimignano, Orvieto, or Pinot Grigio.

Yogurt: This versatile food is milk that has achieved greater glory. It is rich in much-needed calcium and many other nutrients. As far as the ideas of this book are concerned, you should purchase *low-fat* yogurt in one of three flavors: plain, lemon, or vanilla. Each will give the distinct taste you need for any recipe or to eat atop cut fruit. The only exception to this statement is in Frozen Chocolate-Banana Yogurt Pie (page 260) in which a fruited yogurt is acceptable. Otherwise, skip fruited yogurts. They often contain extra sugar or artificial sweeteners that will do you no good. Besides, the fruit you serve with plain, vanilla, or lemon yogurt will always be superior to the stuff on the bottom of the waxed container. If you are in the mood for ice cream, seek out low-fat frozen yogurt instead. Be sure to read the label to check that it has no added sugar, gums, colorants, or artificial flavors or preservatives.

Recipes for Specific
Conditions of Pregnancy

$$\textcircled{10}$$

*I*f you are one of the many women who experience some of the typical conditions and complications of pregnancy, you need to make some adjustments in your eating habits. We have created the following list concerning five typical conditions or complications of pregnancy—morning sickness, the need to gain weight, the need to slow down weight gain, preeclampsia, and gestational diabetes—so that you can select recipes that are suitable for your condition.

Every recipe listed under a particular condition will be suitable for most women experiencing that condition. Of course, you may have special instructions from your doctor, and you should always follow specific advice instead of general guidelines. While each recipe selected for a particular condition is nutritionally sound, there are many other dishes you can prepare using the same ingredients that will probably suit your needs as well.

There are some points to bear in mind regarding the lists of recipes for weight gain and loss:

• Our recommendations are based on the portion sizes indicated with each recipe. Therefore, if you eat small amounts of fattening dishes, your caloric intake will be minimized.

• If your doctor tells you to consume a precise amount of calories each day (whether to gain or lose weight), be sure to eat a wide range of foods to ensure you get the nutrients you need. Each recipe's Doctor's Note indicates the calories contained in a portion.

• Many of the dishes in this book are not specifically indicated for weight gain or loss. They are for the average pregnant woman who needs to gain weight at a normal, gradual pace. Of course, you may feel free to enjoy these as well.

About morning sickness: Each woman has her individual responses to particular foods when she has morning sickness. Our list contains foods that you may find appealing. If other foods please you more, follow your own taste.

Our selections for dishes for gestational diabetics and women with preeclampsia follow the medical guidelines that exist for these conditions. However, if you have these conditions, you should take the time to learn what ingredients you should assiduously avoid. Start by reading about them on page 60.

Morning Sickness

BREAKFAST	•Vitamin B$_6$ Breakfast, 122 •Panettone French Toast, 123 •Apricot Sauce, 131•Berry Sauce, 132•Oat Bran Muffins, 253•Corn Bread, 249•Orange Apricot Nut Loaf, 251•New England Loaf, 252
DRESSINGS AND SAUCES	•Tofu Ranch Dressing, 126 •Faux Hollandaise Sauce, 130 •Apricot Sauce, 131• Berry Sauce, 132
APPETIZERS	•Crudités, 136•Insalata Caprese, 165•P.O.P., 175•Rice Salad, 169
LUNCH AND BRUNCH	•Pita, Pita, Pita, 140 •Stuffed Potato, 227
SOUP	•Chicken Stock, 146•Endive Soup, 148•Rice Soup, 152 •Turkey Rice Soup, 153
SALAD	•Caspian Cucumbers, 160 •Insalata Caprese, 165 •Rice Salad, 169
PASTA	•P.O.P., 175
FISH AND SEAFOOD	•Flounder Florentine, 189 •Broiled Monkfish, 191
POULTRY	•Grilled, sautéed, or poached chicken or turkey supremes, 194–197•Turkey Piccata,198 •Poultry Burgers, 209
MEAT	•Meat Loaf with Chicken Liver, 213•La Milanese (Veal), 214
VEGETABLES	•Carrot-Potato Purée, 225 •Baked Potato, 227 •Boiled Potatoes, 228•Mashed Potatoes, 229 •Creamed Spinach, 232 •Baked Zucchini and Onions, 238
FRUIT	•Apple Sauce, 244•Frozen Bananas (or variations of flavored frozen bananas), 245•Frozen Banana Purée, 258•Frozen Grapes, 246
BAKED GOODS	•Corn Bread, 249•Banana Buttermilk Bread, 250•Orange Apricot Nut Loaf, 251•New England Loaf, 252•Oat Bran Muffins, 253
DESSERTS	•Frozen yogurt (plain or vanilla) •Frozen Banana Purée, 258
BEVERAGES	•Water, Broth, or Herbal Teas.

Weight Gain Needed

BREAKFAST
- Vitamin B$_6$ Breakfast, 122
- Panettone French Toast, 123
- Apricot Sauce, 131•Berry Sauce, 132•Corn Bread, 249•Banana Buttermilk Bread, 250•Orange Apricot Nut Loaf, 251•New England Loaf, 252•Shakes and smoothees, 266

DRESSINGS AND SAUCES
- Classic Vinaigrette, 125
- Vinaigrette aux Fines Herbes, 126•Pesto Presto, 129•Salsa Verde, 130•Apricot Sauce, 131•Berry Sauce, 132

APPETIZERS
- Hummus, 134•Guacamole, 135
- Asparagus Parmesan, 222
- Baked Asparagus Rolls, 223
- Brandade de Morue, 186
- Insalata Petroniana, 166
- Tuna–String Bean Salad, 168•olive purée on toast, 176
- all pastas •Rice Salad, 169

LUNCH AND BRUNCH
- Asparagus Benedict, 222
- Baked Asparagus Rolls, 223
- Stuffed Potato, 227

SOUP
- Endive Soup, 148•Minestrone con Fagioli, 150•Rice Soup, 152
- Scotch Broth, 154

SALAD DAYS
- Waldorf Salad, 164
- Insalata Petroniana, 166
- Tuna–String Bean Salad, 168
- Rice Salad, 169

PASTA
- All pasta, especially Fettuccine with Walnut Sauce, 177

FISH AND SEAFOOD
- Brandade de Morue, 186•Pescado San Sebastian, 188•Grilled Tuna Cancún, 190

POULTRY
- Pollo Castelli Romani, 201
- Chicken aux Fines Herbes, 200
- Chicken Livers, 202

MEAT
- Basic Burgers, 207•La Milanese (Veal), 214•The Perfect Veal Chop, 215•Pan-Fried Steak, 216
- Moroccan Shepherd's Pie, 217
- Simple Lamb Stew, 218

VEGETABLES
- Asparagus aux Fines Herbes, 221•Asparagus Benedict, 222
- Asparagus Parmesan, 222
- Baked Asparagus Rolls 223
- all potatoes•Baked Stuffed Tomatoes, 234•Tomatoes Provençal, 236•Baked Zucchini and Onions, 238

FRUIT
- Frozen Bananas, 245
- Frozen Banana Purée, 258
- Frozen Grapes, 246

BAKED GOODS
- Corn Bread, 249•Banana Buttermilk Bread, 250•Orange Apricot Nut Loaf, 251•New England Loaf, 252

DESSERTS
- Frozen yogurt with Apricot Sauce, 131•or Berry Sauce, 132
- Frozen Chocolate-Banana Yogurt Pie (or any variation), 260
- Frozen Banana Purée, 258

BEVERAGES
- Water, whole milk, juices, smoothees, shakes, broths•sangria, spritzers,267• herbal teas

Excessive Weight Gain

BREAKFAST	•Fruit salad, 239–40•Oat Bran Muffins, 253	**POULTRY**	•Grilled, sautéed, or poached chicken or turkey supremes, 194–97•Turkey Piccata, 198 •Chicken or Turkey Gismonda, 199•Poultry Burgers, 209
DRESSINGS AND SAUCES	•Tofu Ranch Dressing, 126 •The World's Easiest Tomato Sauce, 128 •Faux Hollandaise Sauce, 130	**MEAT**	•Lamb Burgers, 209•Basic Meat Loaf, 211•Meat Loaf with Chicken Liver, 213
APPETIZERS	•Crudités, Marinated Mushrooms and Peppers, 137•Asparagus with Faux Hollandaise Sauce, 221 •Green salad, Orange-Shrimp Salad, 163•Salmon Loaf, 193 •Sprouts Salad, 162	**VEGETABLES**	•Basic Asparagus, 220 •Asparagus au Faux Hollandaise, 221 •Asparagus Bismarck, 222 •Red Cabbage–Green Apples, 223 •Lemon Yogurt Slaw, 224 •Cauliflower-Pepper Crunch, 226•Baked Potato, 227 •Boiled Potatoes, 228 •Creamed Spinach, 232•Baked Stuffed Tomatoes, 234•Broiled Tomatoes, 236
LUNCH AND BRUNCH	•Carrot Peanut Butter, 142 •Asparagus Bismarck, 222 •Baked Stuffed Tomatoes, 234		
SOUP	•Chicken Stock, 146•Orange Chicken Broth, 147•Emerald Soup, 149•Turkey Rice Soup, 153	**FRUIT**	•Fresh Fruit Salad, 239 •Poached Dried Fruit, 243 •Apple Sauce, 244 •Strawberries Modena, 247 •or select any fruit under 100 calories
SALAD	•Green salad, Caspian Cucumbers, 160•Mushrooms and Sprouts, 161•Orange-Shrimp Salad, 163		
PASTA	None	**BAKED GOODS**	•Oat Bran Muffins, 253
FISH AND SEAFOOD	•Flounder Florentine, 189 •Broiled Monkfish, 191 •Poached Salmon, 192 •Salmon Loaf, 193•Salmon Burgers, 210	**DESSERTS**	•Low-fat frozen yogurt (without sugar)•Fruit Crisp, 259
		BEVERAGES	•Water, skim milk, broths• Parsley-Pineapple Smoothee, 266• spritzers, and herbal teas

Preeclampsia

BREAKFAST
- Panettone French Toast, 123
- Apricot Sauce, 131•Berry Sauce 132•Fruit Salad, 239–40•Oat Bran Muffins, 253•Corn Bread, 249

DRESSINGS AND SAUCES
- Classic Vinaigrette, 125
- Vinaigrette aux Fines Herbes, 126•Tofu Ranch Dressing, 126
- Faux Hollandaise Sauce, 130
- Apricot Sauce, 131•Berry Sauce, 132

APPETIZERS
- Guacamole, 135•Crudités, 136
- Asparagus with Faux Hollandaise, 221•Green salad, Insalata Caprese, 165
- Orange-Shrimp Salad, 163
- Rice Salad, 169•Sprouts Salad, 162•Tomatoes Provençal, 236

LUNCH AND BRUNCH
- Pita, Pita, Pita, 140•Asparagus Bismarck, 222 •Stuffed Potato, 227

SOUP
- Emerald Soup, 149•Rice Soup, 152

SALAD
- Green salad, Caspian Cucumbers, 160•Mushrooms and Sprouts, 161•Orange-Shrimp Salad, 163•Insalata Caprese 165•Rice Salad, 169

PASTA
- Spaghetti con Pomodoro Crudo, 174•P.O.P,175•Spaghetti alla Pescatora, 178

FISH AND SEAFOOD
- Brandade de Morue, 186
- Flounder Florentine, 189
- Poached Salmon, 192

POULTRY
- Grilled, sautéed, or poached chicken or turkey supremes, 194–97 •Turkey Piccata, 198
- Chicken or Turkey Gismonda,199•Chicken aux Fines Herbes, 200•Chicken Livers, 202•Poultry Burgers, 209

MEAT
- Beef, Veal, and Lamb Burgers, 207–9•La Milanese (Veal), 214
- The Perfect Veal Chop, 215
- Pan-Fried Steak, 216
- Moroccan Shepherd's Pie, 217

VEGETABLES
- Basic Asparagus, 220•Asparagus au Faux Hollandaise, 221
- Asparagus aux Fines Herbes, 221•Asparagus Bismarck, 222
- Red Cabbage–Green Apples, 223•Lemon Yogurt Slaw, 224
- Carrot-Potato Purée, 225
- Cauliflower-Pepper Crunch, 226
- all potatoes•Creamed Spinach, 232•and all dishes made with *fresh* tomatoes

FRUIT
- Fresh Fruit Salad, 239•Poached Dried Fruit, 243•Frozen Grapes, 246•Strawberries Modena, 247
- most any fresh fruit is acceptable, except bananas and coconut (no cheese)

BAKED GOODS
- Corn Bread, 249•New England Loaf, 252•Oat Bran Muffins, 253

DESSERTS
- Low-fat frozen yogurt
- Fruit Crisp, 259

BEVERAGES
- Water, milk, juices, smoothees, shakes, sangria, spritzers, and herbal teas

BREAKFAST	•Oat Bran Muffins, 253 •Apricot Sauce, 131•Berry Sauce, 132 (omit sugar)
DRESSINGS AND SAUCES	•Classic Vinaigrette, 125 •Vinaigrette au Fines Herbes, 126•Tofu Ranch Dressing, 126 •The World's Easiest Tomato Sauce, 128•Faux Hollandaise Sauce, 130•Salsa Verde, 130 •Apricot Sauce, 131•Berry Sauce, 132 (omit sugar)
APPETIZERS	•Guacamole, 135 •Crudités, 136 •Marinated Mushrooms and Peppers, 137•Asparagus au Faux Hollandaise, 221•Green salad, 155•Insalata Caprese, 165•Insalata Petroniana, 166 •Orange-Shrimp Salad, 163 •Salmon Loaf, 193•Sprouts Salad, 162•Tomatoes Provençal, 236•Tuna–String Bean Salad, 168
LUNCH AND BRUNCH	•Pita, Pita, Pita, 140•Tuna Melt, 141 •Florentine Omelet, 143 •Asparagus Bismarck, 222
SOUP	•Chicken Stock, 146•Orange Chicken Broth, 147•Emerald Soup, 149
SALAD	•Green salad, 155•Caspian Cucumbers, 160•Mushrooms and Sprouts, 161•Orange-Shrimp Salad, 163• Insalata Caprese, 165 •Insalata Petroniana, 166 •Tuna–String Bean Salad, 168
PASTA	None
FISH AND SEAFOOD	•Pescado San Sebastian, 188 •Flounder Florentine, 189 •Grilled Tuna Cancún, 190 •Broiled Monkfish, 191 •Poached Salmon, 192•Salmon Burgers, 210
POULTRY	•Grilled, sautéed, or poached chicken or turkey supremes, 194-97•Turkey Piccata, 198 •Chicken or Turkey Gismonda, 199•Chicken aux Fines Herbes, 200•Chicken Livers, 202•Poultry Burgers, 209
MEAT	•Beef, Veal, and Lamb Burgers, 207–9•The Perfect Veal Chop, 215•Pan-Fried Steak, 216
VEGETABLES	•Basic Asparagus, 220•Asparagus au Faux Hollandaise, 221 •Asparagus aux Fines Herbes, 221•Asparagus Bismarck, 222 •Lemon Yogurt Slaw, 224 •Cauliflower-Pepper Crunch, 226 •Creamed Spinach, 232•Baked Tomatoes (omit bread crumbs), 234 •Broiled Tomatoes, 236 •Tomatoes Provençal, 236 •Insalata Caprese, 165
FRUIT	•Select any fruit with less than 15 g of carbohydrates
BAKED GOODS	•Oat Bran Muffins, 253
DESSERTS	•Plain or vanilla frozen yogurt (without sugar) and any fruit with less than 15 g of carbohydrates
BEVERAGES	•Water, milk, broth, and herbal teas

Tables

TABLE I
RDAs for Pregnant and Lactating Women

VITAMINS	PREGNANT	LACTATING
A	4000–5000 IU	6000–6500 IU
B_1 (thiamine)	1.5 mg	1.6 mg
B_2 (riboflavin)	1.5 mg	1.6 mg
Niacin (nicotinic acid)	17 mg	20 mg
Folate (folic acid)	0.4 mg	0.3 mg
B_6	2.2 mg	2.1 mg
B_7 (biotin) = 0.3 mg (no other standards established for lactation or pregnancy)		
B_{12}	2.2 mcg	2.6 mcg
Pantothenic acid = 7 mg	no specific RDA	no specific RDA
C (ascorbic acid)	70 mg	95 mg
D (calciferol)	400 IU	400 IU
E (tocopherol)	10 mg (75 IU)	12 mg (18 IU)
K	65 mcg	65 mcg
Calcium	1200 mg	1200 mg
Copper	2 mg	2 mg
Fluoride	2 mg	2 mg
Iodine	175 mcg	200 mcg
Iron	30 mg	15 mg
Manganese = 2.2 mg	no specific RDA	no specific RDA
Magnesium	300 mg	355 mg
Phosphorus	1200 mg	1200 mg
Potassium = 2000 mg/day/adult	no specific RDA	no specific RDA
Selenium	75 mcg	75 mcg
Sodium	570 mg	635 mg

Table II
Allocation of Calories

First Trimester: 2200 calories–2500 calories

Second Trimester: 2500 calories–2800 calories

Third Trimester: 2500 calories–2800 calories

Lactation   2700–2800 calories

Optimum Allocation of Calories in Diet

Carbohydrates   55%–60%

    Simple   15%

    Complex   40%–45%

Fat   30%

    Saturated   10%

    Polysaturated   10%

    Monosaturated   10%

Protein   10%-15%

Apportionment of Calories in a 2800-Calorie Diet

	Calories	Grams
Carbohydrates	1540–1680	385–420
Simple	420	105
Complex	1120–1260	280–315
Fat	840	105
Protein	280–240	60–105

Note: You should use this information as a basic guide rather than gospel. This is because every woman is built differently and each body has its precise calorie and energy requirements. The figures here represent a range keeping in mind that the energy requirements increase by 10%–15% with each trimester.

TABLE III

Metric Conversions

LIQUID MEASUREMENTS

1 teaspoon = ⅓ tablespoon = ⅙ fluid ounce = 4.9 ml
3 teaspoons = 1 tablespoon = ½ fluid ounce = 14.8 ml
2 tablespoons = ⅛ cup = 1 fluid ounce = 29.6 ml
4 tablespoons = ¼ cup = 2 fluid ounces = 59.1 ml
8 tablespoons = ½ cup = 4 fluid ounces = 118.3 ml
16 tablespoons = 1 cup = 8 fluid ounces = 236.6 ml
2 cups = 1 pint = 16 fluid ounces = 473.2 ml
4 cups = 1 quart = 32 fluid ounces = 946.4 ml
1 liter = 1.057 quarts = 34 fluid ounces = 1000 ml
4 quarts = 1 gallon = 128 fluid ounces = 3.786 liters (3786 ml)

WEIGHT MEASUREMENTS

1 gram = 0.035 ounce = 0.001 kilograms = 1000 milligrams =
   1,000,000 micrograms
1 milligram = 0.001 gram = 1000 micrograms
1 ounce = 28 grams
4 ounces = 113 grams = ¼ pound
8 ounces = 226 grams = ½ pound
16 ounces = 454 grams = 1 pound
1 kilogram = 1000 grams = 2.2 pounds

OVEN TEMPERATURE EQUIVALENTS

Fahrenheit	Celsius	Gas Mark	Description
225	110	¼	Cool
250	130	½	
275	140	1	Very Slow
300	150	2	
325	170	3	Slow
350	180	4	Moderate
375	190	5	
400	200	6	Moderately Hot
425	220	7	Fairly Hot
450	230	8	Hot
475	240	9	Very Hot
500	250	10	Extremely Hot

Bibliography

This list represents the principal medical references consulted by the authors during the writing of this book. In addition to these books and sources, the most up-to-date information about nutrition and pregnancy was gathered from articles in professional journals and leading newspapers and magazines.

Committee on Maternal Nutrition, Food and Nutrition Board, *Maternal Nutrition and the Course of Pregnancy*, National Academy of Sciences, 1970

Expert Panel on Prenatal Care, *Caring for Our Future*, Public Health Service, 1989

Institute of Medicine, *Preventing Low Birthweight*, National Academy Press, 1985

B. Luke, *Maternal Nutrition*, Little Brown & Co., 1979

Irwin R. Merkatz, et. al., *New Perspective on Prenatal Care*, Elsevier, 1990

National Institute of Medicine, *Nutrition During Pregnancy*, National Academy Press, 1990

National Research Council, *Recommended Dietary Allowances*, 10th edition, National Academy Press, 1989.

Jean A. T. Pennington, *Food Values*, 15th edition, HarperCollins, 1989

Mary Story, Ph.D., *Nutrition Management of the Pregnant Adolescent*, March of Dimes Birth Defects Foundation, U.S. Department of Health and Human Services, U.S. Department of Agriculture, 1990

United States Department of Agriculture, *Nutritive Value of American Foods*, USDA Handbook No. 456, 1988

Myron Winick, M.D., *Nutrition, Pregnancy, and Early Infancy*, Williams and Wilkins, 1989

Index